M000203477

FRENCH ROLL

MISADVENTURES IN LOVE, LIFE, AND ROLLER-SKATING ACROSS THE FRENCH RIVIERA

FRENCH ROLL

MISADVENTURES IN LOVE, LIFE, AND ROLLER-SKATING ACROSS THE FRENCH RIVIERA

BY

J. MICHAEL JARVIS

French Roll is a work of non-fiction.
Some names and identifying details have been changed.

Copyright © 2020 by J. Michael Jarvis
All rights reserved.

Published in the United States by Interseller Inc.

No part of this publication may be re-produced, distributed or transmitted in any form or by any means, including photocopying, recording, or other electronic or mechanical methods, without the prior written permission of the publisher, except in the case of brief quotations embodied in critical reviews and certain other non-commercial uses permitted by copyright law. For permission requests, write to the publisher, addressed "Attention: Permissions Coordinator," at the address below.

Publisher@Interseller.com
Interseller Inc.
2007 Baja, Newport Beach, California 92660 USA
www.InterSeller.com

Jeff Lyons - story consultant
Lisa Poisson - editor & book coach
Robin J Samuels - copy editor
Tanja Prokop - cover designer
Tracy Atkins - interior designer
Pam Sheppard - publishing consultant

French Roll / J. Michael Jarvis — 1st ed.

ISBN 978-1-7345469-0-3 (Paperback)
ISBN 978-1-7345469-2-7 (Hardcover)
ISBN 978-1-7345469-1-0 (Kindle eBook)
ISBN 978-1-7345469-3-4 (eBook)

For Mitch — I climb every flight of stairs with you, except your stairway to heaven.

CONTENTS

Chapter 1 On the Edge 1

Chapter 2 Say When...8

Chapter 3 The Letter...15

Chapter 4 The Party...26

Chapter 5 Mice Will Play...35

Chapter 6 Making Plans...38

Chapter 7 Making Equipment 51

Chapter 8 Is There Anybody Out There?........................61

Chapter 9 Night Train to Italy......................................66

Chapter 10 Day One...72

Chapter 11 Just Say *Non* 81

Chapter 12 Unwelcome to Monaco.................................87

Chapter 13 Nice Feet...95

Chapter 14 Building Character 101

Chapter 15 Ted the Skater.. 110

Chapter 16 Tom the Skater 114

Chapter 17 Ted the Rocker 124

Chapter 18 Late Night with…...................................... 128

Chapter 19 Nice Departure 131

Chapter 20 Lighthouse and Home................................ 136

Chapter 21 Red Carpet 144

Chapter 22 Red Cutter.. 151

Chapter 23 Tropéziennes 160

Chapter 24 End of a Rivi-Era 168

Chapter 25 Shepherds of Squalor............................. 176

Chapter 26 My French Family 179

Chapter 27 Break a Leg 188

Chapter 28 Monaco Grand Prix.............................. 192

Chapter 29 The Last Room in Nice......................... 198

Chapter 30 Breakout 207

Chapter 31 Chez Blanche 213

Chapter 32 Bad Connection...................................... 217

Chapter 33 Lend Me Your Ear 222

Chapter 34 The Camargue 231

Chapter 35 Massacre at Béziers 242

Chapter 36 Red, White, and Blue 258

Chapter 37 Open the Gates 271

Chapter 38 Sit, Cerberus. Stay................................. 279

Chapter 39 Over the Line... 284

A Note on the Text 291

Author Biography 293

Connect with J. Michael Jarvis 294

CHAPTER 1

ON THE EDGE

Do not look for approval, except for the consciousness of doing your best
—Andrew Carnegie

The rucksack of dynamite pulled on my shoulders with each step through the Alpen tunnel. Chilling panic shot up my neck each time I bumped the bomb against the icy rock wall. My mountain boss led the way, his red jacket barely visible in the dim light of the fitfully working bulbs, goading me to keep his pace. The two of us had trekked high into Tyrolean territory through secret passages inside the Zugspitze, Germany's highest mountain, where we would burrow through snow tubes with the explosives and blast off the top of the mountain.

It sounded like the life of some super-spy or special ops soldier, but I was a long-haired California kid still sporting surf trunks under my layers of ice climbing gear, far from the surf and sand I called home. I had always assumed I'd be a smart, sensible man by the time I turned nineteen. Instead, I was volunteering for avalanche duty, another goal in a series of unhinged, self-validating missions, apparently nowhere near to giving up my conviction that

I could do anything, needed no one, could take on the world on my own two feet. The ski season clock was ticking a countdown to summer—I'd already hit that snooze button of growing up several times.

It was time for an awakening.

We climbed for an hour, beginning at the padlocked doors of the Schneefernerhaus, the enigmatic hotel clinging to the limestone cliffs of the Zugspitze. The desolate hideout overlooked a glacier high above the tree line, an ideal supervillain lair for some literary love child of Ian Fleming and Agatha Christie. For that one cloistered winter of 1980 (because surely I never planned to return once the ice released me from its clutches), I was calling it home.

My foot slipped on an icy stair in the tunnel, and I dropped a knee hard to concrete, ripping my pants. I struggled to my feet under the weight of the loaded backpack, changing my gait to favor the nonthrobbing knee. An icy draft rushed into the tear in my pants and froze a smear of blood on the outside.

I should have stayed in bed.

I could have been cozy under piles of down comforters, waiting to watch another sunrise over the Alps through the dorm window, peeking at me from beyond the well-greased machinery of cable car number three. But the magnificence of the five snowcapped countries outside my window begged adventure, and I wasn't one to ignore their demands. I often climbed out the window onto the cable car catwalks to a secret balcony, where I'd dangle my legs and play my harmonica to the Alpen peaks in the distance. Most nights began with two beers and the twelve-bar blues, and ended with six or more letters written by a flickering candle in a wax-covered Chianti bottle.

The letters of my routine days read like cliffhanger adventures for the folks in California. I penned intrepid episodes of a world they could only imagine, a life even I could barely believe I was experiencing. My frank stories surely freaked them out. I scribed loquacious letters to Carla, the stylish San Francisco correspondent

I met in Munich. I declined important invitations such as job offers and being Guy's best man back in California. And I desperately tried to express my helpless sorrow to my sister Julie with a baby boy in her belly and a softball-sized tumor in her head.

But most of my letters were to my darling Carrie. I gushed over how I missed roller-skating the beaches with her. I rambled on about how wonderful our life together would be once I returned, and I dropped hints about making her mine till death do us part.

Even my readers recognized I didn't belong where I was. My mountaineering adventures were a fix, an episodic high for a teenage adrenaline junkie desperately avoiding his greatest fear. I ruminated on these assessments while keeping pace with Der Spiegel's red coat in the tunnel darkness, following the collage of award patches across his broad shoulders.

After my enthusiastic *ja* to volunteering, Der Spiegel sat me down with a couple of forty-year veteran Tyrolean mountain men in a dimly lighted booth at the back of the employee lounge of the Schneefernerhaus.

Trapped in the café booth by these burly figures and feeling rather puny alongside them, I puffed up my chest, drank a warm morning beer, and choked on the secondhand smoke belching from their prized fourth-generation Meerschaum pipes. A round of breakfast Jägermeister arrived at the table, making me wonder if there might ever be an inappropriate time for shots in this mountain life.

It was there they gave me the Avalanche Talk—in German. Though I had become fluent after five years of studying German, the thick accents of the Bavarian and Tyrolean mountaineers left me reading body language for clues. The Avalanche Talk was like planning a bank heist or a *coup d'état*. A storm had hit unseasonably late, and we would be avalanching from an awkward location. Awkward meant dangerous.

Still, the boss was going, and I was comfortable putting my life in his hands. To say the Alps were his home was an understatement. Through my California eyes, he *was* the Alps.

The men methodically explained the coming tasks in throaty, five-syllable words beyond my fourth-year German vocabulary. There was an audible tension in their gruff voices and rare and genuine concern on their ruddy catcher's-mitt faces. I took notes, from which I would later translate unfamiliar phrases from a pocket dictionary: "hazardous duty," "blow up the mountain," "extra pay." I couldn't shake the feeling that I was being set up for something the career alpinists wanted no part of. But I agreed. Der Spiegel gave me his customary heavy slap on the back, and so it was done.

We met before sunrise in the employee lounge. The 1930s hotel was deathly quiet in the predawn dark. Its zoetic gallery of German history, frozen in time with handcrafted furnishings and gilded Nazi-era artifacts, hinted at adventures and dangers, isolation and secrecy. The Schneefernerhaus is the fantasy of every James Bond film location scout, but that morning it was just a place where a grumpy teenager was told to be at five o'clock sharp.

Der Spiegel tucked a flashlight into his armpit, preparing to fill two heavy canvas rucksacks for the hike. I reached for the heavier of the two bags, respectfully offering to carry the load.

"No, this rucksack is for you," he told me in German.

Why would I carry an empty backpack?

Armed with antique keys on a rusted steel ring, he opened the padlocked doors to the far reaches of the Schneefernerhaus, places I had failed to access despite months of late-night snooping. Exposed to the elements, the formerly grand dining room hadn't hosted a party since 1965, when the Great Avalanche had swept an entire section of the hotel, along with ten of its guests, right off the face of the cliff.

The west wing surrounded us in biting cold. I bumped something at every corner, but Der Spiegel slipped through the darkness like a cat. Dim morning light refracted through snow-frosted tables and chairs, haphazardly stacked and perfectly preserved in these hypoxic altitudes. This was long-term storage, an open-air tomb of tragic memory where outdated equipment was left to rest for eternity.

Beside the stacks of furniture lay disaster rescue gear: shovels, locating poles, stretchers, cables, and come-alongs. A wooden casket was propped against the rock wall, a sobering reminder of how fragile life in this numbing climate could be. Snow dusted the casket's cracked black paint, and the way it stood at attention—ready for something to jump out—sent a chill through me that could have frozen a candle in midflicker. A shriek like a ghostly warning filled my head: the last people to enjoy this space, on May 15, 1965, had died a horrible death.

Der Spiegel paused. His sigh was heavy even from across the room. I stood in silence as he gazed down the slope.

"I was your age when it happened," he began. "We were frantic, harpooning the snow with only the most cynical hopes of finding survivors buried deep. There was just so, so much snow. Everywhere snow. White, and nothing else. We used these harpoons. The rescuers yelled at me to lunge deeper into the snow. 'Lunge with all your might!'"

He shook his head. Between deep breaths, he continued. "And I wanted so badly to find a survivor, to save a life. But I was so scared. So much snow. The harpoon, it would go right through a survivor if I hit one. Maybe I would kill them instead of saving them? My father was the boss back then—the job I have now. 'Lunge harder, lunge deeper!' he yelled at me. I still have nightmares of throwing a javelin into a dark crowd from a stage, but to find a survivor, you had to hang onto the javelin, your hand unaware if you would find or kill a survivor."

An awful taste hit the back of my tongue, but I managed to keep it inside.

"It would be days before we found them. Fifteen bodies, no survivors. Their faces were poked with holes, their backs gashed by picks and shovels, arms and legs frozen solid, broken and twisted like mannequins thrown into a box. I was just a boy the day that it happened." He paused, looking me straight in the eye. "But not the next day."

Another sigh, shorter this time. "Some say I dynamite for avalanches too much, but I can't let this happen again. Not after what it did to all those people. Not after that effect on Dad. And not after a storm like last night's."

He straightened. "Okay, Herr Jarvis, this way. The tunnel is in the back."

Heavy steel buttressed a thick wooden gateway to what I could only imagine was some bloody-toothed, wooly monster's cave. Der Spiegel used a ridiculously oversized skeleton key for the padlock and heaved the door open on squeaking hinges; my anticipation of a sinister screech was richly rewarded with a sound right out of an old horror movie. Behind the door lay blackness. He threw the lever for the electricals, a knife switch like in *Frankenstein* movies, illuminating bare bulbs and exposing wiring along the low ceiling tunnel. Cold, stale air wafted from the passage.

My apprehension transformed into huffing, puffing, and a little high-altitude vertigo in the tunnel's twists and turns. After a while, Der Spiegel turned around and stood still as the tunnel air. He pointed at a white line painted across the floor and held up his hand; I was not to cross. Arrows and words were painted on either side of the line: *Deutschland* and *Österreich*. The international border of Germany and Austria apparently ran directly through the center of the mountain.

"We now enter Austria. Did you bring your passport, Herr Jarvis?"

My expression told him I hadn't.

Had I missed something during the Avalanche Talk? Was I breaking international law? Was I ruining the mission? Would they toss me in the clink if I crossed the border without my papers?

Watching the mild panic rise on my face, his expression morphed from deadpan to a huge smile. "Ha ha, Spiegel. Oh, that was a good one. What's next? The Von Trapp Family Singers come out in their drapery costumes?"

But no, not the Von Trapps. He had something even better. The next steel door required the largest of his ridiculously oversized skeleton keys. Acrid funk filled the tunnel, and our flashlights revealed a room full of dynamite.

Only then did I understand why I carried the empty rucksack.

CHAPTER 2

SAY WHEN

Believe you can and you're halfway there.
—Theodore Roosevelt

Der Spiegel packed my pack so full of TNT we could barely close the flap, delicately pulling the leather to catch the last strap hole for the buckle. I got under the deadweight and pressed upward like a powerlifter struggling to take a step. I was the bomb, literally. I was Little Boy, the atomic device dropped on Hiroshima, wobbling on the legs of a newborn foal.

He gave me a fatherly grin, but his squint silently asked if I was okay. I replied with a tough-and-ready grin. At least I avoided the slap on the back.

I could do this. I'd make him proud.

Onward and upward, each step more deliberate than the previous: *kaboom, kaboom, kaboom*—a marching cadence, as I visualized slipping and turning the Zugspitze into an active volcano. I imagined a body at the front of a fireball blasting down the tunnel to the door below like a rocket launchpad, blasting cremains over the glacier and scattering the ashes across the Alps. Moment of death to an ash-scattering Alpen memorial in two seconds—German efficiency at its finest.

Only soldiers, suicide bombers, and a select few nutjobs have ever been strapped to one hundred pounds of dynamite. How many lived to tell about it? Surely not the ones who carelessly slipped on the icy floor or bumped a tunnel wall too hard.

I wiped a different type of sweat from my brow as Der Spiegel stopped at yet another door. This door opened into a tiny cabin of old wood and concrete, deathly quiet yet comfortable as dry socks. He fiddled with an old metal box on the wall. The ancient fixtures flickered, then illuminated the room with electric light.

We dropped our packs—delicately—and flopped on the floor, breath clouds chugging like locomotives in front of our faces. Der Spiegel crossed the room to the door to the outside. I expected crisp, thin air to breathe and an Alpen morning vista; instead, I faced a solid wall of white. It was as if we were sealed inside with concrete. It was snow; everything white was snow.

I shifted uneasily. All that snow would need to be tunneled before we could get outside to do our job. It would be hard work. But that didn't upset the boss—not even a little. He handed me a shovel and sat back down to rest.

I picked and scooped and quickly covered the cabin floor with wall-to-wall firn. I dug inward, then upward, tunneling and climbing with mitts, clawing like a drowning swimmer to reach the surface until I broke into the foggy predawn with a fist. I breached the surface with a false sense of safety, my head just above the surface, gasping for thin air. Cold, cloudy nothingness lay in every direction. I shoveled a path across the cabin's flat roof, digging down and eventually hitting the top of a safety rail. If I fell off the roof, I'd run out of breath screaming before hitting something at the bottom of the cliff.

The irrefutable smell of danger caught my attention: dynamite. Der Spiegel began passing up the sticks he'd taped and fused together. Taking each bundle was unnerving. In the rucksack, it had been cargo, but in my bare hands, the red paper felt like holding the boundaries of a galaxy. At the opposite end of the roof, a huge reel and crank would let us shuttle the dynamite out on a thin cable beyond the clouds. I stacked the sticks at the base of the crank.

This was the antithesis of the sheltered Southern California beach bubble I came from. This was the edge, where life happened. This was the adventure I'd been looking for. I shivered with cold and something else.

Each bundle was a double-handful of dynamite, maybe eight to ten sticks per bundle, tightly wrapped with black tape. A long red fuse connected each bundle to the next. Working methodically, accurately, Der Spiegel hung the TNT bundles from the cable, and I cranked them somewhere into the clouds.

Relief trickled down my neck the moment they were out of sight. I understood most of his German words about dynamite by then, but none of it sounded safe, especially in five-syllable German words like *streichholzschächtelchen* (little box of wooden matches).

"The bundles are connected by the fast red fuse. The red fuse burns at one hundred meters per second, so they all explode at once. But the black fuse is zee slow fuse. It gives us time to get away."

"So how fast does that black fuse burn?" I hoped the answer would be measured in hours. Or kilometers.

"Slow enough to give us time." He winked at me with the grin of a mad scientist.

What the hell did "enough time" mean? Was I not entitled to some intel on how fast to run for my life?

Striking the flare match, he checked his watch as a matter of professional blaster's protocol before lighting the black fuse.

"Herr Jarvis, you can start cranking now," he stated in calm, polite tones—also protocol.

Cranking so much weight uphill required all the muscle I had. I cranked and hoped with every turn the signal would come—a shout of "enough!"—so I could flee from the string of bombs.

Der Spiegel had moved back to the ice tube, prepared to evacuate. "Did you reel to the stop point on the cable?"

"The stop point?"

Uh-oh.

"Ja, there's a red tape on the cable. That's when you stop cranking."

"I didn't see—I wasn't looking… I didn't understand."

Oh dear god, I'd killed us all.

Der Spiegel held his sleeve back, still calmly checking his wristwatch. "Keep cranking."

I cranked furiously, focused on red tape and envisioning imminent death if I stopped cranking. My only explosives experience came from close calls with holiday firecrackers, but when it came to dynamite, it didn't take an expert to hypothesize that farther away was better.

"Okay, Herr Jarvis."

I turned for visual confirmation, but a black hat slipping below the surface was the only sight. I'd expected something more along the lines of "RUN—SHE'S GONNA BLOW!" But Der Spiegel's sensible protocols helped me mirror his calm. I moved across the roof and sat calmly before scrambling down the snow chute.

I landed flat on my back on the cabin floor, Der Spiegel looming over me. "Did you secure the reel with the pin?"

"Oh, *fudge*."

In hindsight, I should have said that chocolaty F-word. My word of choice was regrettably the mother of all four-letter words, spewed into the boss's face.

He checked his watch, but his casual tone was gone. "Without the pin the weight of the charges will come back down to the cabin if the pin ist nicht secured!"

Calm safety protocol was blown out the window. One of us had to go back up.

"I'll fix it," I said.

He cocked his head and considered. "*Ja, auf gehts.*"

I was going, all right. He pushed my feet and launched me up the tube like a submarine missile. I stopped briefly at the top to look for—hell, what was I looking for? My expectations of this moment came from too many movies in which a digital timer counted down the final seconds. But here, there was no timer. There was no telling how much time I had left, no telling if the reel had let the charges slide back down. The bombs could be far away in the clouds or just a few meters away.

I ran across the roof, grabbed the reel, and cranked like hell.

The holes for the locking pin were at the bottom of the reel, but where was the pin? I'd left it right there. An air raid siren screamed in my head: *Yes, Michael, this is the time to panic.*

Still cranking, I found the pin where I had carefully placed it, dusted over by snow.

"I have the pin! I see the red tape! I'll pin the reel now."

"Get out of there, *dummkopf!* IT'S ABOUT TO BLOW!"

Now that was more like it, Boss.

I slammed the pin and sprinted across the roof, then dove headfirst at the ice hole like a seal escaping a white bear. I made no effort to slow myself sliding straight down the frozen tube and shot through the door, sliding across the icy floor and smashing into the far cabin wall.

Der Spiegel slammed the outer door behind me, grabbed my jacket collar, and dragged me into the rock tunnel. He slammed the tunnel door just seconds before the mountain rumbled like an angry god trying to get moist salt from a shaker. We locked eyes in a low-blink-rate intermission, our blood and breath racing with adrenaline.

A pitiful smile came over Der Spiegel's face, shaking his head and mumbling a German word not found in any of my school textbooks. It didn't need translation; the meaning was clear.

So Good. To Be. Alive. My downhill marching cadence easily allowed me to whisk the empty rucksack past the TNT shack, across the Austrian border, out the tunnel past the casket, and back to the employee lounge. The ski lift crew had just assembled for the workday with warm breakfast beers.

Chef poured two shots of Jägermeister for us.

"It's the avalancher's tradition," Der Spiegel explained, raising his shot glass to a mild cheer from the crowd behind us.

They raised their cups in admiration.

Der Spiegel downed his shot without hesitation, smiled, and gave me a sturdy attaboy on the back in front of everyone. "Good work up there today. That was a brave thing you did."

I had earned his approval, validated by public display, as if Dad had told me I was his favorite child in front of all the siblings. My value had increased. My self-worth was elevating, congenital stock skyrocketing.

But nothing had really changed. Underneath it all, I was the same guy in a bathing suit under layers of mountain survival gear, missing Carrie and the beach and wondering where I would go once the snow melted.

I stared at my trophy, the shot glass in my fingertips, questioning why his approval, why his validation held more value than my own. Why was my self-worth attached to Der Spiegel's approval? To anybody's approval, for that matter?

This was no way to live. I could just as easily hold on to the attitude. And I had control over my attitude, right? Why not consider myself valuable every day?

I vowed to keep this change, downed my seventy-proof cough syrup, and gave Der Spiegel a heavy slap on his back.

"Great job up there to you too." I shook his hand as if we were balanced, leveling our ultimate positions as mere humans doing a job.

He'd saved my life. But the humility I should have felt was upstaged by testosterone and hubris. I smiled at the crowd like a big shot, knowing deep inside the question remained if I could make it—really make it—out on my own. Would I always need a Spiegel, a Dad, a coach to keep me on the rails? I'd gone to the edge and made it back. But maybe that hadn't been the edge. Maybe there was something further? What would ever be enough, and how would I know?

I was determined to test my limits, to challenge how far teen invincibility could take me and still live to tell about the next harebrained adventure I could dream up. I had little concern about how I would ultimately find the limit. But with the seasons and my circumstances changing, the limit soon found me.

CHAPTER 3

THE LETTER

I would have written a shorter letter, but I did not have the time.
—Blaise Pascal

The passing storm left clear skies and fresh powder for the morning commute: skiing to our lift assignments. Most of us left breakfast early to enjoy a few runs before the public got their chance to carve fresh powder. And why wasn't this on page one of the employee benefits handbook?

One of the guys called me away from the exit door. "*Ja,* Mike, this way today."

I followed the guys to the upstairs balcony to find the crew clacking like soldiers in a rifle assembly race. Professional skiers assembled along the rail in a tight lineup, laying out skis, snapping boots into bindings, adjusting goggles, and then leaping from the balcony within seconds. Maybe it was the Jägermeister and breakfast beer, but even the stodgy old mountaineers were yelling some gleeful Tyrolean version of "cowabunga" as they leaped. It warmed my heart. Never have men been so excited to commute to their jobs.

The furious hotel manager stomped out on the balcony as the last of us jumped past the *Verboten* signs on the rail. In seconds, his yelling was behind us and laughter was the only sound filtering through feather-light snowflakes.

My über-exciting life as the avalancher came to a halt with my next assignment: skiing from one lift to the next, setting stakes, stringing queues, and sitting by a red button that stopped the lift. Hardly a grind, barely a job, and almost embarrassing to call it work. Most days I'd ski to an assignment, then sit with a beer and a harmonica before skiing back to the Schneefernerhaus for lunch and more of that delicious German beer.

A wooden chair resurrected with baling wire and ski gear stickers leaned against the sunny side of the lift shack. On slow days, I'd sit there for hours practicing Sonny Terry harmonica riffs, occasionally waving to skiers departing the lift.

A young German couple in matching black jackets, black sunglasses, and slicked-back black hair greeted me. "Hallo, Mike— *wie gehts*? Happy birthday!"

"*Danke schöne*, Geralyn." She was a chatty sweetheart who'd introduced herself when I first arrived. Her dude Gerhard? Let's just say opposites attract. "See you guys tonight, *ja*?"

"*Ja*, for sure we will be there. We can't wait—it shall be such fun," Geralyn called out with the excitement of a cheerleader with new pom-poms. Gerhard snapped his slicked head toward me, expressionless behind thin hexagonal shades. "*Ja*. We shall dance like fairies in the night."

"Alisa *und* Franz are right behind us. They're coming too."

"Okay, have a nice *schüss*, you two."

The next couple passed my assembly line of salutations. "Hallo, Alisa. Hallo, Franz."

"*Servus*, Mike, happy birthday to you. See you tonight."

And so my days passed as the greeter, building relationships ten seconds at a time. Some would stop and have lunch at my shack, listen to my harmonica, share their cheeses and breads. We'd talk of

German philosophy or American politics and say we were comrades for life. Honestly, I was a mere acquaintance, the American harmonica kid with the Hollywood cowboy president.

My close friends lived just down the hill. To be clear, "just down the hill" meant a ride up a six-man gondola to the summit, down 14,600 feet in a forty-four-person cable car to a cogwheel train across fields and farms, and then a twenty-minute walk through snow. Only then could I party with my best friends, the people I'd met a few short months ago.

We didn't need a good reason to party. My birthday happened to be this night's excuse, and a get-together before we all left our Alps jobs for summer adventures. Most friends had a plan, a somewhere to go.

I did not.

I waved as the skiers went by, my down slippers propped on an empty propane tank near a tube of sunscreen next to the big red HALT button. Skiers dropped their T-bars as usual, yet one recoil spring didn't retract the rope as expected. I put my harmonica down and readied my hand over the red button. Normally I'd stop the lift, the rope would recoil itself, and I'd hit the green button before the phone rang with a Tyrolean ranter on the line. If I got it right, the lift kept going.

I hit the red button a second too late. The abrupt stop caused the hanging T-bar's momentum to swing forward. The T-bar hit and broke a safety "brittle bar" on the tower, which then allowed the coil to rewind quickly, bouncing off its return guide and wrapping the rope around the sheave train and haul rope at the return terminal—an ugly mess of ropes and towers and T-bar part names. Even uglier were the four-syllable German words when the phone rang.

Der Meehee, the number-two man on the mountain, was on the phone. "*Ja, Mike—was gibts doh?*" was Tyrolean slang for "What's up?"

High German is the pure, refined dialect spoken by the cultured and scholarly North Germans. But in the south, Bavarians are proud of their distinctive dialect, which took me months to understand. Then there's what they speak here in the deep south, the Alps, where the Tyrolean dialect muddles German until it's incomprehensible to foreigners. That's what Der Meehee spoke. Over months of mentoring, the burly Bavarian had taken me under his wing and taught me how to speak Tyrolean, fix ski lifts, turn wrenches on a PistenBully, and play Three-Hand Skat during a two-beer lunch like a proud Tyrolean.

I spoke my best High German into the phone, linking words like sausages to make each part of the ski lift system into one ridiculous, albeit accurate, German term. "Um, *die schnurschächtelchen* (small rope box) *hat selbtsgeeingewickelt* (has self-wrapped), *und* (umm), *gehängend um die sheavezug und geschpinnt…und hat der spröder gebrochen* (hung in the sheave, spun out, and broke the brittle bar)."

The pang in my voice surely made it across the telephone lines to Meehee's ear. I should have stopped talking, but my next nervous babble came out in still more fabulized "ge-thingy-thing" words.

"Tell me in English," Der Meehee barked.

It was as if he'd been speaking English all his life. Turns out he had. He was American—always had been. I'd worked beside him the entire winter and was just now finding this out? Of course. I would have used English as a crutch, lessening my experience in the Alps. He'd guarded his secret carefully.

Der Spiegel appeared like a superhero, as if he'd flown in with a cape or had been waiting there all day for me to screw up. Once again, I explained in German but mostly just pointed to the mess.

"I will tell the skiers on the lift to jump off, this will take some time." He was cool. He'd been down this road this before. It happens. He shook his head and mumbled something in German.

There was that word again.

Der Meehee called back, speaking in clear, calm English. "I sent your roomie Rollan over to help you."

"Thanks, Meehee. By the way, is Meehee your real name?"

"It's Mike Smith, from Idaho. *Meehee* is Tyrol for Mikey."

"Riiight…"

I'd been duped, but Meehee had lived in the Alps long enough to leave his potato peeling past behind. As I donned my work gloves and tool belt, I realized he'd paid me a great a compliment by not being Idahoan with me.

Like Meehee, many things were not as they appeared up on the Zugspitze, a cosmic magnet for the ultrastrange. But Rollan showing up as my roommate was the absolute zenith of bizarre. Rollan Kim and I had been classmates for four years of high school German. Before that, in junior high, we'd had our first two German classes together, and that's when he'd kicked my ass in the seventh-grade schoolyard.

I'd had it coming. I was a jerk. It was the seventies, and I made some stupid comment about his Asian food at the cafeteria table.

"Hey, Rollan, what's that stuff you're eating? Is that kung food?"

I was trying to be funny, a big man impressing my friends with a play on words of the top TV show of the time, *Kung Fu.* Some of my friends laughed, but at Rollan's expense.

Rollan's friends egged him on, and rightly so. The next day in the schoolyard, he put his right heel in my left ear with a roundhouse karate kick, and I got up from the ground seeing stars and a few kids running from the scene of the one-hit grudge match.

Through six years of repudiation, Rollan and I sat at opposite corners of our German classrooms, avoiding eye contact to the bitter end of high school. I didn't hate him. He was a cool, funny guy. He didn't hate me either. Enough water had passed under that bridge, but I didn't have the emotional wherewithal to simply shake hands with him. A pity—had I not been such a butthead and apologized years before, he could have been a great friend. But what's done was done, and technically he was my enemy.

Imagine the crash of my jaw hitting the floor when Der Spiegel walked into my dorm at the top of this hermetic mountain, six thousand miles from German class, and presented new hire Rollan as my roommate. My mortal enemy stood in the doorway with his luggage. I was speechless, breathless, my face was frozen. I looked to heaven involuntarily. Of all the places in the world. Of all the people in the world. *Really, God? Really?*

As a crack formed in the wall around my pride, I began accepting there was a reason for him to be there. Clearly there was some reason. This was no coincidence. How could it possibly be coincidence? How could this possibly happen? Had I not run far enough from my demons? But I was only halfway around the world, isolated by cable cars far above a dinky town no one in all California had ever heard of or could even pronounce. Here in this small cave of a room, hidden within a hotel hanging off the edge of Germany's highest mountain, was the last guy on earth I ever wanted to see.

After a moment, Rollan broke into the biggest smile a person could make without laughing out loud. It was the opposite of when a toddler falls down and the parents judge the baby's pain by the duration of that silent scream. Rollan held his belly, laughing so hard he began to shake in convulsions without a single sound coming out. His Asian eyes beneath big, circular glasses made him look like a Disney animal.

We just stood there repeating "No way!" before Der Spiegel left. "Gentlemen, I'll just let zee two of you get acquainted." He could not have imagined the grenade he'd tossed into the room.

How, God? Why, God?

Talking to God was not part of my daily dialogue. I hadn't been to church or prayed or read a Bible in years. But when a transgression this big comes my way, it's my style to pick up the phone and have it out with the responsible party. Each time I looked to God, I got a smile and a wink, but I still couldn't believe the cosmic karma unpacking in my room. *Our* room. We talked—small talk, of course. Everything was small talk with our unspoken elephant in the room.

And then we went to work.

Days turned into weeks of not talking about that wooly mammoth in our room. We ate dinner together, drank beer together, worked together, and snored together. Six years of water under that bridge had polished the edges of our jagged past. Soon we became mountain buddies, guys who just figured nothing needed to be said. Deny it each day as I would, the silence festered. Something needed to be said, and I would need to become more mature to say it.

But first, we had a ski lift to fix.

Rollan arrived to help untangle my ropes, barely stopping before snowplowing himself into a cushioned pole. Landing this job without a clue how to ski provided me with a constant source of amusement, but I secretly admired the courage it took for an Asian guy with no ear for Tyrolean to be up here with these Alpen roughnecks. He had a great sense of humor about it all.

"That's a fine mess you've gotten us into this time, Ollie."

"Hey Rollan, about Der Meehee. He's American!" I blurted out. "He's Mike Smith from Idaho."

"Yeah—duh. You didn't know that?" He took on a winning gleam of a newbie overshadowing his senior.

"Didn't have a clue. Just found out ten minutes ago when I tried to explain all this mess to him in Tyrol. 'Tell me in English,' he barks. Kinda freaked me out."

Rollan grinned. "You've been here all year. He did that to me on day one, yeah. He yelled at me to shut down the lift. I didn't understand what he was asking and ran as fast as I could to bring him a bucket of grease."

We laughed and got to work on the lift. I climbed the tower as he pulled the tangled ropes. We had experience in what needed to be done, so there wasn't much to say. Except for the big thing to say.

"Mike, there's a letter from Carrie in our mailbox for you," he began. "I figured you'd want me to read it so I—"

My head snapped around to look down at him. "You read my...?"

"Just messin' with ya. I'm not gonna open your girlfriend mail."

I chewed that over. "Big letter?"

"The usual, maybe a few thin pages. No photos. Bummer. It said, 'Big New Inside.' I assume she means news? Oh, and 'Swal cakws.' What's that?"

"Sealed With A Lick 'Cause A Kiss Won't Stick."

"That is so...nice. Cute, I guess?"

I would have described it as lame or mushy, but despite clearly being creeped out, he found a positive word for it. He always did.

I got part of the rope untangled, but it was still stuck. "Okay, Rollan, here's the deal. We could get a PistenBully up here to pull it, but if I hang on this part and you pull me from there, we can tug it clear. Agreed?"

Using the haul cable as a jungle gym, I traversed the cable upside down, Tyrolean style. I wrapped my legs around the coil, pulled the stuck rope, and reached to find Rollan ready to grab my hand. I hung there by my knees, dangling upside down from cables and ropes, locked in a greasy bro handshake, face-to-face with my enemy. I'll never understand why that awkward moment was the time to say it.

"Hey, Rollan, about that thing." Gravity flushed my face. "I've been meaning to tell you for like six years now. I'm sorry."

His face became serious for the second time I'd ever seen the expression on him; the first time had been when he clocked me with his heel.

He continued pulling me in by the hand, but his grip had something more to it. There was no question what "about that thing" meant for us. It was a thing seven years overdue. And now I'd said I was sorry, but there remained an emptiness in his gaze. He needed more. He deserved more.

I stiffened my upper lip—which at that moment would have been my lower lip—and gave it my inverted all.

"I'm sorry for being a jerk to you in seventh grade. Really sorry, for a long time. I'm sorry for saying whatever stupid thing I said. That was wrong, and I've regretted it all these years. I'm sorry you had to kick my ass to defend your honor, and I don't blame you one bit for that. It was the right thing to do. It changed my life; it changed my view of people different than me. Mostly I'm sorry we wasted all those years not being friends in German class, 'cause you're a really cool guy. I'm sorry I didn't say any of this before. And I'm really glad you're here now."

I rather enjoyed his expressionless face with some confidence that my unrehearsed speech had gone well. And as I held his grip, waiting for his reaction, he gazed back through his big round glasses with a sincerity I'd never witnessed before or again. Seven years of clammed-up kung fu fell away with the mass of a spring glacier. There was no characteristic joke to follow.

He was always making faces—it was his thing. But I couldn't understand his next expression. His other hand joined mine for a greasy bro handshake.

"What thing?"

***

Birthday benefits included leaving work a couple of hours early. I grabbed my overnight bag and Carrie's letter and stood in the back of the cable car, ignoring the view to read the letter as we descended: "Hi Mike—I'm so exciting cuz I just found out Mom and Dad have booking a trip to Barcelona to meat Colleen in the end of June. I'm going to Spain after I graduation!"

"She's coming to Spain!" I blurted aloud, which turned a few heads from a glorious view of the Alps.

Carrie's words were angelic music, even as I mentally corrected her grammar with red ticks, desperately hoping that syntax and tagmemics would finally take hold in her last months of high school.

I finished reading the letter out loud to the gondola occupants. Her run-on sentences revealed uncertain travel plans, approximate dates, and a vague span when she might stay in Europe. I spared the riders the two pages of what she planned to wear on the flight.

I could have left Europe to be with her again at any time, but I wasn't done with my adventures. More accurately, I had no plans regarding what I would do once I got home. College? Career? Marriage? Those questions required grown-up-sized answers, and I was scared to death to choose. What if I chose the wrong thing? It was easier to dodge the soul-crushing gravity of those questions.

But by the time I finished the letter, I had a new goal in life: Barcelona by the end of June. Granted, it was only a short-term goal, but it changed the freak-out-about-life questions into a bite-sized issue of what came next. Carrie was coming to me; I didn't need to leave Europe. I just needed a way to get to Barcelona by June. Wheels in my head began to turn.

At the bottom, I stopped to mail a stack of letters and call Carrie from the post office phones. I plunked down a large cash deposit for a phone booth and connected with Carrie's dad, the big-time district attorney.

"Oh hey, Bob. Sir. It's Mike calling from Germany. Is Carrie home?"

"No, Carolyn is not in at the moment."

"Oh, okay. Do you know when she might be in?"

"I'm her dad, not her calendar."

"Um, okay. I'm calling from Germany. Could you leave her a message?"

"As I said, I'm her father, not her secretary. My job is to protect her from things that could harm her, like boys over eighteen."

"I-I was calling her so we could talk today, on my birthday. Today."

"Oh, it's your birthday? That's great news."

"Well, thank you." I smiled, foolishly believing he'd extended a birthday greeting.

"And that means you can be prosecuted as an adult now."

"Actually, I'm nineteen now."

"So I've wasted a year?"

I can't say Bob never liked me, but after I modified the Porsche 914 he bought Carrie and it accidentally burned to the ground, he was surely not a fan.

"You're all coming to Europe," I continued. "That's exciting. Could you tell me the date when Carrie arrives in Barcelona?"

"Carolyn will have to talk with you about that. Carolyn is the name I gave her. Carolyn."

"Do you know the date she—I mean Carolyn—arrives?"

"Yes. Yes, I do." I assumed he was looking at a calendar or something. Or maybe not. "This is a family trip, Mike."

"Maybe I should try calling later. I better go now. This is a very expensive call for me."

"Oh, I'm so sorry about that, Mike. I'd reverse the charges for you, but I'm still making payments on her incinerated Porsche. By the way, how is the weather there in Germany?"

"Well, it's cold, and there's plenty of snow, but the sun is shining today. We've had some storms lately."

"I see. And, uh, are the storms making new snow?"

"It is the Alps. Everything gets covered in snow."

"Is it wet snow? Or is it more of a dry snow? How would you describe it?"

I finally realized he was running out my clock. After a few more Deutsch marks down the drain for the sake of diplomacy, I closed. "Well, it's been nice talking with you, sir. Could you tell Carrie—*Carolyn*—that I miss her? I miss her so much it hurts."

"You should have thought about that before you left her crying for a year."

CHAPTER 4

THE PARTY

It takes a long time to become young.
—Pablo Picasso

Best friends Joel and his girlfriend Cathy—Texas Cath, as we favored her—waited at the pizza joint, where we'd blow our cash on cheap cheese slices before investing in Munich's finest beers in the village bar. It was a last hurrah before Joel left town.

"News from the post: I got a line on a boat job in Italy," Joel said with curbed pride. "It doesn't pay much, but it's a real job on some rich prick's yacht." He described it as if the ad were written this way. "Beats washing dishes here. Sailing to Cannes for the Film Festival, Monaco Grand Prix—and that, my little chum, will look great on a résumé."

His excited hands sailed from side to side, but Cathy's Mona Lisa smile told a different story. I suspected their final hours of being a couple was eating at her heart.

"Is it still Chicago for you, Cath?" I asked, hoping some talk about her plans would take the edge off.

"If Greenpeace still wants me to work for free, I'm off to the Windy City."

"Perhaps you'll save some whales off Italy? Maybe rescue a lonely sailor?" I couldn't tell if she'd be chasing Joel around the world or if this really was their last night together.

"No San Remo for me. Joel will have to get used to a life of celibacy." She looked for solace at the bottom of her beer glass and then got up to use the ladies' room. I assumed Joel was going to follow her, but he only stood habitually because his lady arose.

Joel and Cathy were the It Couple in our circle, the adventurous twosome with humorous, dynamic, winning spirits. She was the towering blond goddess with a Southern drawl, radically different from his West Virginia drawl, or so I was told. They sounded like peas in a pod to me. I was their third wheel, lusting after Cathy's affections while fighting an Oedipal darkness that secretly wanted Joel dead.

Ski bums by day, outlaw dishwashers by night, my friends' fantasy lives had made me green with envy when I first arrived in town as a guest. I'd sleep an occasional night on their greasy linoleum floor until I had enough pseudo-loyalty points to progress to the lumpy vinyl sofa and take pity on the new stray on the floor. Later, when I got my job on Zugspitze, Joel, Mitch, and I would close the local bars, travel to beer festivals, and count the midnight stars over the Alps while trying to figure out what women were thinking—well, mostly Cathy.

Joel was one hell of a writer too. I often reread the inspirational words he wrote inside the cover of a journal he gave me. I carried that journal throughout the rest of my days in Europe. I might have found my way to the top of Maslow's hierarchy of needs, but I didn't realize how much I counted on Joel's wisdom to keep me on top.

I tried changing the conversation with Joel by gushing about Carrie, a buzz he quickly killed. "So what happens after Barcelona? You run off with the girl in Spain. Sounds great, but then what?"

"It's just like you to ruin a perfectly good birthday with your weight-of-the-world questions," I said with a sigh. "Is it too much to want simple banter about my freewheelin', devil-may-care plans? Maybe I'll go get married. My friend Guy is getting married."

Joel was too close a friend to leave me alone with my sophomoric ideals. "This growing up thing, it's horrific. It's downright tragic. You're like a caterpillar, Mike. You've spent your entire life eating leaves, but now your juvenile hormones have wasted away, naturally causing you to hole up in a cocoon. But while you were up there in your Zugspitze cocoon, your maturing body naturally triggered this caterpillar metamorphosis. Your kid brain started to disintegrate. It involuntarily started digesting itself like a caterpillar in a cocoon, in some sort of protein soup, changing your whole composition. Eventually you'll grow wings and come out as a nectar-eating butterfly."

"Geez, you sure know a lot about caterpillars."

"I used to be one."

Cathy came back to the table with a fresh smile and the attitude we'd come to love.

Joel stood and positioned her chair. "And welcome back, my sweet little nectar." He gave me a wink, making sure I got the reference.

"So what are you boys talking about? Did I miss anything?"

"Not much. Just digesting my own brain in primordial protein soup."

"I must have been gone longer than I thought."

"But Mike—you finally wake up," Joel continued, "and eventually you find yourself in a butterfly body with a butterfly mind. Horrific and tragic for the caterpillar, yes, yet somehow all of us species on this planet have to grow up and figure it all out."

"Are you going to start singing 'First There Is A Mountain' by Donovan?" Cathy asked.

"Don't have to. It's already playing in your head."

When we got to the Von Steuben bar, half the people there called me by name. I was flattered, but it said more about Joel and Cathy's popularity than my own. Among them was Mitch, my first real friend in Germany and the only reason I ever made it to this town.

Mitch splashed a little beer off the top of a full-sized jackboot made of glass and carried it to the table. We were about to play a game we called Das Boot, an Oktoberfest drinking game for the whole table. *Das boot* means "the boat" in German and has nothing to do with footwear. When Mitch landed the huge glass boot on the long table, we acted like Mexican children about to bust open a piñata.

"Get us started there, boortday boy." Mitch didn't speak a lick of German but could parody the accent like a true Bavarian. He said everything he needed in the German language came from watching *Hogan's Heroes* reruns.

I took five gulps from the boot, wiped the foam mustache from my peach-fuzz mustache, and passed the boot back to Mitch.

"Don't Bogart Das Boot, bro," I warned. "Just a little sip for you."

I had no real fear that Mitch would down the remaining liters, but the man had drunk me under the table more than once that winter.

"A sip from ol' Mitchy? You forget who you're talkin' to, brutha." Hailing from Escondido, Mitch was the most laid-back dude I'd ever met, even by Californian standards. "Then again, we're playing Das Boot, and this means war."

He chugged a healthy share as the group thumped the thick table, chanting, "Drink, drink!"

Das Boot has one simple rule: finish the beer, and the person who passed it to you pays for it. A few glass boots go around the table each night, and it's usually someone's girlfriend who ends up with the bill. At least until she smiles at her boyfriend with the wallet.

The trick is not to drink with the toe pointing up; you'll get a beer shower when the displaced air splashes two liters of beer from the toe to your face. We never told new players about that part. Marsha from San Francisco, the new girl one night, had gotten a beer shower just moments before I met her. I laughed all the way to the napkin stacks across the room and back, as she dried her flower-adorned hair. I did my best not to get caught looking at her braless form under a T-shirt covered in cold beer. She didn't catch me, but Texas Cath shook her head and chopped her fingers with that horrible *tsk-tsk-tsk* sound.

Nobody got doused tonight, though, and old friends brought by birthday gifts. Mitch gave me a useless wristwatch from a secondhand store. The hands had fallen off, the crystal was gone, and Mitch had inked "NOW" on the face. "Hey man, I'm not into time" was his signature line, a sentiment I teased him about at every opportunity.

Marsha had hand-knotted a hemp-string friendship bracelet for me with beads of peace, courage, vitality, wisdom, and some other hocus-pocus braided into it. She tied it around my wrist, explaining the purpose of each lovingly selected bead and petting my hand while reciting some mystical whammy that was inaudible over the live band. Later we danced, and she told me the bracelet was for luck. When I asked if I'd get lucky on my birthday, she just smiled and kept on dancing like a pretty version of Janis Joplin.

Cathy's voice was true to every Lone Star cliché, and her alpha roar filled the room from across the bar. "Jam some harmonica, Mike!"

I stood in with the band, playing some CCR so Mitch could do his horrible dancing. The applause of friends was more intoxicating than a boot full of beer.

In the back corner, Cathy and Joel were cable knit into a single tight sweater.

I scooted a pesky chair between the lovebirds and wrapped my arms around them. "I can't believe we're all going separate ways. It's going to be different around here. Definitely a birthday to remember."

Cathy snuggled in, sentimental. "That's why we're all here, Mike. Because of you."

"It's also why we're all leaving, Mike—because of you," Joel mimicked.

We laughed before he began waxing philosophical again.

"Look around," he said. "None of us will ever go back to the selves we were before we arrived. And you at—what, nineteen today? You jive turkey, livin' large up there on top of the world, you have a huge head start on life with all this."

Joel's words shaped my world. He made me use my brain, made me work for it, showing me examples of my life's impact on others and how fortunate I was. Like Der Spiegel's appeal, Joel satisfied my yearning for a protector and leader.

I settled back in my chair. "I just want to grow up and be more…like me, I guess? Make it on my own two feet. Not needing anyone."

As casual as it sounded, my self-actualization mantra was actually well rehearsed. Each time I said it out loud, the lie felt less caustic in my gut. Needing others did cause pain, in my limited experience, and was therefore an adversary that needed to be conquered before I could become my own man. In reality, growing up was my greatest fear. Even the word "responsibility" triggered pangs of a potential peptic ulcer. "Fake it till you make it" was my mantra, force-feeding myself a positive mental attitude despite the pain.

They raised their mugs. "Then here's to Mike's feet. Happy birthday, buddy."

"Last call," the bartender yelled from behind a picket fence of Bavarian beer taps.

Mitch landed another big gray mug in front of me and rallied us to go howl at the full moon.

As all great stories with bad endings begin, "Hey buddy, hold my beer and watch this" was the last thing I told Mitch on my way to a lamppost across the street, for reasons I could never begin to justify. Maybe being closer to the moon would be even better for howling? I shimmied the lamppost to the top, stood on the crossbeams, and howled.

Mitch had tied my beer mug handle with a good knot to a long hemp string I dangled from above. He probably didn't realize I had carelessly unraveled the bracelet Marsha gave me earlier, mystical whammy beads of all colors bouncing off his head.

"I'm on top of the world!" I yelled. I howled like a wolf. I drank my beer. I caused someone nearby to call the *Polezei*.

The first patrol car screeched to a stop.

"It's the fuzz, everybody—run!" Mitch muffed his getaway attempt by rolling over a hedge in front of the bar. The patrol car spotlight and the hedge's inability to support any weight more than a beach ball thwarted his ridiculous plan, but he didn't spill a drop of beer. He arose covered in twigs and snow, hands over his head in comedic drama. "I am not a crook," he repeated in a lousy Nixon impression.

I was wobbling with hilarity but couldn't laugh out loud; even a shushed snicker would have landed me in jail. From my perch above, the drama was as crisp as the night air.

Joel began a red herring tale, appropriately raucous for a 2 a.m. drunk. "Officer, we just came out to have a smoke—you know, *rauchers*." He pantomimed puffing.

"Yeah man, we're just tokin' a fatty out here, it's cool." Mitch's lingo was a test to see if they understood California stoner slang.

One officer made routine ID checks on everyone, inspecting troublemaker Mitch's passport photo with a bright flashlight in his squinting face. Mitch kept his arms raised, still preaching peace.

The second officer pulled Joel aside, emptying Joel's pockets and scrutinizing every stamp in his passport. "You came out for a smoke, *ja*? Well, then, Herr Cook, where are the cigarettes?"

Busted.

"A rather astute question, my perceptive plodder." Joel stirred up a pot of southern bullshit and served it with an ear-to-ear grin, politely connecting with the officer by the name on his badge. "Well, ya see, that's just the thing, Officer Wiener."

"It's 'Werner.'"

"Oh, right. Like I was saying, Officer Vermin, we all came out for a cigarette." Joel continued the smoking pantomime. "But…but then…it came to us that, well…none of us smoke. I guess we'll all just go back inside now—and thank god we'll be spared from lung cancer. Thank you for coming out, Officer Vinegar."

The cop shoved a flashlight into Joel's face with one hand, holding his passport with the other. I gulped. A worrisome stopwatch starts ticking the very moment you surrender your passport to any government official. From that moment, your life is literally in their hands. Joel's clock was ticking.

I trembled, trying not to laugh, cough, sneeze, or gasp. But I really, *really* had to pee. Cathy, scared to death for Joel and me, couldn't help but glance toward the light post. One of the officers caught her tell and searched the bushes below me with his powerful light. Twenty feet above him, I'd never held so still in all my life as the light bobbed slowly back and forth. He picked up one of Marsha's beads, inspected it, and began to tip his hat upward.

Mitch raised rebellious hands high. "Hey man, we didn't do it! War's over if you want it, give peace a chance, man. This ain't no party, this ain't no disco, this ain't no foolin' around."

It worked. Mitch got a German lecture with a flashlight tight in his face.

I considered surrendering. I couldn't let my friends take a fall for me. But then the squad car radios rattled out something more important, and the passports were returned as quickly as they had been taken. They police drove away and my friends went back inside. Deathly afraid of getting caught climbing down the post, I stayed put, wondering how long before it was either safe to climb back down or my bladder burst. It was a nice night, after all. I had the city, the stars, and the Alps all to myself.

I drank from my big stein until I couldn't hold my bladder any longer and worked out a safe way to yellow the snow on the sidewalk below. My hands were too busy to pound my chest and Tarzan yell. *Look at me—I'm nineteen and look where I am, look what I'm doing. This amazing moment is the mirror image of my life.*

The heavy beer mug slipped from my numb fingers as I fumbled to zip my fly, tumbling straight down like an elevator—level, steady, not a single drop spilling along the silent descent—until shattering with a thunderous crash on the sidewalk. Ceramics and brew blasted 360 degrees from ground zero.

A mirror image of my life, indeed. I slid down the pole and ran like hell.

CHAPTER 5

MICE WILL PLAY

The most I can do for my friend is simply be his friend.
—Ralph Waldo Emerson

We said our goodbyes over a traditional Bavarian breakfast of white sausage, beer, and pretzels. After back-patting hugs that sent down feathers flying from our jackets, I crossed the street and stuck out my thumb to hitch a ride back to work. Joel headed the opposite way with his thumb held high.

Two guys on opposite sides of the street wiping tears in unison wouldn't have caught most people's eye. Joel always told me, "Look happy and friendly, you'll hitch a ride faster," so I did my best to smile.

"Smile, Jarvis!" came from across the street, right on cue.

"No, *you* smile," I shouted back. "You look like a mortician over there."

As expected, he got picked up by the third car, a hot blond babe in a BMW, and away he went, leaving me with a bittersweet warmth like giving a puppy to a good family. I dropped my thumb and started walking. No blond babes were stopping for me, nor did I want one to question why my eyes were pink as a rabbit's.

Only a few days of work left on top of old Zugspitze. My final nights at the Schneefernerhaus were spent packing up and hauling boxes down by cogwheel train. I shipped all my winter clothes to California over several trips down the mountain, staying at Mitch's place every night.

Except for the night I slept with Cathy.

I stopped by her work to say hello, but she'd called in sick, so I walked to her studio to check on her. I found her at her sickly worst: drop-dead gorgeous in a thin flannel pajama top, surrounded by a sea of scrunched pillows and discarded tissue wads. The gentleman alarm rang in my head: *I shouldn't be here.* The exalted Texas Cath, half-naked and vulnerable in her bed after Joel's departure, did not add up to a good buddy formula. I had to get out of there, and not because I didn't want to catch her cold—dear god, I would have loved to catch her cold. But it just wasn't right.

Yet even as platonic friends, some repressed caveman marauder inside me wanted to grab her.

"I'm so happy it's you," she said around a completely clogged nose. "You're not the Grim Reaper coming to take me. Maybe I was hoping for Grim? I dunno. Well, here I am in all my glory. It's official. I'm dying."

She reached for the usual hug, awkward from the bed, and a boob fell out of her haphazardly buttoned top.

"Oh, good god, I'm a mess," she said through a laugh connected to a whooping cough. She fell back into her pillows and tossed another wadded tissue to the pile.

There was just no way for a gentleman to hug a half-naked girl in bed. What if Joel had walked in from Italy right then?

I shuffled backward. "I'm going to get you some hot soup."

"Thank you, honey. You such a sweetheart." I loved when she called me honey. "And if it's not too much trouble for you, could you pick me up something from the pharmacy, like NyQuil? Or cough syrup? Or a gun?"

"Of course I will." I would have brought her an aircraft carrier if she'd asked.

An hour later I returned with a care package. I kept her company throughout her slurpy dinner and then read her a book until she slipped into a NyQuil coma, upright with plastic spoon in hand.

Now what? I wiped the soup from her chin and cleared dinner from her comforter as she sat like a statue, blond tendrils finding their way deep into her cleavage. Oh, the devious thoughts I worked hard to suppress. With her eyes shut, I no longer needed to suppress the stiffy I'd been hiding in my pants for half the night.

She wasn't going sleep well sitting up with her neck cocked like that. To be helpful, to make her comfortable, I would have to put my hands on her, which made me fearful that she might wake up and believe that I was doing something naughty. I mulled it over and pushed on her shoulder with two fingers. She slumped to one side, pulling most of her bedding with her. I quickly pulled the covers over her now seductively exposed bare butt.

Okay, maybe "quickly" wasn't entirely accurate.

I kissed my fingertips and tapped her head softly. By then it was well after midnight and not a time to be walking all the way across town to Mitch's. Cathy's place was closer to the train station, and I had an early train to Munich to catch—no sense in doubling back at sunrise. And so I slept in Cathy's chair, using knit scarves and a year's worth of her laundry as blankets, pacified by the soft rhythm of her wheezing breath.

CHAPTER 6

MAKING PLANS

A good traveler has no fixed plans, and is not intent on arriving.
—Lao Tzu

The morning train to Munich was empty enough that I could stretch across a row of seats and catch up on the sleep I missed in Cathy's chair. I awoke just minutes outside of the capital of Bavaria, about the time Cathy must have been coming out of her NyQuil coma to find the note I left on top of neatly folded stacks of laundry beside her chair.

My mission began at Sport Scheck, the world's greatest sports store. It was impossible to avoid a certain amount of awe for their five-story climbing wall with alpinists actively ascending a central shaft past departments for every sport ever played. Looking up from the foyer felt like standing at the base of the Eiger or one of nature's boldest granite walls. Each floor featured a different sport or season. This being Europe, the first floor was all about soccer, with shoes, balls, and…well, more shoes, I guess. I rode the elevator to the second floor: CYCLING.

An inspiring method of getting to Barcelona would catch my eye, I was sure of it. It had to be unique. It had to have character. Bravado. Traveling by train? Too touristy. By VW Camper? Too spendy. By tour bus? Come on, I wasn't ninety. Hitchhiking? Walking? The ideas were adventurous and would allow me to experience every inch of the journey, but where was the fun in walking? It was all downhill from the Zugspitze, that was true, but I'd surely run out of snow—and I couldn't ski to Barcelona. The motorcycle idea had merit, but the challenges of buying, licensing, and insuring mounted as high as the Zugspitze itself.

Bigger-than-life posters pitched happy cyclists touring wine valleys and bicycles with stuffed panniers parked beside tents and hot air balloons. It looked like a beautiful lifestyle, but what I'd do with the bike and my stuff when I wanted to stop and use a toilet had me perplexed. I had no buddy and therefore no buddy system. Besides, a tour bicycle was so cliché. Maybe a unicycle—now that would be really different. What would panniers for a unicycle look like? I daydreamed of whisking Carrie away by hot air balloon. That's the bravado I was after.

I proceeded upward, past the scuba diving and kayaking level— Wait, scuba, kayaks? Never mind—and straight to camping. One way or another, I'd be making some investments on the camping floor. Backpacks, stoves, sleeping bags—you name it, they had three dozen choices, everything from survival flint bracelets to battery-operated hair dryers.

I wasn't much of a camper, but two things I knew for sure. If Carrie were along on this trip, she'd have bought that blow-dryer. And I would've been the guy to carry it, along with the five hundred pounds of extra batteries needed to run the darn thing for thirty seconds. That was just the price a guy paid to have the prettiest girl in the world, right?

I was going imaginary broke and deaf listening to the cash register in my head ring up gear, but I wasn't getting closer to Barcelona. I rode up to the top floor: SKI AND WINTER SPORTS.

With winter behind us, not a salesperson or shopper was in sight among the clearance skis, roller sports, and service techs.

Perhaps some desperation from being on the last floor pushed me into my wild idea, but once I hit it, I knew it was the strategy for me.

I formulated my plan.

***

In exactly thirty-four minutes—every time—the S-Bahn would take me from Munich to the Kleins' house, where I'd soon be hugging the down duvet on the bed where I'd slept for two months after arriving in Germany last fall. Safe, secure, comfortable... There are so many ways to describe the feelings of home, but mostly you just want to bury your face in a clean, soft pillow and exhale for a full minute.

The Klein home had been my first destination in Europe eight months ago. I flew from Los Angeles to Frankfurt and arrived with red eyes, not from lack of sleep but from bawling in self-pity through my New York layover. I'd left everyone I loved behind. I'd popped the bubble of parental protection with a jet airliner, flushed all notions of being a child down that stinky New York toilet in JFK International where I cowered for hours. I sat and watched shadowy movements through the door cracks and listened to men from around the world fart, piss, and make disgusting poop sounds. No other kids were hiding or sobbing.

When I arrived in Germany, I had an arrangement to meet the man of the house, Dieter, at the main train station, Munich Hauptbahnhof. Dieter would take me to my new German home and family, and become my German dad. I was invited me for two months but he later extended the invitation to as long as I wanted. Things were going great with my older brother Berhard, younger brother Georg, and Dieter's wife Traude—my new German mom, quickly to be dubbed *Mütti*. Aunt Emmy was also a delightful part of the Bavarian home.

Dieter secured a paid internship for me at his job, got me a work permit and an S-Bahn pass. Within a month, I had the language down pat and felt comfortable mucking around in the foreign land. My parents came to visit while traveling Europe, and I was proud to show them all I had learned about Munich—my town.

My parents and I were hoisting beer steins at Hofbräuhaus when Carla was showing her travel pal Samantha—Sam—"a mere glimpse" of the world of salty radish Slinkys, steering-wheel-sized pretzels, and never-changing oompah music in the world's most famous beer hall. Our über-breasted, dirndl-dressed beer frau had lugged another round of ceramic steins to our table, unloading upon the sixteenth-century hardwood table with festive splashing. Our cheers caught the attention of Carla and Sam.

The young ladies had been traveling together for safety, but, as Carla explained, scanning for cute guys came before safety. "Walk all the way to the back, then we're straight back out," Carla promised her reluctant partner.

Sam was aghast at what she called the Olympics of frat-boy drinking. "Look at the size of that beer. If we lived here a week, the two of us couldn't finish one of those."

That's when Carla caught a glimpse of our all-American table: Mom, Dad, and their travel friend Doctor Jim.

She wiggled her "follow me" finger at Sam. "Maybe we should at least try?"

Dad broke the ice, then casually bowed out and left me blunder on my own—the ultimate wingman. Oh, to be confident and charming enough to just walk up to girls and begin talking with them as if nothing's wrong with that. I studied his every move and memorized every joke, but his style was beyond magical. His opening line got the girls laughing, and before they could say "g'suffa," they were each sitting behind a liter of beer at our table.

Carla and I shared pretzels between long, pining smiles over weeks' worth of beer in her mug. By the end of the night's music and beer games, she'd consumed two.

We said good night, reserving goodbye for the next morning at the Munich main station where I was to meet the folks for a day of Munich sightseeing. I arrived at Track 31, baffled to find Carla and Sam in a goodbye hug. Carla and I waved as the Orient Express whisked Sam away to Paris. This was not the plan.

"It appears you've missed your train," I said lightly.

"I guess I forgot my luggage," she said with a shrug. "Not that I had an inkling of putting my luggage on that train with her."

I raised my eyebrows, waiting.

"Lying in bed last night, I caught on that this town has more to offer than Sam's *Munich in a Minute* pamphlet showed. This town's probably a lot of fun. I just need a guy-d."

Had she just said "guy" or "guide"? Her play was laid upon on the table: terse, deliberate, forward. It excited the hell out of me to meet a girl so dauntless, funny, and flirty.

"Well, my dear, you're in luck," I replied. "There happens to be a personally guided tour of Munich today." I looked for the enormous clock on the train station wall. "And it starts right now. But I caution: this tour might go late into the night."

"Is this the one that ends up getting sloppy drunk at Hofbräuhaus until 2 a.m.? Already been on that one."

I nodded as wisely as a nineteen-year-old could. "The beer tour can be rough for some. But the wine tour, you'll like."

"'In wine, there is wisdom; in beer, there is freedom; in water, there is bacteria,' says the old proverb. I'm free to drink the wine." She took my arm, connecting us like high-voltage electromagnets. "Well, tour guy-d, let's get started."

Mom and Dad's faces lit up to find Carla with me at our meeting point near their hotel. Radiant with class, character and comedy, Carla greeted them with hugs like a Sunday dinner guest. They weren't the type to pry with questions.

"Where's your friend Sam?" Dad's friend blurted, the pry bar of the mature group.

"I'm guessing Stuttgart by now?" Carla painted away the drama with five words and an engaging smile. Something had happened, Carla and Michael were happy, and it was time to tour Munich. Another word about the subject was unnecessary.

They say there aren't enough hours in a day to enjoy the German Technical Museum—or so Dad would have argued after spending the day pondering a giant statue of Goethe from the bench next to the men's room. Apparently, Hofbräuhaus really did him in.

But Carla was frisky as a lamb.

"Five-hundred-year-old churches, centuries of German technology, two-story cuckoo clocks. Is that all Munich has to offer, *mein* tour guy-d?"

"I'd have to check your booking, *Fraulein*, but I think you signed up for the late tour, which includes a little basement *Glühwein* bar. Would you meet me at Sendlinger Tor in an hour, after I walk the folks home?"

"I'll grab a coat and see you there."

A couple of old churches, an oompah beer parade, and a nice lunch watching the Rathaus-Glockenspiel was more than enough excitement for one day. Dad and the others returned to their hotel early, exhausted. I hugged them goodbye, then ran from their hotel to Sendlinger Tor in time to behold Carla's burgundy beret coming up the subway stairs, complete with matching scarf, gloves, and cheeks.

We shared an umbrella in the light rain, winding through cobbled streets of old Munich to a basement bar by the fourteenth-century gothic gate.

At a fireside table over warm mulled *Glühwein*, we chatted, flirted, and eventually dared plan a weekend rendezvous in Carla's town. Returning the tour favor was our guise. Over the following weeks as my letters chased her around Europe by general delivery, we decided on a time and place to meet in Paris, the city of romance.

***

Carla and I continued writing letters for weeks while she toured Italy and I worked in Munich. I eventually found myself stepping off the Orient Express at Paris Est train station. I had detailed instructions from her last letter.

"A cab ride from the train isn't far or expensive," Carla wrote, "and it's your best choice to navigate the new city after an all-nighter on the train."

Those German-to-French lessons I took were put to the test when it came time to pronounce the hotel address to the Parisian cab driver. My friends cautioned that if I butchered the French language in Paris, the retaliation could be particularly harsh. Based on the cabbie's criminal appearance, I'd be wise to have my affairs in order before hacking up his language.

Here's the deal with numbers in French. In ancient times as they were inventing the language, France's royal word creator was so pleased with his creation of *soixante* (for "sixty") that he went on a wine bender and didn't return that afternoon to the Royal Bureau of Making Shit Up. As this well-documented story goes, the royal mathematician had to step in to meet the king's five o'clock deadline for creating words for "seventy," "eighty," and "ninety." Lacking creativity in his engineering mind, the numerical numbskull added sixty to ten (*dix*) to create the word for "seventy" (*soixante-dix)*, then multiplied four twenties for "eighty" (*quatre-vingts)*. For "ninety," I might have gone with three times thirty, but the mathematician came up with the equation of four times twenty plus ten. That's the verbal arithmetic involved in using three words to create the word "ninety" (*quatre-vingt-dix)*, aka "four twenties and ten." It sounds like an impossible hand of cards and requires challenging French elocution plus a pocket calculator. The system is so bad that both the word creator and the mathematician were beheaded by guillotine the very next morning. True story.

The phrase *"quatre-vingt-six rue Vaneau"* was a challenge I accepted, pocket dictionary in hand. The word for "eighty," it told me, was *quatre-vingts*, neither part of which could I say properly. "Six" was just *six*, pronounced "seese." The idea I had was to say the numbers individually, as in "eight, six," but I still wasn't sure how to pronounce *"huit"*—like "wheat," maybe? "Nine," *neuf*—like hoof—I could say correctly. And thus, I formulated a plan as bad as the numerical system: I would ask for a ride to 99 rue Vaneau, then walk a block back to the hotel.

"Neuf neuf rue Vaneau." The driver didn't get it. I raised my voice like foreigners do, as if volume begets comprehension. *"Neuf neuf rue Vaneau,"* I barked repeatedly, *"Neuf neuf."* I sounded like dog with a cleft lip.

Finally, I scribbled the address on paper and was whisked away to 99 rue Vaneau. I still had to walk a block, for I was too deep into my ludicrous plan to write the actual address.

The back of that taxi is the place I sold my soul. I'm pretty sure I had morals and standards at that point but approaching the hotel door was my last chance to back out of meeting a woman at a hotel. I was Meeting a Woman—a beautiful, fascinating, sexy, and passionate woman who sparked a bonfire in my heart—at a Parisian hotel. We would be sharing a room. Did that mean one or two beds? Or maybe I'd have the sofa? No matter the configuration, my naïve simpleton act wouldn't play. I knew damn well what it all meant, and I was kidding myself that it would be all things platonic once we were in the room together with the door closed.

The original plan had been innocent enough. I showed Carla Munich, and she would show me Paris. Just friendly travelers traversing Europe; what could happen? It was all so logical and virtuous as weeks of mail from Venice to Vienna, Prague to Paris, became an actual plan. But who was I kidding? It may even have turned out so chaste if Carla had had pure and innocent intentions about the weekend. She didn't. But as I rode in the taxi, I didn't know that. I still had a chance to choose to remain faithful to my loving, devoted Carrie. And yet here I was in the world capital of romance, soon to be with a sexy woman in a hotel by ourselves for the entire weekend—a bad idea for my devoted soul. Oh, who the hell was I trying to kid?

The streets of Paris were enveloping me like a lover's embrace, and I was slipping into a French affair like a warm bath.

First came the reasoning stage. I'd had no contact from Carrie in a couple of months, so maybe we were on a break? Yeah, we were on a break. We'd had breaks before; in fact, every winter we would break up and get back together like magnets in the Avalon summer nights. The problem with the "on a break" excuse was I hadn't told her that we were on a break. I wasn't buying my half-truth about this affair, and I shouldn't be selling this bullshit to myself either.

The next sanctification was self-pity. What about my lonely, poor, lost, unloved, and desperate heart? Oh, puleeeeease—as if being pitiful would ease my guilt. This stank worse than self-perjury.

I tried denial again. Maybe nothing would happen? Denial was a mental masturbation exercise I was as practiced in as the exercise of skating.

And if something were to happen? I'd just have to keep the secret forever... It wasn't like I'd go write a book about it or anything.

"*Bonjour.* You have a room for Jarvis?"

The hotelier at the desk leaned through his cloud of smoke to check a registry card in a little metal box. "*Oui.* You are Carla Befera Jarvis?"

"No, I am Jarvis. Carla should be here soon."

"*Oui.* And *la Carla*, she is your wife, *non?*"

"Carla is my friend."

He began a gentle nod while suppressing the "yeah, sure she's your friend" smirk. A lifetime of Parisian hotelier instinct told him exactly what was going on, and he sang a few bars of some French love song, joyful like a bubbly champagne, that the spell of his great city was charming the pants off another couple. He stretched for a key hung high on a wall behind his desk and gave me directions to the top floor.

By the fifth floor, the staircase had changed from classy marble and carpet to quaint wood and wrought iron. The final flight creaked to the slant-ceilinged lofts above. The garrets of Hotel Vaneau's sixth floor were budget-friendly attics at best. Slightly taller than crawl space at the top of the building, this room was the least prestigious in the hotel. The door hit the pitched ceiling as I entered. Steep sloped ceilings offered usable walking space for about half the room, and the rest was only accessible by ducking. I slunk about the room avoiding beams and ductwork. Clean, cozy, and economical, with a certain *je ne sais quoi* only a Paris loft could arouse.

I laughed at myself for having been initially impressed by the furnishings. What I'd considered pricey decor from some fancy French antiques store, like the stuff they have in Beverly Hills homes, was simply Parisian garage sale surplus. The streets below bustled with action through leaded glass, and I opened the dormer windows for a breath of crisp January air, once again bumping my head on the ceiling. I turned around while rubbing it. The brass bed was covered in a vestal white duvet, feathery light, a giant soap bubble floating inches over the bed. I was afraid to touch anything and ruin this experience for Carla. I put a cool towel over the lump on my head, took my shirt off, and was freshening up with a bird bath and a clean shave when that sixth flight of stairs started to creak again.

The stairs described someone excited, racing up. I was almost done shaving, standing with my razor in blue jeans, as Carla crossed the finish line through the open door.

She was flushed, intoxicated by endorphins, out of breath from six flights with a suitcase. She burst in like a reporter, the letter I mailed her in hand.

"The hotel proprietor just handed me your letter," she panted, biting cashmere gloves from her fingertips. Their Beaujolais purple matched her nail polish and flushed cheeks. "My heart stopped. My hands started trembling with this idea that I'd traveled from Vienna to Paris for a Dear Jane letter. He just watched me from behind his cloud of Gauloises, then calmly dropped the word that the blond American was up in the room."

She threw her arms and my letter around my neck. Her adorable smile tickled my chest hair. We squeezed tight without a word.

I was first to break the clinch, before her Beaujolais beret could tickle my nose to a sneeze. I lifted her head, raising her chin to my face. The customary French pecks on cheeks quickly flared into the other French kissing. Like starving animals, we stood groping and grinding and kissing until we fell into bed and found ourselves naked under the soap bubble duvet.

We never even shut the door.

***

After moving out to live in the Alps, I would return for dinner at the Klein's and an overnight whenever possible.

"*Alzo*, Mike, how is the job on the Zugspitze?" Dieter asked while plating his dinner.

"Well, I've quit my job."

That was a statement even part-time parents didn't want to hear unless it was followed by news of a college scholarship or lottery winnings. A dramatic pause passed as the family made eye contact around the silent table.

"Ski season's over, and pretty much everyone will be out of work soon anyway," I said. "It's seasonal. It's expected. I'm having Sport Scheck make me a custom pair of roller skates."

"*Ja*, okay. *Und?*" Traude, or *Mütti* as I would call my German mom, was as concerned about what came next as any good mother would be.

I told them about Carrie's letter, about Barcelona. But I wasn't ready to tell them what I'd actually come to tell them, so I described a little of what Carrie would wear on the flight.

"And you and Carrie will roller-skate in Barcelona?" Mütti was agreeable but confused.

I hadn't verbalized my crazy plan out loud yet. Once it came out of my mouth, I would be committed.

"We'll skate in Barcelona when I get there, but first…" I took a deep breath—a last chance to back out—and said it as one huge exhalation. "I'm going to roller-skate to Spain take a train to Italy and spend the summer skating across France through Monaco, Cannes, Saint-Tropez, the whole Riviera every inch of it until I get to Carrie in Barcelona."

There. I'd said it out loud. To humans.

The awkward silence was broken by the sound of a huge ceramic bowl of potatoes moving toward me, pushed by Tante Emmy's feeble fingertips across the dining table. "Eat, Mike, eat," she would goad me at every meal. I couldn't resist her sweet smile and dazzling ninety-year-old glacier-blue eyes, magnified by horn-rimmed glasses. Eating more than I needed was worth seeing her light up with joy.

Older brother Bernhard leaned forward over his plate. "Mike, can you even roller-skate?" Though I fully expected a snicker, he was as sincere as could be.

"I can skate well. I had skates in California so I could skate with Carrie, and then I started summer training for ski season by skating with ski poles, with rubber stoppers for tips instead of the spikes. It's just like skiing. I'd skate downhill, uphill, and long, flat distances. Sometimes I'd get a ride to the highest place in Newport Beach and skate the steep streets like ski slopes. Yeah, I can skate."

They brewed in silence until little brother Georg broke into a titter. The family was trying to swallow my story and their food at once. I had nothing more to add to my ill-conceived plan. Their barrage of questions kept me up all night.

But there it was: I'd said it. It was out there. I was committed. I'd declared my plan, burned the ships, and blown up the bridges behind me. From this point, there was only one possible outcome: to roller-skate across France and meet Carrie in Spain.

CHAPTER 7

MAKING EQUIPMENT

Plans are nothing; planning is everything.
—Dwight D. Eisenhower

One last trip to Garmisch-Partenkirchen, one last duffle bag to cart down from the Zugspitze, and one last chance to say goodbye to my amazing room at the Schneefernerhaus.

A letter from Joel waited in my mailbox, miraculously delivered from Italy in an envelope that read only "Mike Jarvis, The Zugspitze, Germany"—no postal code, no city, no street, no numbers. Just a name and a mountain in a country. The return address was equally preposterous: "Joel, Yacht *Sylvia,* San Remo, Italy," making this the most unimaginable envelope in the history of world postal deliveries. From a guy on a boat to a guy on a mountain.

Hello Mike, your buddy Cook is the new cook. Me. On this 110-foot yacht. We sail from cove to cove, country to country, so writing me back will be next to impossible. However, a rendezvous at the Cannes Film Festival is a sure bet on our schedule. The "Sylvia" hasn't missed it since she was built.

I put the letter away when I heard the heavy breathing of the Schneefernerhaus's manager coming up the stairs to check my room. His mass punished the creaky stairs. Maybe the fat old fart would have a heart attack before he made it up there. Maybe the stairs would finally collapse under all that lard.

I was done being nice to this despicable man. In the months I'd lived there, I had improved the room with fresh paint, electrical repairs, and wood moldings. I'd rearranged the furniture. I moved into a dank, cold storage dorm and was leaving a bright, cheery apartment. But I refused to clean up the pile of someone else's cigarette butts in the hall or the other disgusting chores he constantly suggested were my responsibility.

In his caustic manner, he ducked to enter the room and asked the one question I feared most. "Where are the beds?"

I pointed to two king-size beds, explaining with my best salesman smile that I'd turned the bunks into side-by-side beds.

"*Nein!*" he snapped, his bushy eyebrows pointed like devil's horns.

I backed away.

"There's two beds missing. Where are these beds?" He clapped the back of his hand into his palm, each slap dangerously closer to my face, each word increasingly harsher on my ears. "Where? Are? These? Beds?"

His fat frame blocked the door, enflaming my trapped animal instincts. We counted the thin metal tube beds together, my German purposefully worsening, playing the confused American kid card. He was certain two beds were missing. We counted again.

"No, Herr Manager, only six beds. Eight beds would surely make it difficult to move around this room." It was the same case I'd presented when I moved in.

After more incomprehensible yelling into my face, he grumbled his way down the creaking stairs and out of my life forever. My sigh of relief was followed by my guilty smirk. Once the snow melted, he would find the missing beds neatly cut into pocket-sized bits by a Swiss Army knife, scattered at random around the mountain slopes.

***

Mitch, Marsha, Cathy, and I laughed away that last night in Garmisch-Partenkirchen, leaving Mitch and I with brutal hangovers the next morning on our walk to the rail station. We hurried as we knew the German trains would not—could not possibly—arrive late. A few winks of shut-eye would have done me good, but Mitch got his groove on and started in with the twenty questions as soon as we boarded.

"So how long is it?" he asked.

"That's rather personal, buddy, don't ya think?" I rubbed my forehead in exaggerated exhaustion. "Oh, you mean the roller-skating trip. It's a long, long way. I mean, I could add up all those little ticks on the maps and figure it out, I suppose."

"You're crossing a country on skates without knowing how far it is? Okay, I can dig the whole uncharted routes vibe. I'm just saying it would be nice to know, ya know?" Mitch had a cool way of pointing out where I was being an idiot, yet he was always on my team when it came to doing my own thing.

"Maybe eight hundred miles and some change when you add in the twists and turns through all the little coves. I want to experience every cove. No shortcuts. Hug the shoreline all the way."

"Why not go on a bike? Carry all your stuff on the racks. It's probably easier. Safer, for sure."

The train accelerated past the last tight turn of the Alps near Eschenlohe, both of us pausing without a word for the ride's last view of Zugspitze. I explained how my thinking had evolved from hot air balloons to roller skates. "Besides, a bike's a thing with stuff I gotta babysit and fix."

He nodded. "No attachments, nothing to care for. Maintenance-free. Outta sight, brutha."

"Anyone can ride a bike across the country. They do it all the time. I want to be Zen-like, a caterpillar spreading his wings. As one with the road."

"If you get run over by a bus, you'll be one with the road, that's for sure."

I was convincing myself as much as Mitch. "By train, I'd just be a typical backpacking schmo getting on and off wherever trains can get to. It's that 'every inch of the French Riviera' pitch that's got me hooked."

"It's Carrie that's got you hooked. You'll skate across Western Europe for a girl? She's a hook."

I leaned in with a hint of confrontation. "You're calling my lady a hooker, are ya?"

"I'm simply observing how desperate you are. Make no mistake, it's a bold, daring, dangerous adventure. So yeah, she's a hooker, a siren, a temptress. I'm not saying it's wrong, man. It's romantic—I mean, they say battleships have been pulled across oceans by a single pubic hair. You're just as whipped as the rest of us. So when do I get to meet this foxy babe of yours?"

"Barcelona? Two months?" I watched Mitch weigh the possibility. "That is if I survive the journey. Or we'll just connect when we're all back in California."

He nodded. "Whenever. Wherever that is, I'll meet you guys there. And it'll be totally bitchin'. Right on."

"Totally bitchin'. Yeah." A five-gesture bro handshake sealed the deal.

The train stopped at Lake Starnberg where white swans ate bread crumbs tossed by tourists boarding a ferry. Cerulean blue skies contrasting the white Alps in the distance defined the significance behind the *Blauweiss* Bavarian flags surrounding the landing. Again without cue, I began playing harmonica and Mitch stood and recited the lyrics of *Green River* like a coffee shop poet. Again, we kept the cabin all to ourselves.

As the train pulled away, Mitch was drumming up more questions. "I get it. You're going to see Carrie. No bikes. No trains. Boss. I'm just not getting the rest of it."

I reeled back in my seat. "Jeez, man, have you been talking with Joel? It makes perfect sense." I began counting on my fingers. "The snow's melted, so I can't stay on the Zugspitze. I can't go back to live with the Kleins. They'd say yes 'cause they're awesome, but that's going backward in life. And how long would that last until I'd go do the next thing? I can't crash at their pad forever. I gotta move forward."

"*Ja, das ist* very interesting, Herr Jarvis. *Und* how does zees make you feel?"

I rolled my eyes and shook my head. "That is without a doubt the worst Sigmund Freud ever. And you can't use a Bic pen as a cigar prop."

"Sometimes a Bic is just a Bic. That's quoted by the Ziggy himself. Now there was a cool cat."

The landscape began a gradual shift from country to city. Train crossing bells became more frequent, and my would-be therapy couch became a hot seat. "I wanna go home. But then what? Go to college, get a job, start a family? I'm not ready for that—any of that. I'm not done here, with whatever I'm doing here. And if I run home now, I'll just become…"

Mitch stared me down until I finished.

"I'll have missed something important. Know what I mean?"

He nodded.

"I can't go back and live with the folks. That just says 'loser' all over it. And all my friends now have a year of college behind them. I'm gettin' lapped. I'm nineteen now, and I gotta figure this out, this 'who am I' thing. I can't count on ski jobs, the Kleins' house, Mom and Dad's pad, or Mitch's lumpy vinyl. I gotta stand on my own two feet."

"You'll be doing a shitload of standing on your own two feet when you're skating across France."

"That I will. I guess what I really want is to go home—or be home, wherever home is. Carrie is home, so I'm going home to a city I've never been to. And on the way, I'll have a couple of months to figure out my next adventure."

"Have you figured out what you'll do after Barcelona?"

"Honestly, I'd like to marry her. Not right away—I'm only nineteen—but that's the long-range plan. Of course, I have nothing to support that plan, but I'm looking at an engagement ring to take along with me. She's my everything. I'll figure out what to do with it when I get there. The plan is half-baked."

"But you are completely baked, dude." Mitch was right about that. "Did you tell Miss Everything about your little side trip to Paris?"

"No," I said with a little gulp. "But I will."

"Like, when you get to Barcelona? 'Hi honey, I had an affair in Paris but will you marry me?'" Mitch rubbed his face, looking at me through his fingers. "Dude."

I had hoped I would never have to tell her, but I knew it was wrong. Telling her by mail or phone was wrong too, but I knew I was procrastinating by waiting to see her in person.

"Okay, so maybe you ask her to marry you in Barcelona. Then what?" Mitch continued.

He was trying to be helpful, but my legs jumped up to pace the cabin. "Mellow out, bro, I don't have a clue! I finished high school, my parents set up this trip to Munich, you got me to the Zugspitze, and now I got nowhere to go. It's freaking me out. I can go anywhere I want now, and no one is telling me what to do next— for the first time in my life, it's totally up to me. What are *you* gonna do with *your* life?"

He smoked his Bic pen again. "You are zee one on zee lumpy couch. Stay focused *und* lay it on me, mophead."

My words repeated themselves through my frozen expression. "Nowhere to go. I've saved enough bread to go anywhere in the world. I have some skills, I can get work. For the first time in my life, no one's telling me what to do next. But I've got nowhere to go."

The train slowed and rocked its way across dozens of switches just outside of Bavaria's central train station, filtering us like a pachinko ball to our arrival track. Mitch caught my lost puppy look—withdrawn into industrial scenes. He sat up. "Embrace it, Mike. It's just a season of life. Next season's just around the corner. It always is."

I stared bleakly out the window as he busied himself getting ready to debark. Munich's big station clock ticked to the exact published arrival time as the train came to stop. Such was the accuracy of every detail in Germany that warmed my soul deep to my heritage. I tapped the broken birthday watch strapped to my wrist, showing Mitch "right on time, every time, perfect."

He grinned and shrugged. "If you're not into time, man, ya can't be late."

I wasn't so sure about his philosophy, but I loved his commitment to it.

We whisked our way through the crowds of Marienplatz, occasionally stopping to drop a coin for the buskers. I followed Mitch, several steps behind as he gave a thumbs-up at the Mariensäule, the Virgin Mary balancing on a tall column in front of the new *Rathaus* where the *Glockenspiel* would soon play morning bells. A venerable landmark, but he was alluding to the night we'd met beneath that statue some nine months earlier.

He'd introduced himself during a Neil Young harmonica session I was playing to the night plaza. He told me about Garmisch-Partenkirchen, how a bunch of American ski bums wash dishes there and how I should crash on his lumpy vinyl sofa some weekend and go skiing. I did, and I fell in love with the town. I quit my job in Munich and moved out of the Kleins' house, got a German work permit and an interview with the Bavarian Zugspitzbahn company. Would I like to live at the top of the mountain? A dream job, an amazing home, and a plan for my life? Carrie had been pissed that

I wouldn't make her winter formal dance, but Mom and Dad were proud.

"How'd you ever get me into all this, anyway?" I asked Mitch as he wove through the crowds. "I could be sitting on a boat in Avalon with a six pack, makin' out with Carrie. But nooo, I had to come ski and drink beer from a glass boot with Mitchy."

Sport Scheck was just around the corner. Ski and Roller Sports was on the fifth floor. I tapped the elevator button while Mitch gawked at the climbers on the rock wall. The stainless steel doors opened with a ding.

"Yo, Mitchell. Elevator."

"Yo, Michael. Stairs. If you got the legs, you got the stairs." I held the doors, yet he made no move to enter. "Dude, the elevator is for wheelchairs. It's a climbing store, for cryin' out loud. We're lucky they don't make us climb this wall to the fifth floor. How 'bout we get some of that 'stand on my own two feet' thing going, eh Mikey?"

The yellow claim ticket I'd been carrying in my Velcro wallet was worn, wet, and unnecessary; the ski shop techs recognized me. One tech waved at me and headed toward the back of the shop past another tech, probably mumbling, "He's back." The second tech waved and smiled, as though I'd come to tell him another funny joke. They brought out an Adidas box and opened the lid to reveal white leather high-tops mounted to roller-skate plates with top-of-the-line Kryptonics wheels. No expense was spared: I had the finest German bearings, bushings, and trucks.

To me, they were the red-ribbon Ferrari on a Christmas morning. To Mitch, they were the shoes they'd find on his buddy's dead body along some French highway.

We switched gears to backpacks, an area where Mitch's experience would make the difference between completing the journey and crying for help. Together with backpack expert Jorg-Peter, we analyzed every feasible outcome with various packs.

"This one has number-one-rated suspension," said Jorg-Peter.

"Yeah, but it's too wide for me to swing my arms backward with full motion." Skeptical, I showed them how I would need to use my arms.

"And it's too heavy to skate with," Mitch said. "You need the lightest thing they got with the best suspension system on the market."

"I'll need heavier material like this one in case I have to ditch and skid on my back."

The three of us considered every scenario, but not one pack met all criteria. In the end, I bought a good backpack and modified it with Mütti's sewing machine to make it the best damn cross-country roller skater's backpack the world had ever seen.

Next were ski poles. I needed telescoping poles to adjust for uphills and downhills, toe stoppers for tips, and convertible grips for cross-country propulsion.

Finally, we laid out all the campsite gear on a large table.

"You can cook just about everything in this frying pan: eggs, steak, bread," Mitch said. "It's got this folding handle. You'll cut this plastic spatula down with your Swiss Champion, so it packs inside the pan."

His river guide experience was an enormous help. The pack had gained weight with all the gadgets and gizmos I'd throw in, only to have Mitch toss them back out: "That's too heavy" for this, or "You'll never use it" for that. Every ounce was accounted for in true minimalist fashion. I thought his head might fall off the back of his neck when he found the battery-operated blow-dryer. I laughed myself silly.

Images of French toast and eggs at a beach campsite filled my head with travel-poster excitement. Beef stew from a stove the size of a tuna can, fresh baguettes with butter and marmalade from a toothpaste tube—I'd be living the dream. Now it was time to zip it all up in the backpack and put it to the test.

I laced up and took a lap around the fifth floor. My feet felt as though they were flying; I fell in love with the famous three black stripes of stiff Adidas leather. The narrow backpack allowed my arms to swing the long ski poles behind me, and the weight of the gear was no problem.

I floated easily around the fifth floor.

"That works," Mitch said with grudging approval. "You weren't kidding when you said you could skate."

"You will need to break in the shoes before you go. They will not be friendly to your feet."

I took Jorg-Peter's advice by leaving the skates on, settling the bill, and passing Mitch by at the elevator doors.

"If you got the legs, you got the stairs, Mitchy," I called. "Elevators are for wheelchairs."

I turned my toes down the metal stairs and skated down five flights, backpack and ski poles flying and raising pandemonium throughout the store.

"You're gonna need a wheelchair, ya freak show!"

He followed me down while shoppers gawked upward. Wall climbers swung on their ropes, reaching out for a high-five. I waved to an applauding audience in the foyer and headed out the door.

After lunch, it was time for Mitch to return to Garmisch-Partenkirchen. I would go to the Kleins for a few nights before leaving for Italy. This was goodbye, a smiling farewell in contrast to Joel's tearful send-off.

Mitch disappeared down the U-Bahn stairs, taking with him his wealth of camping knowledge, and leaving me free to solo. I skated through the center of Munich, getting comfortable with my new equipment, and knowing I would need to recall and expand on his short, valuable lessons throughout my journey. But I didn't realize I would need his wisdom so soon, for moments later I would chime a small bell entering a jewelry store and ask the lederhosen-wearing shop owner to show me a diamond ring.

CHAPTER 8

IS THERE ANYBODY OUT THERE?

No one can build you the bridge on which you, and only you,
must cross the river of life.
—Friedrich Nietzsche

The Kleins' house made a welcome home for a couple of nights of preparation. I showed them my new equipment, explaining how it would all work out and trying to convince them (as well as myself) that I would be okay skating across France. None of us were really buying it.

"So on this journey, you will perhaps find yourself?" asked older brother Bernhard at the dinner table.

"Actually, it's quite the opposite. It's more like creating myself."

They were never sure what to make of me but showed unconditional love regardless. "Eat, Mike. Eat."

I couldn't let Tante Emmy down. I loved the joy in her smile as I shoveled calories like snow. I piled on another helping from the potato bowl.

"They say it's in our darkest hours where we learn more about ourselves," I said, broadly gesturing with the serving spoon, "so it's actually these struggles—the right struggles—that I need to find. If I push myself far enough out there, I can never go back to the same person I was. Sounds a bit crazy. But it's in the work, the hard, seemingly never-ending work, that we create ourselves. The idea that we simply find ourselves out there removes ambition and work from the equation."

"It sounds as if you've been reading Nietzsche up on the mountain." Bernhard was an intellectual with philosophies of his own. *"Das was uns nicht umbringt macht uns stärker."*

"'What doesn't kill us makes us stronger.' Nietzsche, right. Something like that. And 'Self-worth cannot be verified by others. You are worthy because you say it is so. If you depend on others for your value, it is other-worth.' Dr. Wayne Dyer."

After dinner, Mütti taught me how to use her sewing machine, and I went to work customizing the backpack. I spent the next couple of days sewing while listening to French lessons on a record player in German. I customized the shoulder straps, added film canister elastic straps, and a clip for hanging a wet bathing suit were a few of the features the Alpine backpackers had failed to think about when creating the ultimate trans-Euro roller-skier rucksack.

I recorded cassettes to listen to, from Bernhard's killer vinyl collection, positioning a microphone in front of a speaker, putting the stylus on the album, and quietly shutting the door while it recorded. I made a summer sleeping bag out of terry cloth, sewing up red, white, and blue panels I dyed myself so the bag itself made a French flag. This would be my beach towel and my bath towel too, showing my French spirit to impress cute girls, angry police, and French tent campers. The only thing I didn't get around to creating was a drag parachute, a concept I had for slowing down if I got going too fast down the hills. It worked for dragsters and jets, but I figured I wouldn't need it.

My last supper with the Kleins had a happy buzz and a sadness, and Tante Emmy made sure I stocked up on enough carbs for the next couple of months. I couldn't resist a last chance to enjoy the tiny ninety-year-old fingers trying to push the behemoth bowl of potatoes in my direction.

I would leave right after doing the dishes to catch the ten o'clock train to Italy. Before I left, Dieter dialed the international operator to make The Big Call to California. Mütti stood beside us at the phone table by the front door as Dieter talked to the operators in German, then English, dictating Carrie's phone number with clarity and accuracy. In all the months I lived with them, this was only the second call I'd made.

Carrie and I had agreed by mail to this call. Eleven o'clock in the morning California time wouldn't awaken my Briar Rose too early.

"It's ringing," Dieter announced, handing the receiver to me with across-the-planet excitement.

I counted the rings, picturing Carrie's hot-pink phone aside the matching bedspread.

"Hello?"

Her voice made me stand a little straighter. "Hello! Carrie, it's Mike. Can you hear me okay?"

"Hello?" Her groggy, listless voice was quite familiar from so many mornings waking beside her.

"Carrie? Hi, babe, are you there? Hey, it's me. I'm heading out to Barcelona, getting on the train to Italy tonight."

She just listened.

"Yeah, babe, so you need to tell me when and where we are meeting in Barcelona. And I need your flight numbers too."

Her breath was soft, deep, and tranquil. A phantom whiff of her plush blond locks enveloped me, recalling the velvety mane draping around her long neck and plunging across her chest.

"Carrie? Hello, Carrie? Wakey-wakey, honey. Hey, wake up! Tell me where I'm going."

Carrie's mom picked up the phone. "Hello?"

"Oh hi, Betty. I was talking with Carrie. Could you put back her on the line, please?"

"She's out cold. She was out really late. How are you? How's Germany? Oh my, the stories I've heard."

"It's all wonderful, yes. But I'm headed to Barcelona now to meet her. I don't have the exact dates or a hotel or a flight or anything. Can you give me the dates and info?"

"Oh, yeah. Bob takes care of all the details. He doesn't tell us anything, we just pack and go."

"Right… He sounds reluctant to share."

"Oh, fiddlesticks. I'll find his papers and get it to you somehow. Carrie has some place she can write to you?"

Betty and I were in cahoots about many things. At times she seemed more excited about my dating Carrie than Carrie was. She loved dressing up her princess and was convinced I was the knight who would sweep her away.

"I took Carrie shopping for the trip. I just hope we're airborne before Bob sees those bills." She giggled guiltily.

"Carrie's just as lovely in a burlap sack. I always tell you that, both of you."

"Hogwash. You just wait until she steps off that airplane." I heard her hand cover the mouthpiece. "And maybe there are some surprises underneath that gorgeous outfit too."

"Bob's not going be happy about that."

"Oh, don't you worry about Bob. He won't really prosecute you."

"Prosecute? No one said anything about prosecution."

"He's just mad Carrie slept with you all summer. Well, and burning her Porsche too. But don't you worry about that."

"I wasn't worried—I mean, ten seconds ago I wasn't. But you said that was all okay with you."

"But dear god, if Bob found out what you were doing to our daughter, he'd have parts of your young manhood removed."

It occurred to me that I would be asking Bob for his daughter's hand in marriage in a few weeks. After a few more brief pleasantries, I said goodbye. Dieter hung up the phone twice, checking a dial tone between.

They all looked at me expectantly.

I explained that I still had no target date or location. "I'll try calling her from France when I get somewhere."

"Where will you go?" Dieter had concerns that I was skating through three countries with no finish line.

I had that same concern.

The three of us stood, puzzled and distraught.

I drew a deep breath and bent to pick up my things. "I'll be fine. I'll write. I'll call again. I'll catch up with her. I have nothing but time—I'll figure it out."

After hugs from Dieter and brothers Bernhard and Georg and small tears from both Mütti and Tante Emmy, I rolled out the front door, backpack and skates on. A final look over my shoulder at my German family showed them receding behind me, waving goodbye in the dark street.

In that moment, rolling along in the dark silence away from all comforts of safety, family, and warm food, I was more alone than ever. I had no boss to make decisions for me, no one to call for help if I didn't show up on time, no safety nets to catch me. Only a fading vision of who I once was and who I might become.

CHAPTER 9

NIGHT TRAIN TO ITALY

Trains, like time and tide, stop for no one.
—Jules Verne

The prospect of connecting with Joel at the Cannes Film Festival kept my spirits high. The idea of skating all the way to Barcelona was still beyond me, but if I could make it just a few days to the safety net of Cannes, I'd be in Joel's benevolent care. But until then, the things on my back, in my hands, and on my feet were now my entire life. There was nothing more, and it scared me to death.

I skated onto the S-Bahn, through Munich's main station, and past hundreds of international travelers probably wondering what the passports looked like on the planet where I came from. A second-class sleeper bunk waited for me. The no-frills cabin had bunks stacked three per side, leaving minimal space to walk between six vertical beds. I crawled into the bottom bunk, clueless that the Italian family sharing the cabin was desperately looking for the ladder to climb into the upper bunks. Drama Mamma, her three adult boys, and her ruddy-faced old Papà argued nonstop, although they may have just been saying their sweet good nights with whole-body Italian sign language.

I fell asleep before the train even left the station but was jarred awake just a few minutes later when a German conductor tapped my shoulder to show the angry Italians the ladder at the back of my bunk. The tired and cranky family yanked the ladder off the wall, pulling me to the floor with it, then stepped on me before I could scramble back into my bunk. I pretended to fall back asleep as the family took turns yelling into my face, Mamma taking a bonus round with a look as nasty as her breath. I couldn't help dwelling on visions of a Mafia hit on the night train to Italy. Not that I could have stopped a knife assault, but there was no sleeping after that. I lay there in fear until the yelling stopped.

The train stopped around 2 a.m., I presumed somewhere in Italy. My traveling bedfellows packed to leave as I played opossum, eyes shut, not moving. They packed and yelled in continued anger at me—or in love with each other, it was hard to say. I peered through one eye, watching as Mamma knocked over my bag, kicked my roller skates to the other side of the cabin, and let the ladder crash to the floor.

Once they were gone, I scrambled out of the bunk and fixed the room back up. I had the cabin to myself, but only for the moment. I was fiddling with my backpack on the floor when a pair of red stiletto heels appeared. They were attached to the long legs of Rosabella, a woman in her early twenties, who found me on all fours in my bathing suit pajamas. I greeted her with a friendly American hello and a handshake, then moved my stuff aside to make room for her suitcase.

"*Buonasera*," she replied. Her gaze lazily crawled up my torso to my eyes, with a smirk.

I turned the lights up bright and watched her feeble attempts to lift her bag to a middle bunk. A man should help a woman—especially a gorgeous woman—with heavy luggage. I heaved the Goliath up for her. Clearly a little tipsy, she bent over for her smaller bag and caught her long black hair in the bottom bunk frame. I helped with that too.

"Hold still," I said, but she kept yanking her head like a trapped animal, squealing as the trap got tighter.

I stepped over her bag and reached into the tight space between bunks, awkwardly leaning over her. There was no gentlemanly way to get at the silky black knot. The train pulled slowly from the station as we continued our struggle.

Out the window, Mamma and Papà walked the platform. Papà did a double take, pointing at the young lady's palms on the glass, giggling pain on her face, and half-naked American guy bent over behind her, yanking her hair. Mamma pulled off Papà's hat and hit him with it before covering his eyes and shaking her fist at me.

"*Grazie!*" she exclaimed, rubbing the back of her freed head. "Where are you go?"

This would be one of few English phrases she would have to share with me.

"I'm headed to Barcelona, but first I'm going to skate across France with my backpack." I paused, figuring I should keep it simple. "Italia."

She lit up. I kept trying to communicate, evading the part about why I was going to Barcelona. Using the only three Italian phrases I knew, I discovered 1) Rosabella had no leather gloves for sale, 2) she could not point me toward the road to France, and 3) this was not a topless beach. She laughed at my ridiculous questions, then stood up and sang a few bars of "Happy Birthday, Mr. President" as Marilyn Monroe. I recited the names of three pasta noodles. We were getting along famously.

She pulled half a bottle of Chianti out of her giant purse. I was pretty sure where the other half of that bottle had gone. She poured us a glass, giggling and spilling as the train rocked its way down the tracks, and handed me the cup, pantomiming our lips will come together.

I finally figured it out while imagining her lips on mine. "Oh, right. We'll share this one glass."

"*Sì, sì, noi condividiamo*," she said, gazing into my eyes, then at the bed. "Uh…we share, *sì*?"

Were we sharing lips, wine, the bed—everything? I smiled happily and told her *sì* to all the above.

"I undress we go to bed, *sì*?"

She rummaged through her suitcase, finally finding some slinky, see-through number. I sat on the bottom bunk, sipping wine as it sank in that she wasn't saying what I'd hoped she was saying. She cleared her throat—*ahem*—then pantomimed her finger stirring the air to get me to turn around.

There was zero chance of complete privacy in the second-class sleeper, so I simply ducked my head, covered my eyes, and stared at the floor. Her white blouse floated to my feet. I was reaching to pick it off the old linoleum floor when a bra fell too, flopping across my hand like two lacy black melon bowls. The weight of it surprised me, the straps and cups and wires and clips. All that hardware… Wow.

Her short black skirt dropped next, covering the red shoes, which she stepped out of with a ballerina's grace. As the train lurched around a bend, she lost her balance. Some part of her soft body pressed against my face. She giggled, but I kept my head down as a gentleman as my hands grabbed to keep her from falling.

"*Completato, amore mio*," she said.

She scooped up her things and sat on the floor wrapped in a blanket and camisole. Then as I perched on the edge of the lower bunk, she finger-fed me cheeses and meats from a paper bag. I fed her wine as she peeled an orange. Her fun, sexy forwardness was a huge turn-on, but I was determined to be a good boy—a seriously tempted good boy. A boy on his way to find a girl he hadn't been with in nine months who would be god only knew where in a town of over a million people at some unknown point in the future. Had

I not been so determined, I might have locked the compartment door and had my way with Rosabella all the way to Milan.

After talking, teasing, and staring at each other for hours, Rosabella invited me to stay at her flat in Milan, where she would make her world-famous, five-in-the-morning spaghetti for me. After the half-bottle of Chianti, I thought it was an excellent idea. I told her I'd sleep on it.

Her tender, unexpected kiss goodnight, followed by the lingerie show up the ladder, didn't strengthen the case of the little white angel perched on my shoulder. The red guy on my other shoulder had my full attention, as did the purple guy in my pants. Did Italian girls really dress like this just for sleeping in a train bunk? Or was I already dreaming?

No spaghetti for this guy. No sausage or meatballs for this girl. I slept right through Rosabella's departure in Milan.

By morning, the train was nearing my destination, Ventimiglia, Italy. I caught a whiff of lingering perfume in Rosabella's bunk before the conductor moved me to a regular train car, where I joined five older Italian men in a six-seater cabin. They didn't know what to make of me. They looked me up and down, making nonverbal and possibly telepathic comments to one another. The locomotion made them look like Armani-suited bobbleheads.

Maybe I really was the irresponsible idiot these men stared at through piercing eyes that silently screamed "Get a job!" Perhaps their apparent disdain was based on a lifetime of regret for having never taken a devil-may-care summer to do something adventurous and amazing, just once in their lives. Maybe these family men came home to the same house they grew up in, except now Mamma lived in the little room upstairs.

My attitude shifted, and I broke into a smile. I would test their English. "Maybe I'm not the idiot here."

No reaction? Good. Blather at will.

"What if I'm the smartest guy on the train? What if I'm not just some crazy kid on roller skates? I might even turn out to be everything I want to be in life. I might get to do anything I want to do, all the things you guys wanted to do before you got locked into your jail cells of responsibility. And that, my flavorless friends, would be cool, right?"

They continued their anesthetized stares, as if they were deaf too.

I got up and prepared to disembark.

CHAPTER 10

DAY ONE

A journey of a thousand miles begins with a single step.
—Lao Tzu

The scent of burning train brakes wafted away, revealing an almost imperceptible salty tang. Like cookies in the oven, the sea air assured my nose that I was home.

How easy it would be to simply stay on the train, arriving at Barcelona Sants station in several hours as the same person I'd always been. But where was the adventure in that? What would I learn by playing it safe? I was taking the road less traveled, living the life of a philosophical adventurer. It felt right.

But drinking beer on top of a German lamppost had felt right too. I questioned my judgment.

A quick stop before I got on the road: gloves, lunch, and dinner. I rolled to a harborside flea market, watching the locals and tourists stare at the abominable skate man rolling by. The skates and ski poles apparently made people stop and ask questions.

"Is it like skiing?"

And "Is it as fun as it looks?"

And my favorite: "Are you crazy?"

Carrie had taught me to roller-skate back in California. She'd skate backward holding my hands, coaching me as we went back and forth across the harbor's Crescent Street. Once I could skate without falling, I added big hills and took it to a whole new level. The idea of using ski poles came to me later as a plan for getting in shape for ski season. Rubber tips helped me spot turns going downhill, and using my arms for propulsion on flats and up inclines helped me nearly keep up with cyclists. It kept me in shape year 'round.

The Italian flea market shoppers clicked photos of me, shooting more film of me this day than my parents had in my entire childhood. A small crowd grew behind me. "*Meraviglioso*" was apparently my new Italian name in town.

"Where did you roller-skate from?" a French woman asked.

"The train station." I pointed up the street.

"*Und* where are you going on the roller skates?" asked a curious German.

"Barcelona."

There were no reactions.

"Ya know, the one in Spain."

I'm pretty sure the word "crazy" was among the international reaction. I heard Der Spiegel's mysterious German word in there too.

I skated away toward the sign reading "French Border Ahead." There was no more preparing. Whatever this trip was going to be, whatever was going to happen, it was happening.

The steep, narrow two-lane road leaving Italy continued uphill for miles. At times it offered some space for a pedestrian on the margins, but I was mostly forced to skate in the traffic lane to make any headway. How would I ever get back down this hill? Topographically, I was crossing the Alps, the sea-level base that rises to fifteen thousand feet and spans eight European countries.

Climbing these hills saturated my visor with sweat so completely that the brim dripped before my face.

Ahead of me were oncoming cars to dodge. Behind me, titanic tour buses charged at a pace I doubted would allow their drivers to stop before squashing anything ahead of them. To my right, waves of purple and orange bougainvillea swelled over the cliffs and covered the Falling Rock signs. Below me, pebbles that could chock a wedge in front of my wheels littered the road. The backpack made me top-heavy, so it would only take one pebble to put me flat on the pavement like a snapping mouse trap. But to my left, ahhh—the glorious Mediterranean Sea. The left side also held a certain fall-off-the-cliff danger.

In my first sweaty hours, I began to fear how long the journey would really take. There was no human on earth to consult about this, no book to read. I had a paper map for navigation and a girlfriend to meet in about eight weeks. I should have figured a way to make this journey raise money for cancer, but the only beneficiary of my efforts would be the Horny Teenager Temporary Relief Foundation—me.

The road finally plateaued near the three-kilometer milestone. By milestone I mean an actual ancient stone on the side of the road with a "3" chiseled into it, probably by hand. The border was all downhill from there.

I sat on a rock and cooled off, prepping for the downhill run with water and energy snacks. I shook the sweat off my visor and strapped on my knee and elbow pads. I'd done this in California so many times that I'd never even considered a helmet. But never once had I done this wearing a backpack. The weight of the backpack would pull me down hills faster than I had ever gone before. More braking turns would be required. I shortened the ski poles by eight inches to keep my center of gravity low, knees bent and slightly forward, while spotting the tight turns that would control my speed

With nothing left to prepare, I began rolling down the wrong side of the road into oncoming traffic. I shared the lane with uphill-bound cars and trucks, dodging them by hugging the cliff's edge. In some sort of feathered fight to the finish, I was playing chicken with the cars and eagle with the cliffs.

Just as when skiing a black diamond slope, tight turns control speed. Like skis, roller skates have no brakes. Unlike skis, my soft wheels were built for traction, making a skidding stop impossible. I was okay with skating on the wrong side of the road for a while, but as the road grew steeper, the shoulder grew narrower and I got going faster. And faster.

At some point, I crossed the line from in control to in trouble.

The better choice became shifting lanes and skating with the flow of traffic at fifty kilometers per hour. I merged and used the right lane to slow. It was working but cars still wanted to pass, so I shifted back to the oncoming lane whenever it was clear to let a car or two go by. This sharing maneuver nearly got me killed a couple of times; I avoided a head-on collision by swerving in front of speeding car at my back. Dancing with tons of rolling steel wasn't wise, and it was time to own the whole damn road and deal with the honking horns.

Another milestone marker flashed past. Only one kilometer to the border. Good god, I hoped I could even stop at the border. I pictured myself shooting the duck under the gate as the border guards blew their whistles and chased me down. The possibility made me chuckle, relieving a bit of my stress.

But there was no time to relax. I was the last pawn in a winner-take-all game of chess against an angry queen: a two-story tour bus on my tail. Each move challenged my existence on the steep chessboard. I was playing for my life, and my opponent could not lose.

The ominous monster rumbled behind its eight-wheeled teenage prey, ready to squash and eat the roadkill. I risked a glance at the predator, an eleven-foot-high impenetrable wall on wheels. The monster wasn't gaining on me, but it was too close for comfort. I waved for it to back off and got three blasts from a horn appropriate for a cruise ship—shots so loud they blasted my spine upright. If I fell, the steel titan would have no chance at stopping in less than fifty feet. It would surely run me over, followed by a couple of other buses behind it, before any of the parade of titans discovered what the speed bump was.

My legs were in shape from a daily skiing routine, but I was acutely aware of the need to perform or perish. My muscles begged for mercy with each agonizing slalom turn. I couldn't be bothered with the pain; I had other limbs and organs to save. Der Meehee's skiing wisdom, "Stick with technique—it's the key," played in my mind. Knees bent, body forward, arms and poles slightly extended for balance, I took imaginary gates as if I were racing a giant slalom course. It was exactly like racing giant slalom, with the exception of the thirty-five-pound backpack, silky shorts, pebbled asphalt, lack of a helmet, and being chased down the course by a double-decker tour bus.

The drivers coming up the road made all sorts of astonished faces and hand gestures. Horns had been honking at me nonstop since the summit. The show was further charged with encouraging yells in French and Italian, flashes of their joy juxtaposed with the face of my sheer terror.

Where was that border? It was close—I might just make it. I would make it. I practiced keeping a positive mental attitude, aware I was in a "fake it till ya make it" stage. I was counting on level ground at the border. What I wasn't counting on was the dark tunnel ahead.

As I raced from intense sunlight into the tunnel entrance, a wall of blackness blinded me instantly. Pulling off my sunglasses didn't help one bit. I was a man with a white cane—two white canes— flying like a jet at night. Echoes of vehicles in the tunnel tortured my ears. I had no idea how far the tunnel went, no chance to stop. No choice but to survive the blackness.

This unsurpassable terror was quickly surpassed—go figure— by the terror of the tour bus entering the tunnel right behind me.

With no warning, I hit rougher pavement. It added friction and slowed me down, but now my wheels began to trip me up. I caught myself innumerable times just before a face-plant in the dark. I slowed more and more, the bus closing the gap on me. He was moving in for the kill.

And then the bus snapped on his bright headlights, probably signaling for me to get out of the way. The lights blinded the oncoming cars, which began honking and flashing their brights back at the bus—and into my eyes. The bus honked back, the reverberations rattling me like a skeleton in the blackness. I shouted into the black noise with all I had, but I couldn't even hear my own voice.

By now, my eyes were adjusting to the blackness, the bus headlights lighting the way. The squealing brakes behind me were maintaining a good distance back—still too close to survive any error, but I became comfortable with their presence, like a remora swimming with a great white shark. I gave the bus a wave to draw closer to me; a light tap from the horn acknowledged my request. As it got closer, the ground ahead of my feet came into view. I swallowed hard. Charging the road ahead could run you into trouble, but go too slow and trouble would get you from behind. That goes for all things in life.

As the first glimpse of light at the end of the tunnel came into view, the road began to level out. If I could just make it out of this tube...

Daylight again. Squinting and tears. My speed returned to a controllable thirty kilometers per hour, and I pushed my sunglasses back on, legs still shaking and burning. It was all I could do to give the bus driver a shaky thumbs-up of gratitude for not running me over and lighting my way through the darkness. The street had become smooth enough to skate backward, and I turned face-to-face with the two-story wall of steel and glass just a few feet behind me. There behind the glass windshield was another wall: a wall of faces, a wall of cameras.

I've yet to figure out how everyone on that bus managed to crush close enough to fill the windshield, but there they were, tourists stacked on top of each other so closely that no space remained for even one more face or camera. The driver peered over a man lying on the dashboard in front of him. He honked at me, and I gave a namaste bow and continued down the hill with an ear-to-ear grin.

The remaining descent to the border was all bunny slopes. Still catching my breath, I slalomed between dozens of vehicles waiting in line to pass the gate. The driver of the first car I cut in front of yelled out his window something in Italian—probably "Hey, you're the guy we almost ran over back there." He gave a honk, which made the next driver look and yell out in French, "Hey, there's that guy—he made it!" and contribute a honk of his own horn too. The ruckus alerted the drivers ahead to stick out their hands for a high-five from the passing skater, a few yelling my Italian moniker *meraviglioso*. A few drivers got out to check out the commotion, and they too started honking and clapping. Apparently, a guy with a backpack doing fifty kilometers per hour down the streets of Italy was a novelty.

I kept the S-turns going down the hill, passing every car that had nearly killed me during the previous few miles. At the bottom, a group of perhaps two dozen drivers stood around their cars, applauding and cheering as I passed. The French border police had their cameras out and joined in the impromptu party.

Car horns and encouraging yells in French and Italian continued from up the hill. I gave them a wave while digging out my passport, excited for the official stamp, eagerly waiting for a guard to hand-lift the red-white-and-blue striped gate.

I'd made it, the first person in history to roller-skate across the border. I should have felt more proud, but the nagging thought that I was lucky to be alive made me feel stupid for doing it.

***

Separated by a line of paint across the road, France was more like a new world than a new country. The streets were smooth, the sidewalks maintained, the gutters absent of trash. Pedestrians dressed in style, and everything around me seemed upgraded by two and a half stars.

People showed excitement as I passed, wanting to start conversations and take photos, but all I wanted was to get the weight off my back, get off my feet, and get to a beach where I could cook some dinner and collapse for the night. The all-nighter with Rosabella and sustained near-death experiences had outlasted my stamina.

I found a bench and my butt hit as hard as the truth. I couldn't keep up this lunacy all the way across France and half of Spain. I was lucky to be alive after only a couple of hours skating between two towns. I looked at the hundreds of miles of forbidding hills ahead, where my luck would inevitably fail me. Call it wimping out or call it becoming responsible, but gambling with my life wasn't worth the risk. Between the curvy roads and curvy women, the challenges and temptations were too great to make it across France with skin attached and a faithful heart.

I held my head in my hands. That was it. I was throwing in the towel.

It all sank in as I rolled through Menton, groaning beneath the five steps of grief raining down on me. I'd made a big mistake. This hubris-fueled journey was the most adventurous thing I'd ever tried to accomplish—perhaps the most adventurous thing I'd ever heard of. Clearly it was time for me to grow up, take responsibility for my well-being, and choose a safe method of travel.

Is this what I'd come here to learn? I'd learned with Rollan to make amends with my past and apologize. I'd learned with Cathy I could take care of a half-naked goddess and remain a gentleman. Was recognizing the limits of invincibility a third test?

Facing these hills and buses had been horrifying. Facing everyone I'd told about the trip and confessing that I wasn't good enough, that I was a quitter, that I was too scared—that humiliation held its own horrors. But if I wanted to tell any story, it wouldn't be on roller skates. I'd camp for the night and catch a train in the morning to Cannes. Maybe I'd hang with Joel for a while, then ride the train to Barcelona, hook up with Carrie…

And then what?

CHAPTER 11

JUST SAY *NON*

It's always too early to quit.
—Norman Vincent Peale

I was told the French police arrest those treating their beaches like campgrounds. The wise and the homeless find other hiding places to get a good night's sleep, and the far end of the Menton harbor had a spot that looked like no one would care if I slept there. I'd get one good night—the poster shot with all my new gear on the beach—and enjoy the great memory before scrapping the adventure.

I set up my Therm-a-Rest mattress and laid out my handmade sleeping bag, the oversized terry cloth French flag which was also my beach towel, shower towel, and display of respect to keep me out of trouble. *Vive la France!* Inside the flag bag was a pocket for money and my passport and a D-ring to clip a thin cable to my pack and skates while I slept. If someone tried to run off with my stuff, I'd wake and scare them off with…what, my Swiss Army knife? Not every eventuality had a solid resolution.

Thanks to Mitch's advice, a propane stove the size of a hockey puck, cleverly folded within two aluminum pots, warmed the macaroni-looking stuff I'd bought in Italy. It looked delicious but made my stomach turn. The translation dictionary revealed *trippa* as tripe, which I then had to look up too. Those were the first and last cattle intestines I'd ever eat.

I learned a few things that night. First, terry cloth cotton makes a lousy insulator and is worthless as a sleeping bag. Second, nights on the Riviera aren't as warm as expected.

Despite shivering through the night, I awoke as refreshed as if I'd slept in a five-star hotel—not that I'd had that experience firsthand. I was a guy waking up in dirt and bushes, hiding from police, connected to his gear by a cable to avoid getting rolled by fellow bums.

Fresh fried eggs sizzled in my camping pan. The folding handle was a gem for reducing space but a turd when trying to wrist-flip eggs in the pan like a chef. I didn't thoroughly lock the handle hinge, and the eggs flipped onto my shirt. My glorious morning included sipping hot tea and dabbing yellow egg goop from my shirt with toast.

My first swim in the Med made it special. Being able to say "I swam in the Med" made me different than I was the day before. So many firsts—I could never go back to living as the same person I used to be. Such is the experience of travel; the adventurer never returns home as the one who left. This is the reason we travel.

I cleaned my mess, packed up, and snuck out of the bushes for the train station. Gare de Menton was abuzz with travelers boarding at last call. The conductor blew his whistle, yelled "*En voiture!*" and away they went—without me, leaving me with the entire day to kill in Menton before the afternoon train.

I skated around the beach, where a few girls stopped to talk with me. Cute, friendly, and flirty, they roused me with their accents. I skated until I found myself at the end of town with two more girls wanting to ask questions.

"I'm heading to Cannes," I said. "My friend there works on a yacht."

"You are roller-skating all the way to Cannes?"

"No, I'm taking the train. It's—" I stopped myself before telling them it was too dangerous to skate that far.

"Where are you skating now?"

"I'll go back to town and ride the train, maybe stop in Monaco."

"Monaco is close. It's only a few minutes by car."

It sounded like a dare, so I pulled out my map. "Yep, I could probably skate to Monaco in an hour."

"You cannot roller-skate to Monaco from here. It is too dangerous."

The exact phrase that brought out my peacock feathers. "Oh no, I just roller-skated from Ventimiglia yesterday."

I refolded the map. My big mouth plus a couple of pretty girls meant I now had to risk my life to impress two strangers. Next stop: Monaco.

At under a square mile, Monaco is the world's second smallest and most densely populated country. It's a monarchy ruled by the Grimaldi family since 1297, with a small army of two hundred fifty men and the world's highest life expectancy rate at nearly ninety years. It boasts the world's most expensive real estate, the lowest poverty rate, and the highest number of millionaires and billionaires in the world. It's a tax haven to the ultrarich and a playboy's playground for the famous. Though the names are practically synonymous, Monte Carlo is a city within Monaco and home of the world's most famous casino. I devoured all these facts in my travel guide and kept my eyes peeled for the Grimaldi girls.

Menton to Monaco was about ten kilometers. After my crazed blaze of glory through the mountains and tunnels of Italy, how bad could it possibly be? The asphalt Alps temperature was a delightful twenty-two degrees centigrade, and now that I was once again in my native element, my T-shirt and shorts reclaimed their freedom after nine months buried beneath snow boots.

The French pavement was noticeably smoother than the Italian roads, but nobody considered space for bike lanes so many centuries ago. The road had probably been a horse-and-buggy trail at the turn of the century. I soaked up the views, but my legs tired quickly. The hill out of Menton made me realize I should have trained harder and stretched more. Using more arm muscle to climb with the ski poles was the answer.

To my left, the Med seemed to change colors from each elevated perspective. Some spaces glistened deep green, then shifted from cobalt blue to turquoise. The sea became a friend and playful partner in keeping me entertained while climbing.

I pulled over to take a break and let a parade of vehicles pass. The occupants showed their support by honking at me, taking photos, and standing through the tops of sunroofs with arms open wide, screaming things in various languages. Dripping with sweat, I used a mental skill called interoception to trick my brain into cooling down. The idea was to concentrate on a time when your body was cold, then let your brain regulate your body temperature. Hiking those icy tunnels with explosives on my back had prepared me for roller-skating with a pack of smelly laundry.

It had to be thirty degrees centigrade in the hills where I finally ditched my egg-gooped T-shirt to cool off. As if a T-shirt would save my skin from being ripped apart on asphalt at fifty kilometers per hour. Only then did it occur to me to loosen the trucks on my skates so I could slalom more sharply. Better to make tight turns and progress at a slow pace, but it was too late for that. I had screwed up again. I was back on the giant slalom course, taking up the whole road, including oncoming lanes, as I approached the speed limit leading a parade of vehicles, the first few cars cheering me on.

Approaching Monaco, I rounded a sharp corner to a glimpse of a green traffic light at the bottom of a steep hill. Yellow and red would come soon, my instincts warned. Stopping was still a possibility, but the light was green and traffic flowed through the intersection like water down a slide. In that moment, I decided the light would stay green.

Just as I pointed my toes downhill for maximum speed, the light changed to yellow. I wasn't far from the intersection. I'd made the decision; I was committed. I prayed to the demigod or patron saint of traffic lights for just a few more seconds of yellow.

Red light; the gods did not hear my prayer. I gauged the momentum of the car just ahead of me, calculating that he'd run the stale yellow light and protect me like a two-ton linebacker hurtling toward the end zone. Instead, he slammed on his brake pedal.

I should have taken the hit there. Slamming into his trunk would have knocked the wind out of me, at worst. But survival reactions made my legs swerve around him and into the crossing traffic, where their light had turned green. An animal-like awareness piqued my senses. With eyes focused on the pavement ahead of me, my consciousness told me the cars in crossing traffic had released their brakes. Engines revved slightly as four cars and a roller skater began a race to the center of the intersection. My best chance was to cross diagonally, forty-five degrees from left to right.

I believed I could make it. I had to. I was all in, skating as fast as I could go.

Brakes squealed to my left as a red car and a silver car reacted. I had it made, at least halfway. My lizard brain shifted to the next threat: the cars from the right. They had a head start on accelerating and weren't expecting a 30-mile-per-hour pedestrian shooting in from their blind spot.

A black Range Rover nearly put an end to it all. Instinct tucked my right leg in preparation for impact with the front bumper. I turned as hard as I could with my left leg. The truck slammed on his brakes, the big rubber tires screeching louder than the car horn from somewhere else. In full crouch position, my right leg desperately reached for traction to make a lifesaving turn.

I found that traction somewhere underneath the Range Rover. My right ski pole pinged his bumper like I'd hit a slalom flag. The truck batted the tip of my pole, jolting my arm and throwing me off balance. My lizard brain got me around the truck and through another second of life, but I was still going fifty kilometers per hour and facing another split-second decision on what to hit: the curb, the brick wall, or the stopped car.

Jumping the curb was the easy choice. But before I reached it, a drainage grate would swallow my wheels. I would have to jump it. Beyond the curb, a flight of concrete stairs dropped to a sidewalk below.

I jumped the whole thing. In a few dizzying seconds, I had sneaked under a truck, pole-hopped a storm drain, and leaped over a curb and down four or five steps. I had no idea where I would land, but I made it with backpack, ski poles, and skates intact, only to find myself flying into the center of a sidewalk café at full speed.

Waiters yelled and women screamed. The shock of a flying backpacker sent patrons rolling back in their chairs as plates and glasses crashed to the floor. I tucked my poles in tight and by some small miracle managed not to hit anyone or anything.

Back on the street and back in control, I left the sounds of recovery behind: car horns, accelerating trucks, and some man screaming in French about flying monkeys in his lunch. I waved an apologetic acknowledgment and skated around the corner and out of sight.

And that was only my first faux pas in Monaco.

CHAPTER 12

UNWELCOME TO MONACO

We believe that the way you dress and the shoes you wear are
not probable cause for questioning or arrest.
—Luis Gutierrez

The prices of the houses, cars, and trophy wives increased exponentially each block closer to the harbor. I had entered the mad world of superrich. Handsome *Monegasques*, the residents of Monaco, passed me in their supercars on their way to their superyachts with their supermodels. They honked and waved and held up their superthumbs. Were they lauding my unique travel method or my tight parallel downhill form? More likely, it was the fact that they were no longer downwind of my superstinky body. One sexy lady rose from her passenger seat, turned around, and blew me a bright red lipstick kiss over the back of her matching red convertible.

As I skated onward, dead Walkman batteries left a silent void between my ears for self-analysis. Who would I be once I reached Barcelona to claim my own trophy wife? The lack of a theoretical safety net was a constant reminder that I didn't own my own independence. If I fell, wouldn't someone else always be there to save me? That put responsibility for my life into the hands of others. Maybe that's why I risked it so often; I had nothing to lose. Out there on the road, I was indestructible, autonomous. My only real confidence was that someone, no matter how distant, would surely be there to save me.

I imagined a high-flying trapeze artist dropping the net before a stunt. That's what I was looking for, the reality that a mistake could equal death. The moments surrounding the words "drop the net" must change a person forever. The choice to do or die, to evolve with such delineation and clarity, staged the performance somewhere between boundless confidence and scared shitless. Once successfully played out, the artist would forever live life as a confident flyer.

But I had no precise moment of dropping the safety net of distant parents. I would have to gnaw those ropes like a rat. How could I ever gain true independence if my confidence was based on someone saving my ass if I screwed up?

The flashy lives of the earth's most affluent humans paled in comparison to the clarity, the raw exposure to self-awareness I was gaining access to. I didn't give a damn about the affluence surrounding me. The glitz of Monaco was exciting, but more exciting to me was the opportunity to tank up on fresh water.

But my first view of the casino against the sea stopped me in my tracks. It really was all that. To get to it, I'd have to skate through the Allée des Boulingrins, a royal garden of sorts overlooking the ostentatious Place du Casino fountain. Boulingrins, a cognate to the English "bowling greens," refers to bowling as in francophone countries. I tried to imagine anyone bowling on the steep slopes of these gardens as I skated down the trails to one of the world's most famous buildings.

A magnificent fountain rained before the casino in stunning grace. All I could imagine was the cascading dome of water on my hot, shirtless body. Just the fantasy of dive-bombing the last hundred meters of hill into the center of the fountain took a sweat bead off my brow.

Smooth marble stairs and curved paths through the bowling greens made for a comfortable slalom down to the casino. Showroom-fresh cars, their price tags higher than most houses, were backed in next to museum classics with price tags comparable to a private island. I gaped at rock stars in leather, sheiks in white robes, Euro-gents in day tuxedo jackets, all with their ladies competing in some contest for the world's largest sunglasses. The ladies led porters with shopping bags among the photographers crowding the Place du Casino, to complain on their yachts that night how popular they were among the paparazzi. A line of fashionably gilded casino guards stood before the main entrance, eyes forward for hours on end.

Enter the shirtless, sweaty, long-haired, bearded, roller-skating backpacking freak onto the scene. It was all so pretentious I could barely hold back my laughter. I was so out of place, and these people's lives were so out of touch with the authentic originality rolling into their town.

I was slaloming down a last flight of marble stairs when two casino guards appeared from nowhere, grabbed my arms, and snatched me off my feet, backpack, ski poles, and all. My legs dangled in the air, feet kicking and ski poles flailing, as they carried me backward to the side of the gardens.

"Hey, what the hell? Put me down!" I yelled.

They soon put me down, but not in the way I was hoping.

"Hey, hey, *hey*! Get off me, man."

My words fell on deaf ears, but the tourists craned to see the tale they'd tell of a great crime on the casino steps. Despite my protests, the guards carried me about a meter or two from a concrete bench, counted "*Un, deux, trois,*" and tossed me back onto the bench. To be clear, they threw me. Surely these finely uniformed gentlemen were skilled at properly seating their guests. But a sweaty, hairy, backpacking roller skater? Tossed.

I hit the bench hard and bounced with a back roll onto the grass. They hauled me up and planted me firmly on the bench. One guard began a face-to-face ass-chewing in French. The other wiped his sweat-soaked hands with a white pocket square; I assumed he would shoot me once his hands were tidy.

After yelling several paragraphs of Monaco laws into my face, the lector finally understood I wasn't getting a word of it. He paused, noticing the assembly of spectators gathering behind him, took a deep breath, squared up his tie and pillbox hat, and crossed his arms.

"*Monsieur*, you will take these, these *patins à roulettes* off your feet *now*, and you will walk out of Monaco. And you will never…ever…come back." He stood firm, looking down over me, pointing out of town.

I wasn't even old enough to have experienced being thrown out of a bar, yet I was being tossed out, ejected from a small country for life?

I read an infinitesimal shift in his posture, indicating the worst might be over.

At that instant, a primal instinct, an unexplainable, deep-seated teenaged hubris to challenge authority, overcame me. I bit my tongue while setting my backpack on the bench. I couldn't help it. The cocky dickhead punk within me was too powerful to fight. *No, don't say it!* screamed in my head.

It was no use.

"But *monsieur*, I was heading in for a coup of baccarat."

His expression changed to infuriated, and he kicked my backpack off the bench with all his might. "You will take off the *patins à roulettes* and leave Monaco. AND YOU WILL PUT ON A T-SHIRT!"

The guards backed away while I unlaced my boots, changed into sandals, and covered my sweaty self with a tee. A crowd of photographers and tourists pressed forward, discussing and ridiculing as my stench-ridden skates and putrid wet socks came off. I only cared that the fresh breeze cooled my flaming feet.

As I walked away from the hovering guards, I stopped to dunk my red bandana in the casino fountain. The guards shot me a disapproving glare. I strolled casually toward the city limits.

It would be my first visit and last legal visit to Monaco.

Within a block, I came to the realization that walking sucked. Without wheels, the fun was gone, the speed rush disappeared, the challenges vanished. The slope from the casino to the marina would have been such fun on skates. This would be the only stretch of the Riviera I had failed so far to travel by roller skates.

I sighed. Carrie would have loved Monaco. All the fanciest things on earth, women dressed to kill at all hours of the day, men apparently walking to or from fashion magazines photo sessions. Ugh. The glamorous life held no fascination for me. I carefully avoided it except when Carrie and her mom fancied me up for a high school dance. They'd get me into some swishy coat with the sleeves rolled up and a belt tied in a knot instead of buckled. Sure, I'd play—anything to make her happy. But we were happiest with our island life in Avalon, spending our days in bathing suits, messing about in boats. To quote the Kenneth Grahame's *Wind in the Willows*, when Ratty says to Mole: "Believe me, my young friend, there is nothing—absolutely nothing—half so much worth doing as simply messing about in boats."

Hollywood fame was Carrie's ambition, but I'd never be that guy. Ratty's words were the gospel of my lifestyle. I was no actor or hairdo rock star. I'd never make the cover of *Tiger Beat*, and I didn't need to be on either end of a camera lens. The joy in my life came from the sea, a sweet girlfriend, and a little boat to mess about in.

Avenue d'Ostende is the street from the Casino de Monte Carlo down to the harbor, the famous stretch where F1 racing tires would be climbing at a blistering 285 kilometers per hour in a couple of weeks. The town had already adorned itself with Grand Prix race regalia, as scheduled annually since 1929. Team flags flapped in the sea breeze over banners for cigarettes, wristwatches, and *parfum* hoisted on streetlamps, palm trees, and just about any semi-solid structure. Megayachts were packing the harbor so tightly there was hardly room for water. The air itself was supercharged. Just driving the race course was a thrill, even for the guy ahead with the yellow BABY AN BORD sign in the back window of his station wagon.

I was all rallied up just walking the road. Imagine the thrill if I could have skated down. But a country where you couldn't even roller-skate… Who needed it?

The harbor area reminded me a little of Avalon, my second home town on Catalina Island, where I met Carrie and fell in love with her. Carrie lived in a house with her older brother, and I lived on a thirty-two-foot boat with my mom, enjoying the best this resort community had to offer. Avalon was Monaco in miniature. Avalon yachts were the size of Monaco dinghies, and the Monaco limos could have held Avalon's golf carts in their trunks. In Monaco, it was Gucci, Hermès, and Valentino; Avalon had Morrow's department store and Piacentini's groceries.

But best of all, you could roller-skate in Avalon.

Still, my eyes stayed busy as I plodded my way to the harbor. The women of Monaco were mostly tens, dripping with diamonds you could've anchored a small boat with. The men sported Armani coats and boat shoes without socks. I passed one *Monegasque* enjoying an afternoon nap with his legs hanging out of the open trunk of his Rolls Royce, snoring like a hibernating bear. What a town!

At the mouth of the harbor, I stopped to gawk at the megayachts, the pretty floating white cities with two crew members for each guest. The motor yacht *Nabila* caught my eye, a stunning megayacht ahead of its time and hailed as one of the ten yachts that changed the world. I had to get a closer look at her.

But my interest tumbled when a topless teen girl ran across my path. She and some boys were having good clean summer fun jumping off the pier, and she had just climbed up the swim ladder for the next jump into apparently cold water. Ripened by sunlight, her C cups bounced shamelessly above a tanned torso and a G-string bottom—three threads away from complete nudity.

I turned my head away and bit into my hand. I had to keep it together, man. But I gawked in amazement as the guys around her responded as if she were just one of the boys frolicking in the afternoon sun. She stood right next to me, laughing, and not one boy stared at her boobs. Were they gay, autistic, blind eunuchs? Were they stupefied, comatose, benumbed by the bourgeois routine of topless girls?

If I were to walk in their Speedos for a moment, I could admire the purity in equality. Or perhaps they were such refined gentlemen that gawking would be grounds for club dismissal. But what did that make me?

Her friends were maintaining eye contact with her; it took me several minutes to notice she had a head. I popped my eyeballs back into their sockets. The blood in my brain, all the fluid that supports logic, rushed to my shorts except for one drop of blood that came out of my nose. I stood catatonic, battling my involuntary stare with the guilt of a total pervert. I moved my unsteady legs to sit on a bollard.

Two questions emerged along with my recovering brain function: *How did these guys do it?* and *What the hell was wrong with me?* I had already been thrown out of the country. Best I move on before getting into more trouble.

So I walked away. More precisely, I backed away slowly.

The famed yacht *Nabila* had vanished from my thoughts. I also forgot to ask the topless teen if she was a Grimaldi girl. In my mind, I had been prepared to propose marriage if she were heir to the country's riches. The fact that I had an engagement ring in my backpack made it even more convenient. *Sorry, Carrie.*

As I trudged out of town, my rubber Flojo sandals began cutting into the tender areas of my arches. By the time I reached the train station, I had the makings of some world-class blisters.

The sorts of places where you had to wear shoes were not for me. I put my skates back on and tossed my only walking shoes into the trash.

CHAPTER 13

NICE FEET

If you lay down, people will step over you. But if you keep scrambling, if you keep going, someone will always, always give you a hand. Always.
—Morgan Freeman

The train station was abuzz with travelers boarding at last call. I arrived as the conductor was blowing his whistle and yelling "*En voiture!*" And just like that morning in Menton, my train pulled away without me. I had stayed too long in Monaco, bamboozled by boats and boobs, and blown my chance at a train ride to Nice.

It was only twenty kilometers—like an hour—to Nice. Why not just skate there?

It wasn't long before I found myself hopelessly lost in the twists and turns of the low route to Nice. The point at Cap-d'Ail would be a dead end, but curiosity pulled me past dozens of parked cars. I followed the people walking to the point. Hiding behind the trees was a little beach café with colorful picnic tables supporting vibrant tangerine-and-fuchsia umbrellas in the sand. French jazz blasted from a jukebox, and not a single sign advertised the name.

Apparently the 270-degree vista of the Med meant they didn't need to spread the word.

This was the Côte d'Azur I'd come for, the France few others with their rail passes and rental cars would ever find. This was the unpublished fantasy of my trip, the destination inaccessible by mass transit.

After a snack, I skated along the Avenue du Trois Septembre, or Avenue Third of September, the day America's Benjamin Franklin and England's John Jay signed the Paris Peace Treaty in 1783, which recognized the United States of America as an independent nation and began the retreat of British troops from the Americas. It hadn't changed much in 156 years and probably wouldn't for another century or two.

Tree-lined streets through the town of Èze kept me cool as I skated toward a short tunnel to Beaulieu-sur-Mer. The pizza shack hanging over the cliff looked like a great place for lunch—I was already hungry again—but I wanted to take in more of the coast's vistas and soak in the crashing sea on rocks as the summer sun melted the frost of the lifestyle I'd left behind. Through a necklace of tiny beach towns, each bump in the pavement further irritated the blisters on my arches. I feigned a smile when sidewalk café patrons cheered me on, but by the time I came through Villefranche-sur-Mer that hot afternoon, I was popping aspirin from my first aid kit.

From that point to Nice it was all downhill, so I shortened my poles, strapped on my pads, and prepared for downhill speed. The Corniche André de Joly gave a smooth, fast ride that hurt like hell, but I would have no idea how bad my feet were until I got into town for help.

Nice had a definitive hustle, a buzz like its posh neighbor Monte Carlo yet doused in organic common sauce. In Monte Carlo, I would have had to ask for a Band-Aid at a Gucci shop; discount pharmacies didn't exist there. Nice had normal stores with normal prices.

A Dr. Scholl's foot store caught my eye—perfect. The only store in the world that specialized in nothing but blistered, ailing feet. An angel's chord played in my mind as someone opened the door, and I resolved to buy every salve, balm, and pain-killing product I could slather on my feet.

An older gentleman offered me a chair before sending me an angel with blond hair, dark eyes, and lab coat to help me.

"*Bonjour*, I have some blisters," I told her. "Do you speak English?"

No acting was required to show her how much pain I was in. I squirmed in the chair as she untied my laces and motioned for me to take the skates off.

Pulling the steaming Adidas leather off my feet was painful, but peeling the goop-soaked socks from my broken blisters was worse. I regretted again not taking enough of those "Learn French Fast" lessons. They must have skipped the session that covered flirting with smokin'-hot chiropody therapists while hemorrhaging through your feet at the franchise podiatry supply store. Not one of those words were in my French vocabulary.

The blisters looked like ping-pong balls. My angel returned with a warm foot bath and poured in some powdered magic.

I tried a little flirty French. "*Je m'appelle Michel. Merci beaucoup pour l'amour.*"

I went with "Michel" as my name because that's just how the French said it. But French podiatry was beyond my vocabulary, so I went with something about thanking for the love.

She gave me the "you're cute" look, but I couldn't keep up the flirting due to the pain.

"*Je m'appelle Rachelle*," she said, massaging up my legs.

If she kept going, I'd buy every product in the store.

She moved her hands up my legs, never breaking eye contact, apparently trying to draw all the blood away from my throbbing feet. I bought a foot bath, some moleskin, Band-Aids, cotton balls, gels, sticks, foams, powders—just about everything she had to offer. Now what could I offer her—dinner?

She summoned the gentleman, apparently to ask him to translate.

"*Monsieur*," he asked, "do you need a ride somewhere?"

Like a penguin waddling over hot coals, my bare-bandaged wrapped feet were worse off than when I skated in. My plan of skating to Cannes was canned.

"I have no place to go," I replied without shame. This was becoming a signature line.

The gentleman and Rachelle exchanged words, quietly, as if I could understand them. His posture was curiously not of an employer speaking with a subordinate.

"*Monsieur*, a good hotel is one block from here. Rachelle will help you."

On the way out, I asked Rachelle if the man was her father. Somewhere in her reply, I caught the French word *oncle*. I assumed from the cognate that she was his niece.

Rachelle had my backpack strapped to her tiny frame. She understood that I had no shoes, so a few doors down, she stopped and helped me choose a pair of canvas espadrilles, which I could not wear due to the glut of gauze and medical tape around my feet. A few more doors and we stopped for wine, salami, pâté, a baguette, and a couple of cheeses to take with us. I bought ample provisions, including an extra bottle of just-in-case wine, hoping she might join me.

We made a strange picture as we entered the hotel lobby together, a backpacker in a lab coat and red stilettos and a shoeless gutter pup toting shopping bags. Rachelle helped by doing the talking at the front desk. After customary cheek kisses with the hotelier, Rachelle's conversation with the desk clerk lingered, drawing a curious woman from the back office and more cheek kisses with her. The hotelier introduced himself.

"*Bon jour, Monsieur,* I am Marcel. I present my wife, Jolie. Welcome to our hotel."

Rachelle handed me a key as the hoteliers stood by as spectators of blossoming young love.

I wasn't the fast and forward type, ready to ask her up to my room, and I couldn't forget my girlfriend, the catalyst for this journey. But I couldn't just say "Thanks, *au revoir,* see ya never again." She'd been so nice, so sexy, so incredibly cute. I wanted to drag her up the stairs and jump her little bones.

Rachelle pulled me to the side of the lobby, alluring eyes captivating me as she took my hands. Something important was about to be said. She spoke slowly, deliberately, close to my face as if that would help me understand her French.

But I didn't.

She waited for my response, any reaction, but was disappointed by my uncomprehending, dumb silence. With a crushed smirk, she glanced at Jolie who was pretending to work, smirking at her defeat. Rachelle dropped my hands, held my face, and gave me two friendly kisses on my cheeks, then closed her eyes and left a big red lipstick mess all over my lips before she left.

My crumbling knees blocked the pain to my feet. Maybe that had been her plan all along, a kind and wonderful person wanting nothing but pleasure for my feet. I was such a loser, a dumbass. I'd *had* her! She'd *wanted* me, and I'd just stood there, too scared to make a move.

The room key nearly dropped from my numb hand. Neither Marcel or Jolie's smirks nor the sad love song playing in the lobby helped. They joined in the song, Jolie amplifying the high notes, crooning until they finally laughed.

"*Ah, l'amour,*" Marcel sighed.

"*Monsieur*, she is a nice girl," Marcel said. "She wanted to come up and help you enjoy your wine and...well, take care of you."

"Why didn't you say so? What the... Is she gone?" I waddled to the door.

Rachelle was gone.

I headed to my room for a night of pain and humiliation. My glimmer of self-pride at roller-skating all the way to Nice had been extinguished by self-doubt and pity.

Would I ever be smooth with the ladies? Welcome to Nice, moron.

CHAPTER 14

BUILDING CHARACTER

Dear Carla,

Turns out they don't allow roller skaters in the casino at Monaco. I got tossed out of the country and told never to come back. Good thing it was just a small country, as I have a long way to go. I've made it a little farther, now healing foot blisters with the help of a nice Nice niece.

Your intrepid overseas correspondent,
Michael

Corny jokes, scenery narratives, and tales of adventure were a joy to write to Carla. But eventually solitude began generating philosophies that should have stayed in my journal instead of airmail paper. I was no Rhodes scholar; I was a barbarian with silk shorts and wheeled feet. My writing was only special because she read it.

Memories of my chilly autumn night with Carla in Munich kept me company as I walked the streets of Nice on swollen heels and the sides of my feet. The blisters raged for two days. My feet were wrapped in gauze and moleskin, cushioned inside the new espadrilles. A series of safety-pin surgeries, saltwater soaks, ice packs, and antibiotic ointments kept the biggest flaps of skin on my soles.

Rachelle had told me to avoid the shoes and activity that had caused the blisters until I healed, which was rather inconvenient for someone traveling by those shoes and the activity they provided. Three to seven days of healing was the heartbreaking prescription; I gave it two. Nothing could keep me down.

Once the blisters had begun receding to the point that a ten-block walk to the sea might be conceivable, I was off. Along the way, I stopped at the American Express office and picked up letters from Carla, Joel, Mom, and various friends back home.

I also placed a telephone call to Carrie.

The line was ringing. *Please don't be Bob, please don't be Bob...*

"Hello?"

"Oh. Hi, Bob. Nice to hear your voice." I hoped I sounded convincing. "It's Mike calling for Carrie. How are you? Is she home?"

"Oh. Hi, Mike. How are you? How was your day? How's the weather in France?"

I was onto his game. I wasn't going to drain my wallet in the name of congeniality. "Is Carrie home?"

"Well, maybe she is, maybe she's not. I can't really say for sure. Hold the line. I'll go look around the house for a while."

"That won't be necessary. I'll call when she can answer her private line. I did call her private line, didn't I? Isn't that why she has a private line?"

"My house, my daughter, my phone bill, my line. Any more questions, smartass?"

"Well, yes sir, since you asked. I'm still looking for a time and place to meet her in Barcelona."

"Oh, really? I have a couple of questions of my own, like why you installed non-Porsche parts that aren't street legal in California."

"You mean about Carrie's car?"

"I'm being asked by the insurance fraud division, so now I'm asking you. By the way, what country are you in right now?"

"France. Yes, it's beautiful here on the Riviera with the sea and the beaches, and the weather is—" It occurred to me he wasn't asking out of curiosity. "Will you be visiting France too?"

"That depends on their extradition treaties."

I said goodbye before he could ask more questions. I had one more to ask, but the moment wasn't quite right to ask for his daughter's hand in marriage. I hung up.

Nice's iconic beach stretches five kilometers along a picturesque walkway, the Promenade des Anglais. The Prom, as they call it, is lined with classic hotels and wide, smooth sidewalks along the beach. Dozens of roller skaters glided past my envious stare as I hobbled my way down the stairs to the beach.

Instead of soft white sand, these beaches have golf-ball-sized rocks—*galets*, as they call them—which pressed every ripped and tender part of my feet and made it impossible to ambulate with dignity across the beach. Time and great determination to reach the sea prevailed, and I soaked in the therapeutic sea until my feet were prunes and grapes. Then I laid out my big French flag towel on the galets to sit and people-watch. Fat, skinny, bald, hairy—they were all packed in tight on the massive beach. Vendors walked the beach yelling sales jingles for T-shirts, jewelry, and ice cream, sneaking in a whisper for whiskey to some.

I lay on my towel and read my letters, savoring these small treasures as connections with my tribe. Joel would be heading for Cannes on a big red sailboat named *Sylvia*. My California buddies were out of college for the summer and drinking beer on boats. And sister Julie would be having brain surgery to remove the tumor. She looked well in the photograph Mom sent, despite the new chemo beanie.

I looked around for anything else that might distract me before carefully opening Carla's letter. I wanted to fully absorb the orphic wisdom I had come to expect, an essential nutrient my mind now craved.

"I'm so proud of you, Mike," she wrote. I "It looks as though you've really grasped life by the hair and are giving it a good shake."

Carla's *belles-lettres* satisfied like warmed honey, like a decree of mental health to counteract my debatable sanity on this journey. Each paragraph was a road sign toward a place called Confidence, a destination that continuously backed away like the summoning coach in a Mommy and Me swimming class.

Carla continued: "Driving into the city at dusk, the sun set so brilliant, finely red and orange. Huge, dramatic clouds stunned me to stop the car to watch. I pulled the Spitfire over, wondering about your challenges and temptations, about how they're forging your spirit, about who you're becoming. Doing things the easy way does not a strong character build. 'What the hammer? What the chain? In what furnace was thy brain?'"

What the hell? My pedestrian grasp of William Blake left me dumbfounded. As if she could hear my commentary, her next line continued, "Look it up. It's from 'The Tyger.'"

Her truth about my spiritual revolution was spot on. There were fierce forces at work on my soul, a tiger-like energy brutally dismantling that lamb of innocence. Only true tests of my character could inspire me to rise against established rules and conventions.

But Carla was about to take me back to our time in Paris.

"We picnic in the shadow of the Tour Eiffel," she wrote. "The air is brisk, the leaves brilliant orange and red. Our lunch: wonderful pâtés and composées (rabbit and vegetable), each so beautifully mosaicked in its gelée. A bottle of wine, each shopkeeper so kind, chuckling 'Ah, young love.' It seems to be the national pastime here, that each Parisian is pledged to do their bit to promote love in this, the cool gray city of love.

"Boat ride down the Seine, then up the Eiffel Tower, then back to our room and—how marvelous—not only does he make love well, but he does it beautifully, gently, masterfully. Such a smooth brown body, strong and covered in soft, golden down—ah, those curling tufts of blond hair that so endear. This towhead a field of shining wheat, of pure sun; I warmed my hands on it."

I read her words a dozen times, yet not once was I comfortable reading that part about myself. Romance is not my genre. But reading her letter pulled out the emotion. Through my squirmy, still-adolescent reactions, I continued reading.

"We finally go to dinner at the Tunisian restaurant, sleepily return through the cold night air and again tumble into bed under our slanting ceiling—flowered fabric walls. Outside, Paris twinkles in conspiracy.

"Early dawn—that warm clover honey envelops me again. Lazy breakfast in bed, then off to Notre Dame—breathless windy heights, the monsters holding forth as we shiver and laugh beneath their stony countenances. Come down—the men's choir, so chilling. Walk to the Louvre, comforted by the sun; its smoothness matches our warm, smooth love.

"Walk up to Place de le Concorde. Bright sailboats on the fountain ocean, piping voices trilling French, chasing their fleets across the pool. Montmartre—ah, Montmartre. Spicy, cold air—black, inky-black sky. Hot crêpes to walk with. Then dinner near Saint-Séverin, quiet from the long day—the exhilaration of the wind, of walking.

"Back to our cozy attic—more love and sleep, so deep and sudden. He wakes at dawn, watches me sleep. His sea-green yet blue eyes immerse me like pale, warm wine. I drift gently toward his sun-drenched shore only to slip again beneath the surface of those blue yet green eyes. The embers of our garret bed cast a glow that encloses us two, suffusing each other's every act with that special charm belonging only to one's child or lover or best-loved pet.

"Tender, sad croissant and warm, frothed chocolate—the last. Can it be over so soon? The *propriétaire* cackles over the house phone: "*Oui, deux chocolats pour les deux amoureux.*" We fiddle in the morning. I stop at the *bureau du poste* to mail some things and he watches amusedly as I parry playfully with the postmaster.

"We barely make the train. It's for the best, for when it pulls too quickly away, I find my eyes misting—surely from the cold—and I almost succeed in blinking back the tears.

"And like an iridescent, breathtakingly fragile bubble, it floated along, higher than most, and with a sudden, delicate burst, it vanished."

My fragile bubble of our Paris affair floated on, delicately folded back into thin airmail paper and slipped carefully into the envelope. An involuntary deep breath came over me, followed by a long sigh to the sea. How could I be so overjoyed by Carla's letter while carrying an engagement ring for another girl? What the hell was I doing?

My next test of character began on cue as a local girl strutted through the crowd on the Prom. I roosted on my elbows, studying the flow of her thick chocolate hair glistening with each springy bounce. I couldn't turn my eyes from her white cotton blouse, transparent enough to reveal a beach-bunny tan. She shared a dynamite white smile with everyone she passed, and her mascara, lipstick, and whatever else it is that drives men crazy were driving men crazy.

I was reminded of a lesson from Carla as I impatiently watched her apply mascara one morning.

"Do all men hate makeup?" I snipped.

"They think they do."

I vowed never to complain about waiting for a woman to look her absolute best again.

The French girl chose a section of beach, descended the stairs, and slinked into my area. All heads turned as she made her way toward the water's edge, and my bingo card hit when she laid her towel to my immediate left.

This was the very temptation Carla was referring to.

From afar, I could stare. At close range, I had to count on my sunglasses to cover my peering eyes as she unbuttoned her blouse and wiggled her shorts down to reveal a G-string bikini bottom. And then, as if every man on the beach had pitched in a few francs for the show, she pulled off her bikini top and rubbed her large, bare breasts with tanning oil.

I had turned away to bite my lip when a woman's voice called my name. My eyes nearly popped out of their sockets. The voice was not the sultry French accent I'd expected from my left. It was a familiar, chipper voice from my right.

It was Marsha from Garmisch-Partenkirchen.

"Mike? It *is* you. Wow, hi! This is unbelievable. I can't believe I ran into you here, of all places."

I would normally have jumped up and hugged her, but after the burlesque beach show to my left, Marsha might have gotten the wrong idea about how happy I was to see her.

"Marsha? No way!" I choked out. "This is so cool. What are you doing here? How did you find me here?"

I stopped myself before asking how soon she'd be leaving, wishing my eyes were in the back of my head.

"Didn't you… I was walking right there up on the Prom. You were staring right at me for like a block or two, and I was like waving my towel and screaming your name. Maybe you were looking at something else. I can't believe I found you down here. This is like so totally amazing."

If she wanted to talk about something totally amazing, she would have mentioned the oiled-up mounds behind me. I couldn't focus for five seconds.

"Excuse me for not getting up for a hug. It's my feet—they're completely ruined from skating. Check out those blisters. I can't even walk."

"Then how did you get down here?"

"I took the train from Germany to Italy and then roller-skated from Ventimiglia."

"But if you can't walk? I don't understand."

"So where are you coming from?" That was good. If I kept asking directional questions, maybe she'd point to something in the topless girl's direction.

"Where are you staying?" Marsha pointed to a hotel behind us.

"Which direction are you going next?"

Marsha pointed behind her, toward Italy.

"Is there any ice cream up on the street?"

Again, she pointed to a vendor behind her.

"Which way is it to Spain?" Still no opportunity to look to my left.

We talked for a while, her sweet, fun attitude embracing whatever life handed her.

"Isn't Joel down here somewhere too?" she asked.

"He's working on some rich prick's yacht, as he says. They'll be at the International Film Festival. I'm going to meet him in Cannes a few days from now."

"And Texas Cath? Where did she end up?"

"Greenpeace—Chicago, she said. Great times just a few short weeks ago, and now we run into each other in France. Small world, huh?"

We talked about Germany and our friends and all the beer we drank at the Von Steuben until I could get off my stomach without embarrassment. My brain was under blitzkrieg. I must be a gentleman. I couldn't look at the enormous boobs to my left or I'd be busted. I must focus on my friend. That was the right thing to do. The challenge was to comport myself as a gentleman while spasms nearly snapped my neck around.

Finally, Marsha told me she was on her way to catch a train.

"It's a shame you have to go now." A captivating performance, delivered with sincerity and timbre—and I'd never had even one acting class.

I took to my feet for a goodbye hug, wished her safe travels, and she was gone.

Not Marsha. *Her*. She was gone. Marsha was still walking away, wondering why I looked so distraught. Somewhere in our conversation, the pinup girl had left the beach. She was nowhere to be found by my extensive scan.

Climbing the stairs to the Prom, Marsha pantomimed crying with a fist rubbing her eye. I may have shed a real tear.

I was grateful for my visit with Marsha, but I had to acknowledge that I was thinking like a pig. I'd just squandered a visit with a dear friend who cared about me while my mind obsessed over a sexy half-naked stranger beside me.

C'est la vie, as the French would say. It wasn't too much guilt for a teenager in his sexual prime.

CHAPTER 15

TED THE SKATER

All truly great thoughts are conceived while walking.
—Friedrich Nietzsche

The open road was still painfully off my list of physical abilities. Mere walking without wheeled feet, like some loser, quashed my adrenaline buzz with each plodding step. The blisters healed for an agonizing two days, finally contracting enough that I could walk with my whole foot on the ground. It was time to get those sensitive soles back into skates.

As though talking to an excited dog going for a walk, I promised my feet a bit of casual skating. Patches of moleskin and bandages made my feet look like well-traveled suitcases with stickers from around the world. Fair enough—they were as ravished as if they'd been around the world.

Slipping back into my boots was gratifying with a measure of anxiety. I could enjoy complete freedom: thirty pounds off my back, hands free of poles, protective pads and T-shirt unnecessary. Just skates, shorts, my Sony Walkman, and miles of perfectly smooth surface beneath my wheels.

"Take it easy now, hotshot." My father's voice played in my head.

I skated an easy mile, fearing the return of pain with every stride, stopping often to adjust laces. The most comfortable movement was side surfing, a style I got accustomed to while skating big downhill runs like Spyglass Hill in Corona del Mar. In side surfing, one foot faces forward while the other toe faces backward. Miles and years of practice had made my legs flexible enough to hold a straight line in this heel-to-heel configuration. The initial tendency is to cramp up and spin out in a circle while your feet naturally creep back into toes-forward form. But with a little speed and a lot of stretching, you can lean into a backside turn, then quickly cut forward and change direction as if you were surfing or skiing a slope. It's unconventional. It's downright weird-looking. And it caused people to point and start conversations as I rolled by.

Ahead on the Prom, people gathered to watch a tall man in tight black slacks, flowing white shirt and a fancy vest, figure skating with leaps, lutzes, and pirouettes. I appreciated the difficulty of his style of "pretty skating," but these were skills I could not consider useful in my life. I was content in the parallel slalom and surf-bum styles I'd picked up. I rolled around the crowd's perimeter, side surfing outside the circle of tourists mesmerized by the show, ice cream melting down their hands.

To my surprise, the showman left his stage and jumped in front of my path.

"American? Are you American? Do you speak English? Hello-hello-hello. Australian? What's your name? Where'd you learn to do *that*?"

His rapid-fire questions required a moment. "Yes, yes, yes. Hello. No. Mike. And California."

He tried to connect my answers like imaginary dots in the air with his finger but quickly gave up.

"Whatever." With dramatic theatrical gestures, he presented me to his audience. "Ladies and gentlemen, presenting Mike from California!"

About half the audience responded "Hello, Mike!"

With that, I was pulled into his show.

"I'm Ted. I'm American too." He was friendly and eccentric, a cocktail of door-to-door salesman with two parts charisma and one part con man. I wasn't buying whatever he had to sell, but I enjoyed the sound of his American accent—a sound I was losing familiarity with.

I opened my mouth to respond, but he blurted his question over me. "Can you show me how you do that?"

"Side surfing? It's just practice." I said it like it was nothing. I didn't tell him it took years and hundreds of miles of practice. "I have a couple of pointers that'll help, if you want to try."

Ted was an animated and gabby gentleman, polite like an Englishman yet indecorous like an Italian. We talked about my journey as he tried side surfing, his legs spinning out every time. His audience disseminated, but he didn't care.

"You're pretty good at doing your thing out here, Ted. Is that just street practice here on the Prom?"

"Ah, my dear boy. It is my distinct pleasure to evince decades of skating and dance and thespian grandeur from the theater."

I might have let "thespian grandeur" slide, but the way he pronounced "thee-yay-tuh" like Katherine Hepburn left me rolling my eyes. Such drama had no place on a sunny beach day. Still trying to side-surf, Ted asked questions too quickly for me to keep up, so I briefed my story from Italy to Nice.

"You did what? A backpack, ski poles? Oh dear lord, Michael. You could die on those hills. You could die right here on the Prom, for that matter."

We moved from his sidewalk stage to a bench overlooking the sea.

"Right you are about those hills. I was going to skate to Barcelona, but I'm pretty sure it would kill me. Better I use my head and take the train than let the buses use my head as a speed bump." I smiled—who's the dramatic one now? I hoped my confession didn't show my shame in defeat. I had conquered many hills and should be proud of my accomplishments, instead of feeling like a quitter.

"Wow," Ted said. A long wow with a deep stare beyond my pupils, like I had found something he still sought as an older fellow—some secret I might reveal through my eyes.

"Well, Ted, gotta go. My hour's up. I told my feet I'd give them an easy day. Got a long way to skate tomorrow." I left him on the bench, staring like a statue.

After skating a block, I looked back to see he was finally leaving the bench. I rolled back toward my hotel, and Ted went back to spinning and leaping for an all-new audience.

CHAPTER 16

TOM THE SKATER

There's not a word yet for old friends who've just met.
—Jim Henson

At the other end of the Prom, a crew was erecting a circus tent in a park across from the beach. I skated a few curious laps of the area, casually gliding sideways, watching the bikini girls flirting with long-haired dudes in black shirts behind a temporary fence. A fellow roller skater and girl watcher, an American-looking guy, joined me, and we circled the girls like sharks around a sinking ship.

The ticket booth displayed a poster: "Ted Nugent Tonight." Ted Nugent, here in Nice? I checked the ticket prices. Sadly, I would have to decline. Not in the budget, with bills for unexpected hotels and only Bob could say how many international calls. I would be wise to save my money for Carrie and Barcelona.

The other American skater approached. "I been a lot of places, but the women here... *Sheesh*! Hey, how do you do that?"

"Side surfing? It's just practice, but I have a couple of pointers that'll help."

No chat, no introductions, no hello. We just started talking, like dogs of the same breed running after a fox. Eventually we connected with a handshake and two words.

"Tom."

"Mike."

We kept skating without missing a *mademoiselle*, eventually arriving at a short form of conversation calling out girls the other person should check out. "Seven o'clock—she's an eight," or "Ten at ten." Tom's baggy shorts, fashionable shades, and clean haircut hinted he was from California, but his shout of "Ho, Daddy!" in comical panic at each fail of side surfing confirmed his heritage.

I took a bench to rest my feet. Tom joined me.

Turned out Tom was a surfer, which allowed him to pick up the side surfing thing faster than most skaters. It was the backside turn lingo that really pulled it together for him. I'd like to take some credit, but he just got it. Perhaps it was no big deal in the first place.

"I'm just getting out of the RV a while, getting in a little exercise in before the show," he explained.

I eventually put it together that he was part of the Ted Nugent show, not a roadie or groupie or musician but something more managerial, more technical, I guessed.

"I produce the lights and staging for the show," he said. "So yeah, I travel in the RV, make sure all the lighting is done right, then run it all at showtime. I pretty much live in the RV and get out to skate whenever I get a break. Meet some people, check out the local talent. Get some fresh air."

"Wow, now that's a cool job," I blurted with corn-fed enthusiasm.

He nodded. My reaction must not have seemed new. But after most likely (and rightfully) bragging about his job for years, now he drank the antidote of rock stardom as his cocktail of choice.

"Meh."

Careers—and specifically, cool and unusual careers like Tom's— fascinated me. The constant tug, if I'd had a sleeve to tug on, reminded me that one day soon I'd have to choose a career myself. Roller-skating from town to town was no sustainable future. How could I support Carrie with this life? We'd certainly had our own vagabond experiences, but she wasn't the durable sort of girl who could survive on orts from harmonica busking if we found ourselves completely down and out. Only a real job would support the comforts she'd want, and the comforts I guessed I'd want for her as well. So I had wonder about my career, but not worry. It would all work out.

I took my skates off and stuffed the dirty socks in the boots.

"Whoa, dude," Tom said. "Shark attack, or foot massage in a blender?"

We talked a while before he asked me about the concert.

"I'm a big fan of Nugent," was what I said, but I could see that my broke traveler expression tipped him off. "Honestly though, it's not in the budget."

He offered anyway. "Come to the show with me tonight, backstage, as my guest. It's all free—drinks, food, chicks. You'll dig it."

My eyes lit up like Tom's spotlights. Free backstage passes to Ted Nugent in Nice? This would be insane. I nodded like a hungry little mouse.

"Come to the bus and party with us first, about seven. The roadies like to get some local talent on board, and it could get interesting. Whaddaya say?"

"Duh—of course I'll come" filled my brain but didn't make it out of my mouth. The mouse nods kept coming.

"Yeah, cool man," I replied. "See ya at seven. Thank you."

I walked casually around the corner, out of his sight, before jumping up and down and yelling. "Yes, *yes*! I'm partying backstage with the roadies at a Ted Freakin' Nugent concert on the beach in France!"

Tom had confided that he wasn't a big fan of Nugent's music, something about the work making the nightly performance stale. I couldn't feel more different. I owned all Nugent's albums. I spent long nights cleaning my vinyl records and listening to every analog click of the needle with my big can earphones. I studied Nugent's album jacket stories instead of textbooks. I played air guitar until my air fingers bled, banging long hair with buddies on the headrests of my '72 Ranchero, my badass eight-track player cranking out *Double Live Gonzo*.

I walked back to my hotel and gushed a postcard full of exclamation points to Carla.

Nightfall on the Prom sent the ice cream eaters and poodle walkers home as evening scenes took over. Street vendors turned their music up, girls walked arm in arm, and dodgy characters did their deeds in the shadows. The Prom transformed into a five-kilometer pickup bar.

The Théâtre de Verdure, an amphitheater covered with Nugent's circus tent, was surrounded by security. I arrived in a bathing suit and the one shirt with buttons I kept clean for special occasions. I was such a dope, bringing only two bathing suits to live in for two months. I'd tried to spruce up, but who was I kidding with my wrinkled backpack clothes, hat hair, and untrimmed beard? I looked shabby.

I worked my way through the crowd, and the security team recognized Tom's cool friend and welcomed me when I reached the gate. I was relieved I didn't have to jump like a groupie screaming "I know a guy, I know a guy."

"Mike—hell, yeah!" The bouncer's massive bro-shake pulled me through the mosh pit and set the evening's tone. "Grab yourself something at the bar. Tom's here somewhere, I'll tell him you're in. Hell, yeah!"

The RV awning covered a full bar and carpeted sofa seating. A skinny Australian roadie handed me a cup of something sweet and strong.

"You're Tom's friend, eh?"

I took a gulp, nodded, and shook his hand.

"Grab yourself a buzz, mate. I'll fetch 'im. 'E's around 'ere somewhere. Hell, yeah!"

Before I could answer, he disappeared around the RV.

A huge bearded roadie put a lanyard badge around my neck. "Tom's buddy?"

"Yep."

"Hell, yeah." He straightened out my collar, gave me a pat on the back that made me belch, and walked away without another word.

The world inside the fence was not of my planet. Groupies surrounding the RV looked like walking ads from *Vogue* magazine: Paris chic, dressed to kill, leather and lace, sexy as sexy gets. On my planet, they'd have looked like big-ticket hookers, but here they were Friday night teens hanging out.

I pretended to sip my drink, covering my face to whisper "Oh my god" into my cup, holding it underneath my chin in case my eyes fell out.

Outside the fence, no one had looked at me, but inside, the girls took notice. I was now a guy with clout. A tall gal approached, babbling in French and turning my badge to check the color; I had purple, she had yellow. She smiled, put her arm around me, and positioned for me to light her cigarette.

I stood a little taller.

Tom interrupted.

"Hey Mike, you made it. Hell, yeah!"

We did a bro handshake with a little flair—four or five hand positions with an explosion bump finish.

"C'mon, let's go meet some people." He guided me into the RV, but my tall clingy gal with the wrong-colored badge was stopped at the RV door.

I coughed my way through dense pot and tobacco smoke to the back of the RV. The party was crowded with roadies, flirty girls, and some dope-dealing derelict rolling joints on a silver tray. Tom coughed and cranked open a vent in the ceiling. A little fan sucked smoke out through the roof so we could breathe.

I moved close so he could hear me over the music. "Are you sending smoke signals to the cops?"

He chuckled a moment, then looked out the back window in a moment of paranoia.

"Yeah, we're cool," he yelled back.

It wasn't cool to smoke pot in France in 1981, even inside the fence. The penalties would be harsh. But the smokers had a sense of immunity aboard their little Ministry of Marijuana.

"I gotta check something out," Tom said. "Hang tight. I'll be back."

I looked out the back windows, paranoid the police might be trying to raid the security barrier, expecting to spot one of them showing a photo of some backpacker on roller skates in front of the Monaco casino. Tom talked with security until he was mobbed by gorgeous groupies. Word must have leaked that he was the guy in charge of purple badges.

Trapped in the back of the drug bus, I gasped for air. If my own face was tingling from the secondhand smoke, the stoners up front must have lost all sensation in their faces. The tiny fan pulled all the smoke to the back of the bus, where it passed through my lungs before exhausting through the vent above me. I got too stoned baking in this marijuana sauna to even care about fresh air.

The dope dealer rolled joint after joint. With brown from a baggie, green from a tin can, and several rolling papers attached to some sort of cardboard straw, he rolled a long, megaphone-shaped joint. A French guy puffed hard, causing the cigar-sized end to flare up and drop a chunk of burning ash on the upholstered sofa. There went the RV deposit. The partiers laughed without a care.

The French guy passed it around, but I held a hand up and shook my head, which was already spinning like a Ted Nugent album from the cloudy RV.

I had to get out of there. I found a pack of gum by the beds to wash the pungent reek of unfiltered tobacco from my mouth, eyes, and throat.

A commotion at the door caught my attention. The roadies sat up, the excitement in their voices elevating. Five new A-list groupies, even hotter than the nines already on the bus, had arrived. Two of the girls were now headed through the stench cloud to the back of the bus to meet the weird American guy in surf trunks talking to himself. At least my breath will be minty-fresh.

Of all the most provocative girls on the French Riviera, these five ladies had won the lottery. These select five, similar in figure, hairstyle, and attire, made it past security, past roadie scrutiny, and finally past Tom. The chosen few had done enough to win the coveted privilege of hanging out on the roadie bus: primped their hair enough, invested enough time at the makeup mirror, and spent a small fortune at lingerie and leather shops. Being there could be one of the biggest victories of their young lives, but all I wanted to do was go outside to get a breath of fresh air.

Amid it all, I couldn't stop thinking of Carrie. Not because I pictured her on that A-list, but because she too was a smoker. The one thing that should have kept me away from her I carried instead as some badge of honor that love could endure all things. But the towering pedestal I set her upon cracked and crumbled a little more with each flick of her lighter. Would all the positives I loved about her, all the green flags, outweigh that one red flag? Maybe she'd have quit smoking by the time I got to Barcelona. Maybe I wouldn't get lung cancer before I got out of this bus.

One of the A-listers stopped to pose with her cigarette for an excited roadie to light. The other came straight for me, straight for the bedroom at the back of the bus.

She was assertive, forward, domineering. Her straight black hair guided my eyes down past a chasm of cleavage, diving down her bare torso and tickling her skin between unbuttoned jeans and hot-pink lace. I calculated about ten minutes of tugging to get those jeans off. My stoned nerdiness ruined the sexual excitement, and I laughed out loud. What the hell was the matter with me, man?

Her Cleopatra eyes stared at my crotch. She said something in French and put her arm around me, holding up a cigarette for me to light.

I had no idea what she was saying, but I did recognize my name in the dialogue. She said my name. How did she—

She rubbed my back with her hand up my shirt, squishing her firm breasts against my shoulder. Her sexy, nonsensical French continued softly in my ear. I didn't care what she said as long as she kept talking and breathing heavy. I told her I was *américain* and smiled at just about everything she said. Baked, seduced, and hard as a rock—getting it on in the back of the RV was in the air.

And then her younger, shorter partner came to flirt with my other side, rubbing the bulge in my shorts, sliding her tongue up my neck and into my ear. She was less imperious, more playful, and perhaps a little sweet while still asserting her goal. The fantasy of every hetero guy on earth, effortless sex with two hot girls, was imminent.

As excited as a guy can be, I grew even more awkward and unsophisticated. Should I just do nothing, let them run the show? Should I play a part in this act? What if they closed the door—was I committed? What if they didn't close it—would the others watch? I wasn't some back-of-the-van spectator, so I had zero experience in this fast and libertine trade. I dreaded botching the opportunity and becoming That Guy.

Cleopatra Eyes wagged her unlit cigarette at me, and I recognized a word: *fumer*, like the signs at the Dr. Scholl store that said No Smoking. I tried repeating the signage words and ended up telling her it was a no-smoking area. That's when she gave up. Stopped talking, stopped waving her cigarette, and stopped rubbing her hands and breasts on me. I hoped she was only walking to the front of the RV for a light, but she kept on walking.

Short and Sweet kept her resolve with her hand up my shorts. I knew I should've studied more French. Her fun-loving expression turned me on; she was like a girl I'd take home to meet Mom and Dad. What a jackass—I had to stop thinking of Mom and Dad. How did these idiotic thoughts enter my head at a time like this?

She ran her finger across my lips, murmuring "schwing goom," her eyes submissive. "Schwing goom," over and over, so soft and suggestive. I had no clue what she wanted to do, but I was about to burst with schwing goom, and she was ready to schwing goom the pants off me. Her classic French pouty lip stuck out, her thick, shoulder-length hair tousled over her leather coat. She unzipped her coat—my god, there was nothing under it. She jiggled without restraint, intimating with her finger that I should schwing goom her mouth.

What the hell was schwing goom?

She backed me up against the bed and pulled my hips in for a grind to the music, moving my hands up into her open jacket while hers slid from my hips to my face, pulling our faces closer. She softly opened my mouth with one finger, cocked her head to the side, and once again asked: "Schwing goom?"

I surrendered. "*Oui*, schwing goom."

Her eyelashes tickled my face, her lips still whispering the words while nibbling my ear.

And that's when I got it. She was trying to say an English word. The English word must have started with ch- as in "cherry," but the French would pronounce it as sh- as in "ship." It wasn't "schwing" she was trying to say; it was "chwing." A split second later, the second part of the puzzle came to me. "Chwing gum"? "Schwing goom" was chewing gum!

As if I'd hit the big red game show buzzer, I raised my arms and shouted "Chewing gum!" with a burst of laughter.

"*Oui, oui*, schwing goom." She was thrilled that I might have a stick of gum for her.

With so much pot and nicotine in the air, I couldn't stop laughing—partly at the way she pronounced chewing gum but also at how ridiculous I was, believing for a second that these girls were sincerely attracted to me. By the authority of a team of seasoned professional roadies, these two had been voted the hottest girls in the south of France, the most likely to perform, then sent to the back of the bus to find the stoned, drunk, and lonely buddy of the boss. I had repelled them both within minutes.

I handed over the pack of gum I had in my pocket and walked out, laughing hysterically at what a complete buffoon I was.

I was *so* That Guy.

CHAPTER 17

TED THE ROCKER

I surround myself with positive, productive people of good will and decency.
—Ted Nugent

Outside the RV, I pulled up a camping chair next to Tom and tried to explain what had happened through tears of laughter, lack of coherence, and coughing—a useless you-had-to-be-there story. I drank a beer and sobered up on fresh air, concluding that watching the marginally innocent yellow badge groupies through predatory eyes was a better idea than being the prey of professional purple badgers.

Tom pulled a radio from his belt. "Tom to Snake… Snake, ya out there?"

"Yeah, Tom, go," came the voice of a thousand years of smoking in roadie buses and gargling with gravel and glass chips.

"Yeah, Snake, set me up with a guest chair in my booth up there for tonight, will ya?"

"All over it, boss man."

My personal stock was rising. As if sending a pack of sex-crazed French groupies to the back of the bus to seduce me wasn't enough, now Tom had a special chair set up for me somewhere in the tent.

I mock-clinked our red Solo cups. "Dude, you rock so much."

"Showtime. Let's get going."

I yanked him out of his chair with a bro-shake and proudly paraded my purple pass in step with Tom and his regiment. These weren't the chair-folding, amp-carrying roadies from the RV; this was an elite squad wearing safety harnesses, head lamps, and two-way radio headsets. I was an unarmed civilian being escorted to the front lines.

Inside the tent, the squad scattered in all directions. I followed Tom through the darkness, house music overpowering whatever he tried to yell to me. I cupped an ear and leaned in.

"If it's too bright and quiet, the show has no buildup," he shouted. "You watch. I'll start adjusting the lights and control the crowd. It's a power trip, for sure."

A guard at the king pole of the big top checked my badge before we climbed to the techno-treehouse above. Cables with shackles and trusses with heavy wires branched in every direction. On the platform, twenty feet of switches, dials, sliders, blinking lights, and bouncing needles looked something like a sound mixing board, but this was all about lighting.

"Sit back here."

Tom directed me to a camping chair stuffed in the back of the platform, grabbed his headset, and offered me a cup of earplugs. His crew climbed their poles and flashed laser pointer signals our way. Tom ran through final checklists for all systems and spotlights in all locations, each controlled from his panel. As the stage lights illuminated, dimmed, flashed, and changed colors, the crowd screamed and wooed. The onstage crew performed their last-minute sound checks.

Tom sat back and locked his fingers behind his head. "Okay, the talent's here now. Just waiting for Ted."

The French crowd began yelling "Nu-gent! Nu-gent!" Only their French pronunciation made it sound like "Noo-zhon! Noo-zhon!" Tom fed their hunger with luminous appetizers, finally dropping the house lights to create an exhilaration bomb below us. I held the treehouse rails, shaking like an astronaut on lift-off.

Nugent walked out onto the dark stage, a single spotlight on a big man with big hair, strutting into the iconic solo intro of *Stranglehold* like an anthem. He put on an amazing two-and-a-half-hour show as both a visionary musician and crazy-ass performer. My contorted face and overworked vocal chords barely survived the first couple of songs. One of my favorite rockers. One of my favorite tunes. An unprecedented seat.

Equally awe-inspiring was Tom, his fantastic setup, and the way it enhanced the performance. I quickly became more fascinated by the tech than the talent. Maybe this was the real me. I should accept the techno-junkie I was and choose a career with all the glitz, glamour, excitement, and rock-star appeal of Tom's position.

Tom pulled his headphone aside. "This one's a color scroller. That's Snake's spot number two up there. This wheel runs the color gels on those trusses and Showbiz's rig—the guy over there. It's not an exact science. Just hit parts of songs with certain lights, add drama—pow."

He washed the stage in green during a solo, and Nugent gave the booth a nod.

Near the end of the song, Tom had me on the switch panel. "Play with these three. Tap 'em fast, in any random order. Match the beat if you can."

Now I was a light board operator. This would look great on my résumé.

The show moved along its scheduled lineup, each lighting cue met as the crew performed their duties just as they had night after sleepless night. What a night, what a show.

Two more beers with the groupies and roadies at the RV later, and the after-show party collapsed into the breakdown frenzy. I lost

Tom in the commotion so I left. I told myself I'd come back in the morning to offer thanks and a goodbye, but I never ran into Tom again.

I stumbled the few blocks back to my hotel, arriving at the door only to find it locked for the night. What the hell? Who locks a hotel lobby? I would never get used to the European hotel norms. No one answered my knock, so I walked back to a pay phone to call the manager, who would undoubtedly be asleep.

CHAPTER 18

LATE NIGHT WITH...

Wherever you go, go with all your heart.
—Confucius

Calling Marcel after hours felt like so many nights in Avalon, skulking from Carrie's house in the middle of the night to go sleep in my own bed on Mom's boat. The shore boat drivers went home at 1 a.m. After that, you had to ask the harbor patrol for a ride out to your boat if your parents had tied the dinghy out at the boat, and you'd get a lecture from the patrolman about staying out so late. I'd listen respectfully, mumbling "yes sir" in appropriate pauses, and pray he would sneak up quietly and not bump the boat, waking my parents. Typically, the patrolman would rev his engine, bump my parents' boat, and bellow out, "Enjoy the rest of your evening, kid!" before floating away with a vindictive smirk.

Some nights I'd stay on shore with Carrie, and some nights she'd stay on the boat with me. As long as we made it to one of our homes before 2 a.m., there wouldn't be any trouble. If we fooled around and stayed out too late, we couldn't go to either home without getting into trouble for staying out too late. The next morning, we'd tell each parent we'd stayed at the other house, but that left us walking around Avalon until daylight.

With damp swimsuits and T-shirts, we'd borrow a beach towel from a neighbor's clothesline and I'd hold Carrie tight underneath. We shivered through the coldest hours on a terrace road bench, as the harbor lights and casino twinkled in complicity. They were nights of romantic misery, teen lovers choosing outcast togetherness over the comforts of a warm home and a little trouble. We were crazy in love.

Once our shivering embrace was warmed by the first sliver of sunlight, we'd get free donuts and cocoa from my buddy Guy before he opened the donut shop, leading to at least one joke about how I introduced him to his girlfriend-turned-fiancée. "You have to meet this girl," I'd told him. "She's so dumb." Now they were getting married.

I couldn't bear a night like that alone in Nice, so I kept ringing the hotel phone and eventually woke Marcel. He awaited me in his bathrobe holding my room key—but no lecture, no punishments, and no huddling for warmth under damp towels and bright stars. Just a dirty look from a sleepy, grumpy man, and a warm soft bed to crash into.

Morning came with a clattering knock at my thin mahogany door.

"*Un moment, s'il vous plaît*," I called.

Marcel made sure I understood it was past checkout time. I begged for another hour of sleep. I could have slept for days. My hangover made everything a confusing struggle. How had I gotten back here? Why was the TV upside down? Was that schwing goom in my hair?

Another tap on the door interrupted my confusion.

"*Oui?*" I asked, as in "Yes, what is it?" Apparently, it came out sounding like "Come on in."

Jolie stepped into the room. She held a pot of coffee and a plate of butter croissants, but she wore a cocktail dress and a classic pouty French lip.

"*Bonjour, Monsieur Michel.*"

In time, I'd accept the fact that not all words spoken by gorgeous French women were a come-on. I rubbed my sleepy face, mumbling my thanks and taking the tray. She exited with a coy grin, her eyes dropping to the morning boner in my boxers. I was such an idiot.

An hour later, a cleaner and nicer-smelling roller skater came downstairs with fresh clothes and rehabilitated feet, excited to return to the streets of the Côte d'Azur. Travelers checking in to the hotel eyed my equipment as I breezed across the lobby's marble floor, avoiding the claw feet of a mahogany pedestal with fragrant flora in a huge glass vase. They snapped some pictures and quizzed Marcel. I adjusted my gear without looking into the cameras, a zoetic oxymoron of posing for candid shots.

It was time for my exit.

"*Au revoir!*" called Marcel.

"*Bon voyage!*" added Jolie.

They stepped forward and held the front doors, gesturing for a grand aerial departure down the entry steps.

This ham on wheels took the bait. I would deliver for my audience.

With a little speed rounding the flower table, I took a flying leap out the doors, a slalom racer flying through the starting gates. A perfect landing three steps below in the courtyard sent me rocketing toward the gate to the sidewalk, where I crashed square into a guy on a ten-speed bike.

I hadn't just hit the guy; I'd left us twisted in a wreckage of bike parts, ski poles, and spinning spokes.

CHAPTER 19

NICE DEPARTURE

Everywhere is walking distance if you have the time.
—Steven Wright

Midday sun toasted the bronze bodies spread evenly across the Nice *galets*. Roller skaters dressed in electric blues and Day-Glo greens drifted through the crowds walking the Prom. One skater—the one with the backpack and ski poles—had a nasty black friction burn in the shape of a bicycle tire down one leg and a series of scrapes and smeared blood down the other.

The bike collision hurt more than the blisters, a positive sign that my feet were healing nicely. My body was wounded, but my ego had taken the brunt of damage. I recalled the burning embarrassment as the hotel guests helped disassemble the mix of tangled bike and ski hardware. Could I not have walked out and waved goodbye like a normal human? It doesn't take much to egg me on, but do I have to fall for it every time? The cyclist took the fall with me this time, but at least he rode away without a scratch.

My gear was reorganized and fastened like a suit of armor, and I was off again to conquer a small segment of afternoon road, albeit cautious about destroying my feet again. Van Morrison was playing "Into the Mystic" in my headphones, and the groove would take me to the next harbor, where I could catch a train to Cannes and find Joel. I rolled along, satisfied that he was going to love my travel stories, and I was going to love his encouragement, ego boost, and advice.

The trance was broken by the sound of my name.

"Michael! Hello, Michael." I recognized the voice; it was Ted doing pirouettes for tourists.

He rushed over from the entourage. "Oh my god, your legs are bleeding. You've been hurt. Quick, somebody call a doctor! For god's sake, we need a medic."

I shook my head at the crowd before someone took him seriously. "It's just some scrapes, Ted."

"You're not leaving town, are you?"

"That's what the backpack's all about."

He acted surprised, maybe even sad. "So where are you off to, my fine young man?"

"Just down the road to Antibes. Then I'll hop the train to Cannes."

"But you're hurt. Let me drive you there. I have a nice convertible Mercedes just around the corner."

"I'm fine, Ted. Thank you, but no. I want to skate."

"Okay. And then you're off to Spain, right? You are roller-skating to Glory Hallelujah Spain? Wow. I cannot conceive of the courage, the spirit it must take to—" He stopped short, staring at me like a lost old dog. "Take me with you."

"Grab your backpack, string bean. Let's make some tracks."

I wasn't serious. This was the last guy I'd want along on this trip. But as soon as the words left my mouth, I could see he had confused my sarcasm for sincere civility. Disturbing.

"But I don't have a backpack like that," he said. "I just have my little fanny pack."

I needed to get out of there before he made a spectacle, but I was too late.

"Ladies and gentlemen," he announced to the entourage, rolling to his stage for another ceremonial speech. "The brave and daring Michael here is setting a course to roller-skate to Barcelona. That's right, the one in Spain. Five, eight hundred—oh dear god, it's hundreds of miles, or kilometers, or whatever. But it's a long, long... It's a very long way. And I'd like you all to join me in wishing him well on his gallant adventures."

By the time he'd finished I had already left, rolling away from the applause of fifty strangers in favor of one "Brown-Eyed Girl" in my headphones.

The Prom stretched for miles past beachfront hotels where famous people's outrageous secrets would forever be kept by career concierges. To my left, beach clubs overflowed with obese old men in enormous sunglasses reading newspapers, drinking Kir Royale, and smoking Gitanes as they fried their skin in the afternoon sun. God lavished His amazing grace upon the women of France, but He was not so kind to the men.

The outer boundaries of perfect sidewalk and asphalt road drew nearer, and the hotels got progressively shorter until a last seedy tear-down motel marked the bitter end of the Prom and the return of black asphalt with white lines. I broke free of the city, returning to a simpler and more purposeful existence. I was returning to the hunt, to breathing fresh air and doing what my mind and body were genetically programmed to do. I was back to moving through my day in lieu of planning a time for movement. College, career, and building wealth continued gnawing at my adolescent goals, but the sustenance of solitude and experiences to come would surely hold as much weight.

Beyond the international airport and the horse track on the beach, the biggest attraction ahead was a flat, coastal route that hugged the sand, consistent as the Med's surface glistening to my left. Sidewalk cafés and their prattling tourists capturing photos of the backpacking curio on wheels were equally predictable. I was no celebrity, but a guy cross-country skiing down the beach made quality people watching, I had to admit.

Sleeping in, a late start, the crash with a cyclist, and my crackpot conversation with Ted had slowed my progress so much that I couldn't justify a meal yet. But the paralyzing smells of *espagnole* over *boeuf* wafting from the cafés crippled my progress.

I finally plunked down at a café table next to a young couple and their two preschoolers. The kids tried desperately to contain their excitement about my method of travel, pushing their boundaries, staying in their chairs as instructed—if only by a toe—as the rest of their littleness scrambled closer to my table.

Their father and I exchanged pleasantries, and I answered the obvious questions: what was I doing, what was my name, where was I going, was I flippin' crazy? The usual stuff. Bjorn's Swedish accent was clear, yet his translations called for creative interpretation.

"Maka asks from where are you living?"

"Uh, I skated here from Italy. I'm from California."

Most Euros had met a Californian; our stereotypes were more notorious than those of many entire countries. Bjorn translated to Maka and they repressed laughter, nodding as if I'd just told an inside joke.

"No, really. I'm from Southern California."

"This is where Los Angeles to living, yes?"

It was my turn to repress laughter. "Actually, it's about fifty miles south of Los Angeles in a little suburb of Orange County called…"

Bjorn tensed up with the effort of translating English to Swedish and miles to kilometers, recalling a world map from a schoolroom wall, and keeping his kids out of his cassoulet.

"Yes, where Los Angeles is living." I loathed saying I was from Los Angeles.

"Maka asks how much heavy in your backpack."

"About fifteen kilograms of heavy in there." I slid the bag to Bjorn to test the heft.

Maka tried a test lift too, giggling when she couldn't pick it up. The kids got permission to leave their chairs and try. Maka fired off another question to her husband as she pulled equipment from a camera case.

"Maka asks how many kilometers are there in a day?" Bjorn asked.

It was like a quiz show. Repeatedly pulling her blond hair aside, Maka slid behind a 35mm lens, whizzing through the film. I wasn't moving or making expressions, so I found it curious how each photo could get any better. Was there even film in that camera? She looked like a pro, locked behind her lens while her boy plowed a toy truck through her *crêpes complète*.

I was still nursing a hangover, not on my A-game, and likely a dull conversationalist. I changed the subject to their lives, asked a few questions, and sat back as Bjorn shared details of the last thirty days of his children's development, backstory about Maka's mother, and the many places his brother had traveled. Listening was easier; I could eat and formulate my next question. I nodded and enjoyed the rich shallot and herb sauce of *onglet à l'échalote*, catching about half what he said.

The kids were excused from their table and came over to join mine with the toy car and some sort of ketchup-covered magic wand the little girl waved aimlessly. I hunched over my lunch, devouring what I could before she turned salt and sugar packets into pixie dust.

When they were done, I gratefully accepted Bjorn's offer to buy my lunch without a trace of prideful argument. Moments after they left, a bohemian couple slid into their vacated seats.

"To what far are you go this day?"

CHAPTER 20

LIGHTHOUSE AND HOME

One of the most beautiful qualities of true friendship
is to understand and to be understood.
—Lucius Annaeus Seneca

Port Vauban, the harbor for the city of Antibes, is the less pretentious cousin of Monte Carlo. The slightly larger marina—at roughly 1,500 boats—holds its front door open and invites you to join old friends inside. The mellow social vibe paralleled my enervated energy. My stamina said I could go further that day, but my fragile feet told me to slow down. Twenty kilometers was enough for the day.

I nearly overlooked a small market. Vivid fruits, vegetables, and flowers overflowed wooden crates that had likely been displaying fresh color and scents on this sidewalk for generations. My mouth watered for a juicy warm Double-Double from In-N-Out Burger, but it was time to stop being so typically teen, so eager for instant gratification. So American.

How about I try my own French cooking? Maybe some fresh seafood and vegetables? What else did I have to do tonight?

I tossed my backpack into a shopping cart and skated the aisles of the old market, avoiding the center of the store where canned and processed goods were dusted by a small boy in a red, white, and blue apron. He was probably the third or fourth generation to work in this family market; one day he too would chew a cigar at the cash register while his great-grandson dusted cans of tripe.

I transferred my groceries from cart to backpack and rolled out to find a suitable campsite. Along the beaches, pictograms on old metal signs with images of a tent beneath the familiar slashed red circle warned me NO CAMPING. The metal signs were evidently losing their battle with the salt air, being replaced by plastic signs that clinched their message by listing fines for camping plus a friendly little handcuffs graphic.

I stopped for lunch on the seawall. Two officers in a patrol car watched every bite of baguette, profiling their criminal with forensic precision. The backpack, the mode of travel, the absence of a recent shower—all signs of a caper soon to be in progress. As they suspected, I was casing the joint for a decent night's sleep.

The hills were too far inland; I didn't want to go the distance for a good hiding place among the trees. City parks were useless due to night sprinklers, early lawnmowers, and brother bums.

A helicopter resting atop a megayacht lured me to the harbor entrance. Like some giant bird perched for flight, its rotors hung over the decks below, where the crew launched dinghies the size of the boat I lived on in Avalon. Another five megayachts were backed in, their gangplanks bridging from yacht to harbor mole. The massive gangplanks with mirror-polished stainless steel and teak safety rails extended hydraulically to the pier from their transoms, allowing ladies in heels to cross safely. Further down the line, the smaller boats relied on narrow wooden planks that made walking to and from shore a precarious balancing act—comical after a night of cocktails.

Vivid nautical colors dappled the brilliant street scenes. I dodged tourists gawking at the yachts in the hot sun and local scooters zipping around them. The patrol car continued tailing me. I hoped, with a touch of guilt, that some more serious crime elsewhere might draw them away.

The nautical activities behind the megayachts comforted me with the senses of home. I skated past uniformed crews in embroidered polo shirts: young, glamorous guys and girls polishing stainless steel, oiling teak, and otherwise looking busy while flirting with crew members on neighboring yachts. These yachts were their floating mansions as they waited for news that the owners' private jets were inbound. Yes, the rich prick's yacht job looked like a cool gig, and I was happy Joel was enjoying this lifestyle not far from there.

Across the harbor loomed Fort Carré, a star-shaped bastion of sixteenth-century power guarding the entrance to Port Vauban. A half-assed translation of the French plaque left me with vague understanding; the fort had been built in the 1500s and once imprisoned Napoleon Bonaparte. The gravity of that date sank into my consciousness; a time when North America was a fresh discovery. I was immersed in magnificent history, an awareness that can only be felt in its proximity—and often thousand-year-old details required me to contemplate the changes these societies must have gone through to become what they are today. My struggles today shriveled in comparison to the battles Fort Carré endured over five centuries.

Past the plaque and beyond the megayachts at the end of the jetty stood my prospective home for the night. I peeled off my sweaty socks and took my tender white feet down the jetty boulders for a soak in the salty sea, the water permeating my senses with the comfort of warm Avalon donuts. The lighthouse stood on a small section of level concrete, a perfect space to lay out my pack and cook a meal as the last of the day's sunlight painted the yachts orange, dimmed the fort, and darkened the sea.

A fisherman made the long walk along the jetty and joined me at the lighthouse. The crags in his face narrated a life story of sun, sea, and smoke. Yellowed fingers baited his rusty fish hooks as he puffed a cigarette glued to his lips.

We each sized up the other. He scrutinized my camp gear, skates, and ski poles as I assessed his potential as a threat, wondering if my anxiety over a benign stranger showed healthy animal instinct or cowardly cynicism. As my feet soaked, I came to understand that his every action was routine, choreographed over years of performance. I was an uninvited guest, a kid cooking dinner in the middle of his refuge.

I took a chance, adopted a welcoming posture, and exhausted my French vocabulary in a couple of poorly worded attempts at asking if he caught big fish here. He answered with garrulous intensity, cigarette bouncing in his mouth like an orchestra conductor's white baton, raving and rambling while rubbing fallen ashes into badly stained pants. My lousy French made it clear to both of us that I wouldn't understand his words, yet he modulated his volume as he walked near and far so I wouldn't miss a thing between casting his bait and jump-starting each yellow cigarette from the lighted butt of the previous. Was it a political rant? Perhaps a tirade at the fish to take bait, or a cry to the sea about his cantankerous wife? Whatever his woes, the salt air worked its magic swiftly and surely. The success of his hour of nature therapy was assured.

After packing his old wooden tackle box as quickly as it had come apart, he lit another cigarette and approached to shake my hand as if to thank me for listening. I used my right hand to stand up, my palm pressed flat into the chalky guano. The white on my hand didn't bother him. He tossed the last bits of mussel meat to the sea, casually wiping the jiggly bits from his right hand on his pants before presenting it in manly fashion. Like blood brothers, we sealed our bond with filthy hands amid the seabirds and the crustaceans, abating all ailments of mind, body, and soul with our salty antidote.

Fort Carré's spotlights illuminated its bastions. Instead, I pulled a cork from a Bergerac with my Swiss Army knife and stared out to sea, sipping sweet freedom from a tin cup as the stench of gull guano wafted from the jagged rocks—five-star accommodations that no money could buy.

A candle in a small jar offered dim light to write in my journal, a going-away gift from Joel. I opened the green paisley cover to his inscription on the inner flap: "Mike, you're experiencing stuff others couldn't even imagine. And to think this is only the inception. Just a few words a day in this 'whatever you make it' diary will be kept for all to share someday. Life offers so many riches. I admire the way you go for the gold. Don't hold back on the adventures. Don't forget to give it that vivid description, like a sunset over the Alpines, or that audacious run down the slopes, or that wine-and-dine at the rustic Bavarian joint. Shiiit, Mike, this will become a vice. You're out there and involved. I love it; I love you. You're a total individual. I covet your style. Have a merry Christmas—and the New Year, well, like I said, just another inception. My sincere regards, Joel."

I was taking the advice to heart. The journal had become my new best friend while there were so few others to talk to. It was an extension of my friendship with Joel. How we'd grown up across the world with different mothers remained a mystery, yet he was the brother and mentor who demanded that these very words made it onto the page.

A summer's evening of French wine, blues harmonica, and passing fishing boats made an easy transition to slumber. The temperature differential from the cooling land brought cooler breezes in from the sea. I awoke from the cold later, balled up like a fetus in surf shorts. This crisis required the emergency space blanket. I unfolded it with anticipation, my miracle duvet in a sandwich baggie, but it turned out to be a crappy little slice of aluminum foil too small to wrap myself in. The days of hypothermia survival tactics in the Alps came to mind. There was no chance an avalanche dog would find me frozen beside a lighthouse, though, and shivering was a bad sign. I needed to warm my core. The foil blanket should have reflected what was left of my body heat, but the little miracle from space did the exact opposite, conducting heat from my skin and wicking it away to the wet terrycloth sleeping bag where the convective breeze worked like a swamp cooler.

During every miserable night I'd spent cold or sick, broken or drunk, there was that come-to-Jesus moment when I realized falling asleep to make the pain go away was not going to happen. An actual fix, moving to a sheltered area, would require getting out bed and maybe even relocating. The inherent problem with lighthouses as a shelter is that they're engineered for laminar flow of cold, damp wind around their cylindrical structure. The Coandă effect, another fluid dynamic, ensured that the airflow encircled the lighthouse, leaving me no place to hide.

I considered crawling down into the jetty rocks for shelter, but the prospect of sleeping with the crabs and rats and monsters in the darkness was worse than freezing. I considered getting back on the road, skating my body heat back to life at 3 a.m. Finally, too lazy to do jumping jacks and too tired to use my brain for interoceptive heat, I put on every bit of clothing I had, covered myself with the backpack, and got an agonizingly few winks of sleep.

Each hard-won degree of increase at dawn thawed my blood and slowed my shivering. I made tea on my camp stove drank it so hot my nose nearly whistled like a tea kettle. Crews on fishing boats returning from a night at sea waved. They must have been wondering if I'd been crazy enough to sleep there all night.

My fisherman friend returned with his handmade tackle box and a white paper bag and a steaming hot paper cup. A yellow cigarette with long ash dangled from his lips.

"*Bonjour, monsieur, bienvenue.*" My voice quivered; I even sounded cold.

"*Ça va?*" he called back.

This French expression, possibly the most common in the entire language, is both a question and an answer: "How's it going?" It can also mean "My dog was abducted by aliens" or "I just got married"—truly an all-purpose expression.

I tried a little French again. "*Ça va bien, mais le nuit c'est très froid.*"

Correct grammar or not, there was no mistaking how cold I was. He approached as if to shake hands but presented me the hot cup and white pastry bag with a "*Bonjour!*" and a bow of respect. This total stranger had taken it upon himself to deliver coffee and a croissant to the stupid, frigid derelict at the lighthouse. Huh. I guess I had a friend.

Mankind itself had been reborn, my faith in French-kind skyrocketing. My frozen face matched my paralyzed posture, holding my arm out, white baggie hanging exactly as it was handed to me.

He walked away too soon to catch my grand smile.

"*Merci! Merci beaucoup.*" I wondered if my gratitude showed in my bewildered response.

A simple hand gesture told me I was welcome, and he proceeded to casting bait.

I walked down the rocks to hang with my new buddy as he mumbled around the bouncing yellow baton in his mouth. I interrupted to shake his nicotine-stained, fish-slimed hand.

"Sir, this is the nicest thing a stranger has ever done for me, and my faith in the French and mankind itself is renewed and elevated to new heights."

I could see he grasped the sincerity in my grip, my eyes, my tone.

"Sir, I am grateful there are people like you in this world. Thank you for being on this planet with me."

His half-smile told me he understood exactly what I said.

I sat on a rock near him, watching him fish, enjoying my pastry with appreciative sounds loud enough to mask the slapping of the sea on the rocks.

I wasn't alone in this world. I could always make new friends. And the friend I wanted most, now that I was warm again, was just down the road. It was time to connect with Joel.

CHAPTER 21

RED CARPET

The two most important days in your life are the
day you are born and the day you find out why.
—Mark Twain

In times of desperation, "practically healed" can still get you out of town. Once the size of ping-pong balls, the blisters on my arches carried me through rush-hour traffic to the outskirts of Antibes, putting distance and good memories behind me. Excitement at seeing my buddy in the next town drove me through the pain with an increasing buzz in each stride I made toward Cannes. On average, I was skating about twelve kilometers per hour, not quite bicycle speed but triple the pace of walking. In an hour or so, I'd be talking with Joel, sharing stories of my latest adventures.

The crowds of people gawking and taking photographs of me all day didn't fill my social cup. Connecting with someone became a craving as strong as the craving I'd felt for breakfast. Although I was turning thousands of heads and hundreds of cameras in the life of a minor celebrity, I had no one to share my adventures with. It wasn't enough for my soul. You could be popular, I was finding out, and still be a recluse. I had my journal for sharing my thoughts and Carla's letters to boost my spirits, but a voice without a listener is lost in the vastness of the sea.

Golfe-Juan looked like a nice beach town, but there was no need to stop. I'd be in Cannes before lunch. Golfe-Juan was typical of undiscovered sandy hideouts, with sidewalk bars and hotels to the right and topless girls and pizza kiosks to the left—typical in an unreal, utopian sense. A parade of supercars flowed casually along the "Promenade de Whatever," heading for another harbor full of megayachts. As jaw-dropping as it was, it was the daily bread, *le pain quotidien*, of the French Riviera. My backpack was so saturated, it too dripped with sweat. I pushed toward my goal, stopping for self-lecture under the shade of a tree. I squirted water from my bota bag into my mouth and all over my sweaty face. I had to slow down to take in these not-so-famous towns, these golden coves out of the popular spotlight.

One more peninsula to cross before I would be in view of Cannes, sharing sidewalks with scooters and trains and pedestrians. Songs by Steely Dan, Johnny Winter, Van Halen, and Dire Straits detached my head from my feet, zoned me so far out of the milieu that I didn't notice the train creeping up on my right.

I was close enough to board it when the engineer blasted his horn behind me. The shock took a few years off my life. The deafening sound waves and my scared-out-of-my-wits reflexes combined to pitch me off the sidewalk into a flower bush.

As I caught my breath, the engineer looked back, laughing his ass off. I wasn't mad; on the contrary, I laughed too as I brushed the leaves and flowers out of my hair. I would have done the same if I'd been in his denim overalls. He got me good.

Still, I'd better turn the music down a bit and pay attention. I stood a few moments longer, waving back to the tourists on the train, letting them collect their nice snapshots of the crazy roller-skating, backpacking skier with legs quivering in fear. At times it was exhilarating to be the center of attention. Celebrities—and hams like me—thrive on it. I'd been a ham all my life, the class clown, the entertainer with the God-given (or cursed) wit. I hoped to bring levity into the lives of the analytical brainiacs who did all the hard work on genius things like engineering my Sony Walkman. Those geniuses hadn't been cracking jokes as they created the brilliant device that played my cassette tapes from a small pouch attached to my hip. Well, maybe they were, but nobody else without a calculator in their shirt pocket would've laughed. People of this world, I was learning, were balanced, each having a gift to share.

Leaving the gift of undiscovered beach towns, I rolled into the megaworld of Cannes. Finding Joel aboard the *Sylvia* took top priority, above even thoughts of Carrie. She would have loved the glamorous life of Cannes. In my mind, she'd be skating beside me in a bikini top and short-shorts; in her mind, she'd be sweeping out of a limousine in her ball gown onto a red carpet. I longed to make her dreams come true, but few at the top of the pyramid had that gift to give, let alone a lighthouse-lounging roller hobo. The flocks of fans in their film festival frenzy were dull as dishwater to me. I'd skated into the biggest day of the year in Cannes, the start of the International Film Festival, the most respected film festival in the world. The world's biggest stars, film producers, media buyers, and screenwriters were packed into this sleepy little beach town, besieged by the desperate paparazzi.

Scanning the tallest masts of the harbor for the red-hulled *Sylvia*, moored deep somewhere in an overcrowded anchorage, I rolled from the Boulevard de la Croisette to the Promenade de Something. The Cannes Prom was lined with movie posters and Rolls Royces driven by men in black suits chauffeuring overdressed women. Traffic was lined up tight as brickwork. Tourists waltzed around and between the cars and the madness.

I was oblivious to it all, skating with the sole intention of finding the harbormaster's office and learning where to find the big red boat. It would be the most boring government building on the waterfront, with nautical flags rather than Cinzano umbrellas. My best guess was the far end of the harbor, and the only way to get there was directly through the insanity. Skating the streets alongside the cars would be the best way to get past the mess of tourists, reporters, news vans, and fans clogging the sidewalks. In hindsight, I should have stayed off the street on the pedestrian side of the blockades, but I was focused on my mission.

In typical teenage fashion, my attention snapped aside when I caught a whiff of food. That had to be grilled Camembert sandwiches—with a big bowl of ketchup to dip in! My blossoming palate for French cuisine was still in infancy. I fantasized that Joel was cooking lunch for the crew of the *Sylvia*, saving a plate for me. My stomach had become my primary emotion. Maybe someone would pass some caviar on a cracker out the window of their limo? It was certainly not out of the realm of possibility—and no crazier than the scene ahead.

A flurry of paparazzi had hopped the barricade and were standing in nonmoving traffic. Scandalmongers and news crews fought for an angle, desperate for a shot at some star. I didn't care which big movie star was behind the tinted limo windows; my own struggle involved a red boat and a cheese sandwich.

But then it dawned on me that for a few moments, the backpacking roller skater *was* the news at the International Film Festival. These paps needed a kicker, a bumper, some B-roll for their stories. They may have scored interviews from the occupants of the limos, but there was something about the sweaty streaks across the limo windows after the madman squeezed through traffic.

Getting trapped in the thick of the festival's opulent opening hadn't crossed my mind, but by then it was too late. I had slipped past the white-gloved traffic cops to tangle with the bodyguards who shopped for their black suits at "big and tall" stores. They weren't sure what to do with me. They couldn't tell me to go back into oncoming traffic, they couldn't have me climb the barricades, and they certainly didn't want to grab me.

As hundreds of fans behind the barricades waved and yelled to the stars, I recognized words about a roller skater too. My gut recognized what was happening: I was about to be picked up and thrown out of another town on the French Riviera. I should have worn a T-shirt.

My exit was a path past the red carpet zone where the A-listers loosened up and the limos departed. I crossed my ski poles behind my back and side-surfed through a narrow gap between limos. A black suit barked at me, and the crowd went wild with cheers. Maybe they were cheering someone famous behind me, but I'd noticed my fancy footwork often seemed connected to the crowd's volume. Like Tom and Ted Nugent's concert lights, I rallied the crowd with a little skating shuffle. Thank god I made it out of there without falling on my ass.

The harbormaster's office was easily found. I'd passed several of these offices in other towns, and they were all bureaucratic, uninspired, boring. Cannes's office was surely designed by the same insipid architect, a blasé cube as aesthetically pleasing as stick figure art in the Louvre.

I climbed the stairs and rolled across the old wood floor into the office. *"Bonjour. Parlez-vous anglais?"*

The young guy at the front desk called to the old guy in the back. The portly harbormaster put on his hat, twirled his long mustache, and habitually checked his sidearm, a pistol so small he would need to empty every chamber to take down a felonious squirrel.

He scrutinized my appearance, his face contorted by confusion and a hint of pain. His face formed a smile as if he were sliding into a warm bath. *"Oui, monsieur,* how may I help you?"

"I'm looking for the sailing vessel *Sylvia.* I'm meeting a friend on board. She's supposed to be here. She, the boat. He, the friend."

"Ah, la *Sylvia…*la *Sylvia…*" He exhaled with the passion of a lost lover. *"Oui, monsieur, la Sylvia,* the red Italian cutter, proud tall mast reaching to the heavens, tight fantail, smooth lines to her stem."

Each detail was defined with hand gestures as though describing a fantasy lover. "Ah, a vision of beauty, *la Sylvia,* to be sure."

I love boats too, but this guy was having sex with the yacht in his mind.

"That's the one, Monsieur Harbormaster. Yep, that's the boat I'm looking for. Where can I find her?"

He dropped the theatrics, returning to the role of droll civil servant. "Sadly, she no coming here. She cancel her reservation in Cannes. She leave me, not come for first time in twenty-seven years, she…"

Hopelessness cracked his voice, and he sulked back to his desk like a man jilted at the altar.

I stood heartbroken at the counter.

He returned, his voice hushed as though he were leaking top-secret information. "I believe *la Sylvia*, she is still in San Remo, Italy. *Sylvia* called a couple of days ago and said she could not make the trip. Perhaps your he-friend is with *la Sylvia* in San Remo?"

"Perhaps." I turned away and mumbled on the down-low, "Or perhaps it wasn't the boat that called."

I left the office, my head hanging low.

"*Monsieur!*" the harbormaster yelled from his window. He was stretching a telephone cord out the window, pointing at the receiver, and giving me a thumbs-up. Like an opera singer, he belted out, "Saaaaaan Reeeeeemooooooo!"

That's all he said; that was all I needed.

After a tin cup full of red wine, a baguette, and some brie on the seawall, my vision of Cannes, Joel, the yacht, and the cheese sandwiches evaporated in the afternoon sun. There would be no cannonballs off the yacht, no cold beer, no napping in a hammock hanging over the deck. The original plan had been to stay in Cannes a while, maybe call it home for a few days—home in this case being defined by the simple notion that someone waited for me, worried if I didn't show up, cared. The warmth of coming home, even to a place I've never been, had been shattered. No friend, no yacht, and no direction.

If there was a single place I traditionally went to make decisions, it was a seawall overlooking a harbor. Many of my life's big decisions had been made while eating donuts with a quart of milk on the Avalon seawall, looking out at the boats in the harbor. Turns out the same strategy works with a baguette and a bottle of wine in Cannes. The sea cures all maladies.

I wasn't about to roller-skate back to Italy. The agony of tackling those hills and tunnels again would be overwhelming. They wouldn't let me skate through Monaco, anyway. My internal compass spun like a toy ship in a flushed toilet. Any direction I wanted to take was possible, and grokking absolute freedom was like trying to grasp the totality of our universe.

Maybe Mom and Dad were right; maybe I really could do anything I wanted in life. My internal battle of courage and confidence finally overcame my doubt and distress. I made my decision; immediate action was required.

I tossed the picnic leftovers into my pack, grabbed my poles off the seawall, and skated as fast as I could to the Cannes train station. The conductor chirped his whistle for the engineer to get moving, yelled "*En voiture!*" and off to San Remo the train rolled—this time with me on board.

CHAPTER 22

RED CUTTER

In any moment of decision, the best thing you can do is the right thing. The worst thing you can do is nothing.
—Theodore Roosevelt

Trusting that little voice in your head can be risky, but the odds stack up nicely once you learn to trust that voice. As the train moved toward Italy, I analyzed my intuition to pack and run.

Italy by train was a short distance but a long ride, stopping at every one-bench train depot on the Riviera. I leaned out the window to watch a slow, gray-haired porter schlepping mailbags from the train to his tiny station. As he walked away, suitcases and mailbags continued to be thrown from the baggage car, crashing onto the platform in a way I expected would break them open. One of the mailbags did come undone, scattering dozens of envelopes. The old porter didn't notice; the baggage thrower didn't care. As the train pulled away, whirling airflow sent envelopes under the train, over the train, out onto the beach. I had to laugh at the Italian postal service. But the joke was on me: these were the men who'd delivered

151

the letter from "a guy on a boat in Italy" to "a guy on a mountain in Germany."

The Italian train conductor delivered an operatic announcement of our arrival: "Saaan Reeemooooooo!" Evidently, his brothers were the Cannes harbormaster and the guy at soccer matches that yells "goal" until he's out of breath. It was clearly his favorite stop of the day.

In contrast, the San Remo harbormaster showed no signs of flamboyance. He leaned into the window of a lackluster building adorned with nautical flags, fixated on the sea while his long, straight pipe filled the room with smoke. A bell attached to the door had no effect on his focus.

"Hi ya, mister," I said, as noisy and sprightly as a young skater could be.

The statue with the unruly beard and captain's hat fiddled with a pouch of Cherry Cavendish. The warm, luxurious smoke filled the room with a light sweet aroma.

"Excuse me... Uh, *scusami?* I am looking for the yacht *Sylvia*. Is she in the harbor? She's a big, red-hulled schooner. *Dov'è la grande barca rossa?*" My Italian was weak, but I had memorized the key sentence during the train ride.

Without a twitch of his head, he pointed the stem of his pipe to the big yachts on the far side of the harbor. "*Sí, la Sylvia,*" resounded from the baritone depths.

"Okay, well, thank you, sir. *Grazie.* I'll just roller-skate over that way now." I was pretty sure he wouldn't understand, so I got a bit cheeky. "It's been a fine pleasure making your acquaintance, Mr. Harbormaster." I rang the bell twice on my way out. What arrogance I had for authority, especially the petulant ones.

The hull of the impressive cutter cast crimson reflections across the still waters of the San Remo harbor. Just as I imagined, the *Sylvia*'s mast reached for the hot sun at the tip of megayacht row. And though she was physically only a couple of hundred yards from where I stood, there was a good two miles between one side of the horseshoe-shaped harbor around to the other.

Anticipation tweaked my impatient synapses, likely the same ones that fire when you're approaching a long-awaited bathroom. It got worse as I got closer, only minutes before I'd surprise Joel.

Harbor towns in Italy were different than France. The changes were subtle, like sweet tomato sauce wafting from cafés, Neapolitan songs playing in the streets, and ladies riding scooters in stiletto heels. It felt more like a party than France. The City of Flowers, San Remo's moniker, had similar fancy beach club restaurants and touristy curios shops, many adorned with light pink chrysanthemums and roses in various blushes of wine. The former home to Alfred Nobel (like the prizes) and Pyotr Ilyich Tchaikovsky, I imagine they both left San Remo for a beach where girls skipped the bikini tops.

I made my way around Porto Vecchio, the old port, until I found *Sylvia*. I slipped my skates off at the docks of the mole behind *Sylvia* and stalked the boat for signs of life aboard. Her companionways were open; mambo music softly entertained her vacant fantail, but there was no one on board. Fine, then. I'd walk the wharf and wait.

The beautiful people with their magnificent megayachts shared moorings abeam crusty old fishing boats and their crustier captains. Crab traps stacked six high filtered what might have been a fresh breeze, distributing mariner stench all across town. Fishnets sprawled on the dock awaiting repairs next to a fever of Ferraris, a leap of Lamborghinis, and a flock of seagulls. The wharf pavement and pilings formed a canvas of bottom paint, a *plein air* of drips and spills from centuries of boat work and bird art.

I waited for hours, playing harmonica, watching *Sylvia* and human yacht babes. Logic dictated that since Rosabella was Italian and I was in Italy, chances were good I'd run into her. Then again, this was the same logic that had gotten me to urinate from atop a German lamppost and roller-skate in front of a tour bus—but I kept looking.

In the midst of an especially fine harmonica riff, a red pickup drove up the wharf. *Sylvia* was painted on the door in gold leaf, just like on her teak transom. It wasn't Joel's blond mophead in the truck, but surely these black-haired Italians worked with him.

"*Buonasera. Parli inglese?*" The sailor in the red beanie and white *Sylvia* shirt stopped to talk.

"*Sì.* Hello. Some English to speak, yes."

"Hello, my name is Mike. I'm a friend of Joel Cook. I came from Germany, and, well, I came from Cannes just this morning to visit Joel. Is he on board?"

With an accent thicker than Mamma's Bolognese, his voice rang the first of a death knell. "I'm a-sorry, friend, you just a-missed him."

"Oh. Okay, so when does he get back?"

He lifted his sunglasses. "*Signore* Mike, you no understand. You just a-miss him. Perhaps one hour. He leave by train. He go to Paris."

I froze. Numbness overcame my body and mind as if I'd been hit by a torpedo. I was taking on water fast. I'd missed Joel by an hour! Joel and I had likely both been at the San Remo train station an hour ago as I'd bolted out of there to find him.

The sailor yelled something belowdecks to a crew member, who came up to speak with me.

"*Ciao,* I am named Nico. Antony say you a friend of Joel?"

"*Ciao,* Nico. *Sì,* I am Joel's friend Mike." I looked upon him in hope that he might have better news.

"Joel say he go maybe Paris, but where he go, I know nothing. He quit. He leave. *Addio.*"

My besieged life, the *USS Bummer,* continued sinking as Nico continued talking.

"Joel want to sail to Cannes, but *Sylvia,* she no sailing. Maybe Joel go to Cannes?"

He may be where I just left? The *Bummer* began launching lifeboats.

Nico took a step closer. "Mike? You are perhaps famous Zugspitze Mike?"

Someone in Italy knew my name. And that made it all worth the trip.

Nico and Antony welcomed me aboard and treated me as their honored guest. The three of us drank cold beer on the fantail between stories of life at sea and a few good laughs at Joel's expense. They'd never really expected Joel's West Virginia roots to nurture much of a seaman, but "he cooked a hamburger *magnifico*—pasta, not so much." Of course, I had to rat out my good buddy with a few stories Joel hadn't told them. After all, what good friend wouldn't dig up your most embarrassing moments?

We lounged like rich pricks, laughing, translating, and drinking in the cockpit usually reserved for the *Sylvia*'s owners and affluent friends. As night fell, I helped the guys adjust the dock lines and fit canvas. I tied proper cleat hitches and whipped a two-second bowline around a stanchion. Nico casually inspected my bowline, raising an eyebrow.

"*La Sylvia's* owner change-a his mind about Cannes," Nico said. "The mistress, she visit Cannes, and the wife, she on boat... Not-a so good. So we a-working on *la Sylvia* until for go to Monaco Grand Prix."

The setting sun triggered a customary change to red wine. Antony handed me a glass and insisted I stay for dinner. "Mike, do you have a bed to sleep tonight?"

I'd learned so much about graciously accepting charity since my lie about not needing a room at the Schneefernerhaus. Turning a warm, dry bed away in the name of pride would be idiotic, especially considering the alternative was cold wharf guano.

"Yeah, I have a place." Overpowered once again by prideful stupidity.

"Because you can have a bed on the boat tonight if you want."

"I'll take it."

I helped with dinner dishes, habitually conserving fresh water on board and getting a nod from Nico for the effort. After doing my part, I didn't feel like such a mooch asking for another splash of Chianti. They didn't care how much I drank or ate; it was all on the owner's tab. Aside from diving off the deck into crystal-blue coves with Joel, I was living the dream.

We retired to the fantail to watch the stars. Antony and Nico smoked through a discussion in Italian; I'm pretty sure I was the subject. They seemed to be good guys, but I was still concerned about leaving my entire worldly belongings in the backpack downstairs.

"Say, Mike, Joel didn't give us much a-warning before he go," Nico finally said. "A letter from the Texas Cath come. Joel read letter. Joel pack and go."

Yep, that was Joel. They may have split up in the Alps, but their hearts continued to rattle a chain of love all the way across Europe.

"We guess he going to leave. He no happy. All he talk about, Texas Cath and Zugspitze Mike." The sentiments were comforting. "And please not to misunderstand, we glad you here, but we really, *really* hoping Texas Cath show up instead of you."

We all had a laugh.

"But Mike, Antony and I, we have a talk. Texas Cath no tie a bowline, and we no have a cook. We sail Grand Prix Monaco in two weeks then sail Barcelona *in Spagna*. You like maybe have job on *la Sylvia?*"

Holy crap—a rich prick yacht job for me? Monaco, Barcelona? Everything and everywhere I wanted to go? It was an amazing offer, considering "lousy cook" was listed at the top of my résumé. But Chef Renée had taught me to speed-slice a zucchini while bussing tables at Prego Restaurant on Catalina Island, and my half-assed Italian kitchen experience was legit. But I'd been a busboy at Prego, and schlepping plates to the dishwasher was a far cry from cooking gourmet meals for guests on a yacht.

"Gentlemen, my father—*mio padre*—always told me 'Don't make big decisions while drinking,' so I'll have an answer for you by the sober light of dawn."

"This perhaps big opportunity for you, Mike," said Antony. He seemed perplexed, likely that I had not jumped at saying yes. "This is how job go; Chianti, Chianti, Chianti, sail," he continued.

"Tonight you enjoy. We not talk business and drink. Tomorrow you and *padre* do business," said Nico. He closed with something in Italian, I surmised it to be the word for respect.

Another glass of wine ensured that sober light came a little later than dawn.

A ray of sunlight found its way below decks to wake me and launch the battle between enjoying the soft, clean pillow a few more moments against everything else I felt compelled to do while on a boat. After detailing my bunk—as if a naval officer would inspect it—I joined the crew in the galley. Nico handed me a demitasse of espresso with a cube of brown sugar and a tiny spoon on the saucer.

"*Zucchero.* Sugar. *Uno o due?*"

"Just one, *grazie.*" I replied, realizing I was somewhere between excited that I would learn Italian by taking the job, and fearful that I would need to learn quickly. Was there some other reason Joel left so quickly? I carried my sip of coffee up the seven steps, its rich aroma enhancing the warmth of bespoke teak cabinetry, fine upholstery, and perfectly polished brass surrounding the space. The ship was the immaculate statement of how two meticulous men would live if their full-time job was to clean and facilitate every imaginable upgrade or repair.

"*Buongiorno,*" I said to Antony, who was back-splicing the end of a braided rope with a fid. He answered in Italian, possibly forgetting I did not speak his language, or believing I had magically acquired the skill in my sleep. More likely, he felt I should begin Italian lessons immediately. I temperately repeated my greeting; "*buongiorno,*" and sipped my espresso.

To experience the job—and be a helpful guest—I cooked a titanic breakfast for the crew, flipping eggs as I considered their offer. How often did an amazing opportunity like this come up in one's life? Over the last year, I'd worked as a theatrical scuba diver under a glass-bottomed boat, an electrical tech in a Munich factory, and an avalancher on the highest mountain in Germany. Adding the position of rich prick's yacht crew member fit me snug as a boat shoe. I could enjoy amazing experiences in places I wanted to go and end up where I wanted to be. It couldn't get any easier.

But Carla's words from the letter in Nice held wisdom that changed the course of my life. "Doing things the easy way doesn't build character." I needed to heed the calling to complete my original skating journey. Without Joel, the *Sylvia* was just another red boat. I hadn't come to San Remo for beer and cannonballs off the deck. I'd come for replenishment, for love and respect and esteem, to fill my acceptance cup and reassure my ego that I'd be okay. Joel was supposed to be here to affirm my achievements, validate my goals, and remind me of the unique individual I was in his eyes. My desperate need to bond with Joel had been shattered like broken glass. Pain shot through my heart. I craved the freedom of a child and the independence of a grown-up—and now I realized the two couldn't co-exist in the same space. He'd abandoned ship, and he'd abandoned me.

Over French toast, fried eggs, and bacon, I gave my answer. "I cannot take the job."

They kept eating. An almost imperceptible nod from Antony, and a glance Nico shot to him across the mess, was all there was. Maybe my cooking was that good. I gulped my juice, then washed the dishes in reflection. I was losing it, sliding down Maslow's hierarchy. With Joel gone, I'd lost my self-esteem and was now seeking self-worth through the eyes of others. I wanted to skate farther and faster than I ever had before.

The train to Cannes would be leaving soon. I thanked the guys for their hospitality and skated away as they waved and Antony yelled, "More wine in Monaco or Barcelona—see you there!"

"And bring Texas Cath with you next time!" Nico shouted.

I skated off the wharf, passed the parked Ferraris over paint spills and seagull art, thinking Mom and Dad were right about that "anything I put my mind to" concept. It wasn't just a line parents tell their kids. Still, the confidence wasn't the hard part. Deciding what my anything would be was a tightening clamp on my head. I wanted wild, unaccountable fun with a reliable paycheck to help me afford those freedoms—crazy, aimless adventures plus a loving home life. Could a man not have it all?

"Choose wisely, Michael, or you'll mess up your whole life," I whispered to myself as I turned off the wharf onto the pavement. "Have a 'why,' and you can bear any 'how.' Do something you love, and you'll never work a day in your life."

Quotes and cliché poured over my brain like waves on the beach, crumbling my wall of indecision into a pile of sand. Gliding along the rails, hanging out the window, waving to topless girls on the beaches—this was happiness. This was what I wanted to do with my life. Why would I want anything else?

I boarded the train. This life wasn't reality. I hadn't made any progress by going backward to San Remo. Looking out the train window began to disturb me. I'd already skated all the way to Cannes, and this was like sitting through a movie twice. It was too easy to stand in one spot and have the world presented to me. What did I gain by exploring the world without effort? I'd wasted valuable time going back to San Remo; the breathtaking views couldn't change that.

I was done doing things the easy way. What I needed was to move beyond Cannes, to go the next step. And I would do it on my own two feet.

CHAPTER 23

TROPÉZIENNES

I think onstage nudity is disgusting, shameful, and damaging to all things American. But if I were twenty-two with a great body, it would be artistic, tasteful, patriotic, and a progressive religious experience.
—Shelley Winters

Cannes lighthouse. One sleepy eye watched as the sunrise defined silver linings on distant purple clouds at sea. The other eye hid from the light under my thin terry cloth blanket and rolled-up T-shirt pillow. The pocket alarm clock inside my backpack was the only sound. I lay on my camping mattress wondering what the clock said, wondering why I even cared. Why had I brought a clock in the first place? My days had no meaningful beginning or end, regulated only loosely by sunlight and a date which I measured by adding a number to a blank journal page. I surprised myself, quoting Mitch: "I'm not into time, man."

I fried up bacon and eggs into a respectable breakfast. The magic of sizzling bacon outdoors could be the best part of camping, if not quite an equivalent trade-off for sleeping in dirt or guano. The aroma attracted two fishermen and a dozen gulls, all of them inching their way closer. A man sipping coffee, gold chains hanging from his tanned neck, leaned over the varnished rail of a yacht, looking down upon my simple world. When our eyes met, he sent me a thumbs-up with a cool wink. I raised my aluminum cup his direction, pointed at his yacht, and signaled an "okay sign: *You're not doing so bad yourself there, fella.*

By the time I laced up and rolled down the jetty sidewalk, the town was coming alive with the first sounds of traffic. I wasn't sure how far I'd make it that day. I had no goal other than Barcelona, weeks away. The next destination of any note would be Saint-Tropez, a seventy-five-kilometer journey.

The road outside town was an eight on the skater's scale, points mostly gained by the amazing view and enjoyability. This was the road from sports car ads, the one you'd pick for a relaxing drive. The flat, curving asphalt often wound just a few meters from the water past some of the most gorgeous coves and seascapes on our planet.

The creative energy in the air crackled with ion-free purity, the same mystical air that inspired classic writers to write, master painters to paint, and legendary lovers to love. I skated effortlessly down the open road, spotting each alpine turn with the tap of my rubber stopper ski tips. This was a bunny slope at best, and maintaining perfect form was easy: feet parallel, knees slightly bent, the mantra of ski instructors playing in my head: *tap-turn-glide …* *tap-turn—*

CLUNK!

The rubber stopper on my left ski pole tip separated from the pole and rolled off the cliff to oblivion. Damn! My blissful buzz had been jacked, replaced by the galling sound of metal hitting asphalt and the reverberation up my arm with every turn.

I stopped at the next photo opportunity road sign and spread my gear on a bench to figure out my ski tip situation. Since I used the same toe stoppers on my skates and poles, I could sacrifice my left skate toe stopper to the ski pole. I'd been smart enough to bring a skate tool, but the extra weight of spare parts was not a luxury I could afford. Unfortunately, out here in the countryside, a replacement toe stopper could be days away. Still, I wasn't worried about stopping. The term "toe stopper" is a misnomer, as they only help you start quickly and climb stairs.

I'd been salivating over a can of fruit cocktail in my backpack, so I dug in. I told the road a can of sugary fruit would be fine.

"You hear that, Road?" I said. "I'm using you. I'm lying to you too. That's right—you'll just help me forget about my cheap, crappy diet."

It occurred to me that I'd stopped talking with myself and started talking to the road.

"Whaddaya think of that, huh, Road? You probably don't even care that I'm cracking up."

So many hours I spent talking with the road, silent stretches when the road would judge me harshly for cheating on my girlfriend. How would I tell Carrie about the affair? Would I tell Carrie about the affair? Not confessing was a lie, an omission of truth, and a burden I'd have to carry as we started our lives together. My legs weren't strong enough to carry that much guilt.

My arrival in Saint-Tropez was a welcome diversion from such serious thoughts. I learned a writer never abbreviates a city name with "St." or "Ft." or some other prefix. Three fewer letters to write in my journal would be exciting after I passed Saint-Tropez. *Woot, woot.*

The mission was clear: find food for dinner, a lighthouse to sleep on, and that famous nude beach to visit the next day. I could have gone without the food and sleep, but the suntan oil jingle of the late seventies replayed endlessly in my head: "Bain de Soleil for the Saint-Tropez tan," and I was just another American guy hoping to live that fantasy.

People laughing and live music on Quai Jean Jaurès, the front street of the Saint-Tropez harbor, was enticing, but I didn't dare walk any further than I could keep an eye on my things at the lighthouse. The problem with urban camping was you could never leave your campsite. In the mountains, there was no one around; in the city, your entire life was up for grabs. I'd had a hella day on wheels, probably eighty kilometers since the sunrise in Cannes, so I surrendered to the joys of leaning on the lighthouse, playing the harmonica, and writing journal pages after a fine meal from a can. In a strange way, I was home.

The sunrise the next morning painted a harbor of white-hulled yachts in faded purple. The terra-cotta tiles blanketing the town began a ritualistic color transformation as awning-covered windows reflected the bright oranges of sunrise.

With all this beauty, it was an underappreciated fact that Saint-Tropez is named after a headless guy who floated up on the beach in a rowboat back in the fifties. By the fifties, I mean 50 AD, when the Christian martyr Saint Torpes of Pisa was beheaded by Roman Emperor Nero and cast out to sea in a rotting row boat with a rooster and a dog to eat the remains of his body. They could really punish a guy back then.

Little did Emperor Nero realize the joke would be on him when, after weeks or months of drifting at sea, a boat with Torpses's half-eaten, headless, decomposing corpse washed up on the beach at Saint-Tropez. The villagers resolved to name the town after him. To this day, most Tropéziennes and tourists are unaware that the tradition of going topless in Saint-Tropez honors the headless patron saint of sailors found on this very same beach. Okay, so the part about going topless in his honor was my personal theory, but the other point really happened on this world-famous nude beach.

The little village awoke, from the delicate waft of a seabird's feathers to the sandwich boards hitting the sidewalk outside waterfront cafés. In harmony with the ocean surge rippling through jetty rocks, the sound created an airy melody. It was yet another stunning town where I would awake to two thousand years' worth of art, culture, fishing—and tragedy, namely my cold, wet sleeping bag. Poetic and magical was the moment, but something smelled like shit.

Ugh! Torpes's rotting corpse must be back. I looked around for a sewer pipe that opened near me. Every few minutes, it grew a little worse until it became intolerable. Even the pigeons lost their appetites. I had to get out of there, and fast.

I stuffed my backpack as quickly as I stuffed syrup-dipped bread into my mouth and walked barefoot off the jetty just as two policemen arrived to case the jetty for campers to arrest. Without any criminal evidence, they stared down the guilty-looking suspect with roller skates hurrying past. I gave thanks to Saint Torpes for repelling me with his ghostly stench, saving me from a day in jail or a topless boat ride with a dog and a chicken.

On the south side of the harbor, a concrete bollard served as my new office. I laid out my map, hardly noticing the amazing yachts or charm of the city. Now, where exactly would all those naked girls be? Half a dozen older women swept the sidewalks in front of their cafés and coffee shops. Their tired and shriveled skin told of a time long ago when they were the hot brown babes, slathered in quick-tan baby oil, frolicking naked under the sun.

My map showed the route out of town would take me west. But my dirty little desires on the nude beach were to the east. The morning was cool and overcast with a little drizzle. It would be hours, maybe half the day, before any female would be walking around without a jacket. Was I really going to wait around?

I had built up my beach fantasy over years of boyhood sneaking peeks of everything from Pygmy boobs in *National Geographic* to undergarments in the Sears catalog. I'd been waiting my whole life to see the world's most beautiful girls running around naked on that beach, dancing around in nothing but a few grains of sand. The sad realization that none of those erotic fantasies were on that beach yet this morning pecked and chewed at me like Saint Torpes's boat crew.

The little cartoon devil on my shoulder kept selling me my own adolescent fantasies, desperately closing with any conceivable crap he could drop. "Just sign the dotted line and those babes are yours, hundreds of 'em just around that corner. Huge boobs, small butts, all nude. All day. All yours. Step right up…" What was a few hours of waiting out of a journey this long?

The angel on the other shoulder, ironically boasting the same balding hairline as my father, calmly voiced respectable truths into my ear. Why was I waiting hours in the rain for a chance to ogle a few women I didn't know and would never meet?

I skated away, depressed. Ripped off. I felt a little proud for making the right choice and choosing gentlemanly behavior—but mostly ripped off, dammit.

With growth comes pain. The more it hurt, the more I knew I was doing the right thing. I was closer to becoming the man I needed to be, shaping my life to show the respect for women that my father had always shown by example.

My attitude finally shifted to gratitude on a perfect-ten road out of town. Like some cosmic reward for demonstrating good judgment, the road was smooth as if God himself were driving an asphalt steamroller just ahead.

After lunch, I unfolded my map to catch my bearings in Le Lavandou, about a third of the way from Saint-Tropez to Toulon. The seventy-five-kilometer run would take all day. A newspaper at a market showed me it was May 25, and a weather graphic showed me some raindrops were coming.

The good: the road was smooth, the trees were lovely, the traffic was light.

The bad: it started misting, the roads got wet, my wheels began slipping in turns. I stayed inside the white line, about a shoulder's width between the guard rail and the trucks whizzing past me at ninety kilometers per hour.

The ugly: rain-specked sunglasses impaired my vision, and the trucks were not looking for a pedestrian on the freeway. And my stomach was starting to growl like imminent diarrhea too.

My new mantra... This. Is. So. Much. Fun.

I repeated the mantra with each perjurious stride. I didn't begrudge the road, the weather, or my choice to be there. Why fight it? It was entirely my attitude that made it good, bad, or ugly.

An overpass offered a moment's shelter and the temptation to stay put and get dry. But these clouds would produce light rain that would keep falling for the rest of the miserable day. I ducked back out into the mist.

Toulon at last. My body and backpack were soaked through. The tops of my feet were numb, a two-centimeter blood blister on my right foot screamed for relief, and my crotch had developed a horrible rash. I was completely thrashed and ready for a real hotel room.

With its quaint cobblestone alleys leading from café-lined sidewalks to plazas canopied in old oaks, Toulon is rich with history dating back to the seventh century BC. I chugged along, convinced the old roads hadn't been repaved since then. The stalls at the colorful outdoor market at Place Louis Blanc were piled high with fruits and vegetables and flowers, reminding me I'd left quaint seaside villages behind for Toulon's big-city views, including the naval stockyards and graffiti-decorated underpasses.

I found a decent-looking hotel inland just outside the historical quarter, where prices for nice hotels were inversely proportional to the likelihood of getting robbed. I didn't care if muggers attacked me, as long as they did it after I was dry and clean. Besides, I probably looked more like a mugger than a muggee at that point. Even muggers must have a sense of when to say no.

I requested a room at the front desk, signed a card, and paid the manager for one night. The man looked over his reading glasses and handed me a key.

"*Oui, monsieur*. This is the key to the bath. It is up these stairs and to the right."

"This is not my room key?"

"Your room key, *monsieur*, I will give you after you bathe."

Every aching muscle under my filthy, sweaty arms and legs moaned in euphoric pleasure as I slipped into the tub. Days of washing my pits in public beach bathrooms, gas station restrooms, and outdoor camp showers slipped away like the car-slung mud caked over my legs and face. I had to drain and refill the brownish bathwater twice.

The luxury allowed me to reflect on my less than luxurious world. Out there on the road, in those conditions, none of it felt like a hardship. It was just life. You had what you had, and that was that. There was always something better and always something worse, so the situations and moments you were in always seemed...well, perfect.

I picked up my room key and brought some food upstairs, wrote about two words in my journal while soaking my feet in the bidet with Epsom salts, and passed out on top of the clean sheets. Good thing. I would need a full recovery for what was coming next.

CHAPTER 24

END OF A RIVI-ERA

*The middle of the road is where the white line is—
and that's the worst place to drive.*
—Robert Frost

I left Toulon, the unofficial end of the French Riviera, hoping to make Marseille in a day. A sign on the side of the freeway told me it was fifty-eight kilometers to reach my next family-and-friends stop along the journey. Not true family, but truly my people—but not people I'd met. Julie'd had an au pair from Marseille living with her in California, helping with light housework and child care in exchange for room and board and some pay. I never met the au pair, Frederique, or Freddie as they called her, but she'd become a beloved member of Julie's family and was therefore considered extended family.

Julie had contacted Freddie's family in Marseille, announcing that a trans-European skater might stop by at some point. I imagined the letter: "Dear Extended French Family, My crazy little brother is roller-skating across your country. Please extend some courtesy because we've taken care of your daughter for a year. P.S. He probably stinks."

I called ahead and spoke with Freddie's mom, Régine, who struggled through an English translation to invite me to lunch. There was no offer to stay at their house, but no need to be pushy and ask. I had money for a hotel room, although without an income, every bit spent made me less powerful.

Throughout the day of skating, a few cars stopped to ask if I wanted a ride. I did want a ride. I wanted to jump in the back of their cars and drink their cold drinks and soak up their air conditioning. I wanted to say yes.

A tiny Fiat stopped ahead of me. An older, overweight woman rolled down her passenger window.

"Would you like a ride?" she asked in French-accented English.

She and her husband engulfed the front seats as though a lifeboat had been tossed into the car and the quick-inflate cord had been pulled. The back seat would have no way of receiving air conditioning; they sealed it like an air lock.

I smiled and waved them on—"*Non, merci*"—and rolled past their snack-filled beater.

I mulled over the passing cars. Would I accept a ride from a car full of French girls? Doubtful; I wanted to skate. I wanted the experience. I needed the accomplishment.

If I could do this thing, I could do anything. I wouldn't need anyone. I'd be on my own, moving forward, working hard, and living my life. Somewhere ahead, this road would flatten out and things would get easier. I had to say "I did it" without cutting corners.

It was painful to achieve, but independence is the greatest revelation for a teenager—that is, if you were ready for it.

At the top of a two-and-a-half-hour hill climb, I prepared for the equal and opposite downhill run. Downhill can be just as much work. Stretching, hydrating, and resting are the keys to not burning out of energy when rolling at fifty kilometers per hour. It's impossible to stop to rest at those speeds. There was really no stopping at all once momentum took over, even with a new toe stopper from Toulon. Dragging one skate sideways, the usual method for stopping on flat ground, puts all the weight on one leg while the other becomes a dragging brake. It takes practice, finesse, and perfect balance to roll on one skate and apply enough pressure with the other skate, at ninety degrees to its rolling axis, to slow yourself down. The maneuver is challenging on a smooth promenade, horrifying on rough asphalt, and a death sentence with a heavy backpack and a truck chasing you.

I stopped at a gas station bench, resting joyfully under a tree with chilled water from an old yet amazingly functional refrigerated water fountain on the side of the building. I sat a while, hydrating, using the toilet, studying the map, and catching my breath. It was time to strap on knee and elbow pads.

Rolling downhill into a cooling breeze was easy. Gravity quickly converted my weight into road behind me. But within only a few moments of lazing my way down that slick slope, control slipped away. It was too late to recover by dragging a foot sideways. I went from passive to panic, flying down the hill with no choice but to go "banzai" and hope to live until the road leveled out.

Cars stopped passing me, not out of kindness but because they simply weren't driving fast enough to pass me on my sixty-five-millimeter wheels. I once did the math to learn each of my eight wheels were spinning at nearly five thousand rpm, the ball bearings in intense heat. Those calculations didn't help calm me down now.

Sure, I'd gone that fast before, but not with a fifty-pound backpack and hours of hill climbing on my sorry legs. Fifty kilometers per hour is not downhill-skier fast, but it's nowhere near downhill-skier safe like falling on fluffy snow. At least on the slopes, your skis fell off and you slid down the hill with maybe a broken bone. On asphalt, the uncompromising opposite of powder snow in both density and color, any wipeout could be my last.

To give me some form of hope, I'd calculated how far the downhill would go from a formula of the distance I'd climbed this morning. As my mind flashed back to those figures, the infinitesimal change in focus was enough to cause my already faltering legs to quiver, starting a speed wobble in my skates. A split second would determine if I would react properly or end up on my helmetless head and leaving me as one long, red skid mark down the asphalt.

Speed wobbles, or "death wobbles" if you're a skateboarder, are a harmonic oscillation of the skate's steering mechanism, called trucks. Skateboarders dread "the wobs," but few quad skaters ever roll that fast. At high speed, a roller skate's front wheels can oscillate uncontrollably, sending a horrific shiver up your legs and triggering an involuntary reflex to do exactly the wrong thing: lean back.

Logically, slowing down is the answer. But leaning forward aggressively, tucking your posture, making turns, and relaxing are the only things that can save your roadkill ass. It takes strength and mental effort, and it's counterintuitive.

My chattering feet had stopped communicating with my body. Any remaining strength for pulling off a superhuman act had long been exhausted; I'd cashed in all my athletic chips on the way up the hill. Maybe I could fall on my back and side on my backpack? Maybe I could dive over the guard rail and fly over the cliff into the soft-looking cactus?

The hill showed no sign of leveling out.

My only chance of survival was to come out of my petrified posture and get aggressive with the hill. That meant picking up my feet, leaning forward, taking control of the wheels, and dancing with the road. With the wind rushing by and cars and trucks honking at me to get my ass out of the way, picking up my feet called for that last bit of heroic strength normally reserved for mothers who lift cars to pull their babies from accidents.

I had to use my brain. It was the most powerful organ in my body, and it would control my legs. I could do this.

"I'm going to make it!"

I yelled it over and over. The affirmations ignited a booster rocket within me. Despite the excruciating pain in my legs, it was working. The wobbles subsided; my feet were solid. With no other vision but success, my body was forced to realize that vision. The body is an amazing thing when you feed your mind a positive diet.

Back on the flats and cruising safely, I had plenty of time to contemplate the what-ifs back on that hill. What if I'd killed myself—or worse yet, permanently hurt myself—on the side of that road? How long would it have taken for someone to find me or for the news of my broken body to travel back to California? Or what if I'd fallen and lived?

Maybe I should be a little more careful with my life. It might come in handy one day.

Hedged by thousand-year-old stacked stone walls, the gorgeous little town of Cassis was a rewarding treat. Finally, seawater again, and not from hundreds of feet high. Cassis was much like the hundreds of coves I've wandered through, boats arranged from small to large and a handful of sidewalk cafés lining the front street. But Cassis had some mystical attraction. Azure waters lapping onto white sandy beaches and royal purple bougainvillea cascading over the cliffs turned the cove into a vibrant art palette.

Lovely as it was, I was excited about my contact in Marseille. Road signs told me the road was curvy ahead, and curvy means steep. Uphill steep. I was appreciating this beautiful day more than others, but why? How were this view, this road, this day preferable over any other? It was all perfect, every moment of it.

Signs for "*Centre Ville*" led down through narrow roads, making it easy to find a store for food. The pathetic buzz of a Vespa scooter puttered from behind me. Two cute girls, both about my age, slowly passed. They might have been checking me out, but more likely they were checking out what the hell I was doing trying to ski up a road. Since settlers had first climbed this hill in 500 BC with donkeys and wagons, I had to believe I was the first to do it as a backpacking roller skater.

The girls passed me, then came coasting back down the hill with long flowing hair and delicious French dialogue. They did a couple of circles on the vacant road, flipping their helmetless hairdos and snapping photos from a 110 compact camera.

Of course, I was all smiles from the attention. I was also a sweaty mess, shirtless and aglow with sweat. They circled while trying to make conversation in French. My conversational French lessons would get me to a train station or allow me to order a baguette at the *boulangerie*, but understanding the words from those pouty lips was a skill that could benefit my life.

"Bonjour. Je suis américain. Je m'appelle Michel."

They giggled as if to say, "Duh, only an American would do such a crazy, ridiculous thing."

Where had my confidence gone? These girls could have been saying anything. I'd held a solid celebrity status for most of this trip, so why was I beating myself up with self-loathing when it came to girls? Get some confidence, loser! They were no better than me, and I was no better than them.

Without much vocabulary to speak of, I smiled awkwardly and skated slowly away.

They continued talking, keeping up with me. *"Bonjour, Michel. Où allez-vous?"*

I figured they were asking where I was going, like everyone else did. I didn't understand; I didn't care. Dear Lord, why did their language have to sound so damn sexy? I continued skating up the hill, focused, indifferent to them.

The giggling stopped and their manner became interested.

"Je m'appelle Monique," said the blonde on the back of the bike. *"Elle s'appelle Cosette."*

Monique took a moment to brush Cosette's hair from her face, returning her hands to cling to her driver's bare torso, nearly touching her bulging bikini top. *"Pouvons-nous vous aider?"*

It looked as though they wanted to help, but their French banter was unintelligible. I suppose Monique was giving Cosette orders to go faster, slower, hold the bike straight. Cosette, seemingly new to riding a scooter, would yell back at her, perhaps to shut up and let her do her best. I joined them in giggling at their antics.

They came up slowly from behind. Monique put her hand on my backpack and tried to push me up the hill, but the angle was too awkward. They went around, coming from behind again, and Monique grabbed my ski poles to pull me, but she had to release before she twisted her arm. On the next pass, she planted her foot on my butt, which ended in uncontrollable laughter for us all. She tried grabbing my bicep to pull, but her small hands couldn't catch a grip around my slippery, saturated skin.

She jokingly offered her hair as a rope.

"Tee-ray?" they repeated as a question.

It sounded like tee-ray. Or was it T rey? *"El rey"* in Spanish is "the king," so what the hell was a "T rey"?

I shrugged to show I didn't understand. *"Je ne comprends pas."*

Monique tucked the ski poles into her lap and reached behind the scooter until our hands connected. She pulled my hands and placed them smack on her ass, ensuring I grabbed her tight thighs just below her pink thong as she leaned forward.

"Oui. Tee-ray. Tee-ray!"

Oh yeah, tee-ray. And then we'd schwing goom. With these two bonuses to my French vocabulary, I was practically ready for a French girlfriend. Considering where my hands were, I should have had nothing else on my mind. We rolled along for a few meters with my hands on her perfect butt when it all came to me: the French use a silent z in many words. R-e-z would sound like "ray," and I recalled the word *"tirez"* on a door handle. Aha! *"Tirez"* meant to pull.

"Oui, oui! Tirez. Pull. Yes!" I cried out.

They giggled with the joy that we'd verbally connected. Monique turned around with a sultry look, slowly removed my hands from her buttocks, and placed them on the rear scooter handle. It wasn't in a "get your damn hands off my ass" way—no, far from it. She was toying with me. She guided my hands to the bar, then back to her butt, asking which was better with her eyes.

Sure, holding the scooter handle was smarter, safer, more efficient. Whatever. I would have gladly skated holding her butt even if I'd had to push her and that Vespa uphill all the way to Spain. With ski poles back in my left hand and Monique's soft skin in my right, we climbed the hill downright sluggishly. The poor little scooter barely had the power to carry two skinny French chicks up the steep hill. Adding the backpack and me, a one-hundred-and-ninety-pound eight-wheeled trailer, proved the scooter didn't have the juice.

I tried pushing the scooter so the bike could make some headway. Nothing. I was pushing the scooter while being their training wheels, doing all I could to maintain their balance at the slow speed. Pushing two girls plus the scooter and carrying my backpack and keeping it all level up the impossibly steep hill on roller skates, I began to question if I was wrong about that sign I'd read on the door. Maybe *tirez* really meant "push"?

The top of the hill was just ahead. I did my best to keep up with the scooter, but it was no use. I had to let go. They looked sad, which wasn't helping, as they pulled away slowly up the hill, blowing kisses before cresting the point at the top.

CHAPTER 25

SHEPHERDS OF SQUALOR

This is an elegant hotel! Room service has an unlisted number.
—Henny Youngman

Marseille was too large of a city for lighthouse camping. As the second largest city in France, Marseille had its share of crime stories and staying indoors after hours was a good way to stay alive. Also, Marseille's Plainer lighthouse is on an island about ten kilometers off the coast, and swimming out there with roller skates on my feet would have been a poor way to stay alive. But Marseille would have cheap hotels where I could get cleaned up before meeting the family.

It was after dark when I finally arrived at Vieux-Port, the old harbor. Fishing boat lights twinkled across the harbor. The volume of city noise increased with each block I drew closer to the town center. After a lap around the fancy waterfront hotels, I started up the famous boulevard, La Canebiere, where prices and safety dropped proportionately with distance from the water. Sailors used to call it the Can o' Beer, and with good reason. The boulevard is lined with bars, cafés, and seedy nightclubs. The trick was to go far enough inland to get a good deal but not so far to get mugged.

I went too far.

I didn't mind the first derelict asking if I was looking for a place to stay. His friendly manner stalled my prejudice about his appearance, and I gave him the benefit of the doubt. A former Marseille tour guide down on his luck? I was likely the most naïve stranger ever, which attracted still more of these tour guides. After the third or fourth gutter pup approached me as a concierge of chicanery, it was clear they were up to no good. I escaped what was becoming a zombie apocalypse—the monsters closing in slowly from all sides—and headed back toward the harbor.

"Are you looking for a hotel?" A French gentleman, apparently from a home with an operable shower, curiously studied my roller skates, backpack, ski poles, and silky shorts. His cigarette smoke floated up around his baseball cap.

"*Oui, monsieur.*"

"Up this hill is rue de Something Something. The Something Something Hotel has a good price. It is clean, if they have a room. A little further is the Whatever-Ever Hotel, and this is cheap and nice too."

"*Merci. Bonne nuit.*"

He was helpful—as in he didn't seem interested in harvesting and selling my organs—so I had two things to go on; directions to two affordable hotels up the road and a personal recommendation from a friend.

The first hotel I passed looked okay, but I decided to check the other one and then decide. Inside its graffiti-sprayed walls and warehouse doors, the second hotel manager was happy to show me one of his so-called "great price rooms." The lobby facade had a door leading to a dark hallway, where a questionably live dog lay on the last surviving patch of wall-to-wall carpet. Stepping over the dog, the manager filled the hall with cigarette smoke, then ground the butt onto the floor as he struggled to unlock the handle. The dog awoke and nudged his nose through a huge gap in the door frame, obviously trying to get back into his comfort zone.

The great price was steep for the windowless cage. The mattress, which probably had the word "free" spray-painted on the bottom, lay directly on the floor next to a wooden crate, where an ashtray full of butts sat next to a lamp without a shade. Had I guessed, a junkie might have overdosed there in moments prior, giving the housekeeper little time to drag the corpse and drug paraphernalia to the back-alley dumpster.

The dog yelped as the manager pinned him to the wall with his knee. I backed slowly away.

I escaped and headed down the street to the first hotel my good friend had recommended. It was worse. In the full glimmer of night, I skated back down the hill to spend a small fortune on a nicer hotel, patting my safe organs with a confident grin before falling asleep between fresh sheets.

CHAPTER 26

MY FRENCH FAMILY

Happiness is having a large, loving, caring, close-knit family in another city.
—George Burns

Mission: coffee, croissants, and a pay phone. *Patisseries* with fresh and fantastic treats lined the Canebiere, and busy city folk rushed to work with white paper bags and coffee cups. Through the perplexing effort of using a French pay phone, I finally secured a lunch date with Freddie's mother, Mme Régine Blanche. Régine expected my call at her home and was wonderfully accommodating, requesting that I arrive by 11:30 at her jewelry store on the harbor promenade. I spent the morning hours skating Marseille without a backpack, learning the lay of the city.

A poster on a bus station advised that Le Grand Prix de Monaco was only a couple of days away. Maybe I could take the train back and watch the race? The concept of the Monaco weekend developed as I climbed the staircase to the Marseille-Saint-Charles train station. A round trip ticket to Monaco was reasonable. I'd just never considered I might go to the most famous car race in the world. The opportunity was rare, and I decided I was going.

179

Perched high above the city, Le Grand Escalier brasserie overlooked larger-than-life sculptures of women and lions and children catching fish. The city and sea were enveloped by an impossibly blue sky. All that beauty was reduced to my values: a marble-smooth ski run to street level. I half expected some Monaco guards to be hiding behind the statues to pluck me off the monumental stairway and toss me over the side. Without my backpack, the downhill run was pure fun, spotting each turn with a pole tip and treating each step like a mogul.

After a long, hot shower at the hotel, I arrived at Madame Régine's jewelry store wearing shoes. Freddie had been gorgeous in the photos Julie had shown me, so my expectations of Freddie's mom were high. She did not disappoint.

Régine greeted me with kisses on both cheeks. I reminded myself that kissing is a French hello, not an American come-on. I was right on time, and she was ready with car keys in hand.

"Bonjour, Michel. Comment allez-vous?" This was the strongest sense of home and welcome I'd felt for quite some time, and a first for my understanding French so well.

"Bien! Très bien, merci. Et vous?" With that, my French dialogue was exhausted, but it was enough to give Régine the impression that I spoke French.

With barely a breath, she chattered her way to the car while I followed her and her gigantic purse. Her car, parked with two wheels on the sidewalk, had a parking ticket, which she crammed into a glove box full of identical tickets. The Renault R5 Turbo, a rally racer with abundant midengine power, handled the curves around the city like a slot car. Régine demonstrated why she would need such a car in the city, and we made it to the other side of town in a matter of life-before-your-eyes minutes.

Le Cercle des Nageurs, the Circle of Swimmers, was a classy 1920s swimming club at the furthest point of the Marseille harbor. It overlooked a gorgeous cove with views of the sea and Marseille's islands. Passing the Olympic-sized pool, Régine paused to introduce me to a few of her club fellows, friends who had invested small fortunes for the opportunity to label one another friends. It was more of a circle of snobs than swimmers.

What story was she spinning to her friends about me? Their faces morphed from panic-stricken disgust to sympathetic fascination. *Patins à roulettes*, French for roller skates, was mentioned a couple of times, but why were they laughing? Perhaps she was joking that she couldn't afford a better gigolo, or maybe she was paying her high-society debt by feeding the homeless.

As a teenaged guest, I scanned the menu to order by lowest price, but there were no printed numbers. For that matter, there were no words I could read either. Life on the cheap had taught me that the items I should order would be at the bottom right, so I ordered by pointing at the menu where I recognized a word, *poulet*. That means chicken, and chicken means cheap. I pointed at the menu, my eyes begged the waiter for English help. Instead he delivered a long, lovely narrative of French cuisine—or possibly it was an extended monologue about automatic transmissions or insurance documents. I really couldn't say.

"It's chicken," Régine said.

I gave a confident *oui* with a friendly smile, a facial expression somewhat uncommon for the club. Régine followed with three words to the waiter and held her menu for him to take, with not a moment of eye contact with the help.

This brusque trend continued around the restaurant. Did the wealthy French encourage their entitled offspring to treat servers as inferiors? Was it inherent in the charm of membership to show your friends that you were better than these irrelevant serfs? Did they need to raise their own esteem by lowering that of others? I tried to understand, making a true effort to learn and respect how the members' conduct might be morally appropriate. I found nothing.

"So, Michael, how far have you skated?"

"About three hundred kilometers so far, maybe five hundred more to reach the Spanish border. I'll skate through the Camargue, across the Pyrénées mountains…"

She fidgeted through her giant purse, heedless of my words.

"…and then I'll go through a magical time tunnel and end up at a used appliance store on Mars."

The waiter poured red wine.

"Uh-huh, I see." She grabbed her glass as the waiter poured.

Not that my life is all that interesting, but most people I've met along the road have found at least something intriguing about the adventure. She couldn't have been less interested. And why would she be? I was just some long-haired, bearded kid in a fancy restaurant, grateful for a fabulous lunch. It was buzzkill.

"So how is your daughter Freddie?" I asked. "Where is she now?"

Régine lit up like a sparkler. "She's very well. She left Dana Point and is traveling up the California coast with a girlfriend. They will go to San Francisco, and then she will fly to New York from there."

"Will she go to school in New York?"

"She's all done with school now." She looked at me like I should know that. I hadn't let on that I'd never met Freddie.

"I see. Will she be staying in New York?"

"She's coming back to Marseille. You came to Marseille to visit her, no?" Confused, she looked deeper into my eyes, silently questioning who was sitting at her table.

"I wasn't sure if Freddie would be here or not. I was in town to visit with extended family, so to speak."

"And because your sister employed Freddie, you think we are family?" Her words were harsh yet accurate. She cut a bite of meat, staring into the distance as she chewed. Her body language remained calm and accepting.

I drank my wine, nervous that my body language might say I needed to drink. I was hypersensitive to my every move, on edge about my manners, my etiquette. My social graces. The fact that I was wearing a swimsuit in a fine restaurant.

"Freddie's been a wonderful addition to Julie's house," I continued. "She's been a big sister to Julie's kids, Katie and Patrick. Julie tells me she's helpful cleaning the house and how the neighbors have enjoyed Freddie. Sounds like she's part of the family."

"So you have not met Freddie?" She waved her steak knife in sync with her question.

The jig was up. "Not actually, no."

I reached for my wine again, this time revealing my fear as I tipped the glass over and soaked our white tablecloth in red.

The waiter and I scrambled to clear and cover the spill. As I died of embarrassment, her diamond watch ticked away each mortifying second.

But the food was the best damn meal I'd had since I left Germany. The funny thing is, I had no idea what I ordered. It was French food, it didn't matter. Régine cut and chewed as quickly as she could, signed a card, finished her wine, and put her purse on the table before I was done eating. The waiter brought me a salad, which sat untouched next to a section of chicken I shoveled in as fast as I could. When she pulled her car keys out of her purse, it was time to go. I wiped my face, covered the leftover food with the napkin, and walked out chewing and longing for the half-bottle of wine we left on the table.

Another hair-raising road rally back to the jewelry shop ended with Régine skidding like a stunt driver into a spot beside the red painted curb. An attractive brown-haired girl in front of the shop watched, unalarmed by the screeching tires. I made it a point to say hello once I said goodbye to Régine.

She greeted me with kisses on both cheeks. "*Bonjour. Vous devez être Michel.*"

The beautiful girl called me by name and kissed me twice. This day was looking up.

"Michel, this is my daughter Marion, little sister of Freddie."

The surplus of beauty in this family was overwhelming. Marion's English was no better than her mother's, and after they argued a moment in whispers, Régine translated.

"Marion would like to invite you to her house for a dinner party tonight."

"*Oui*, merci, Marion," I replied.

Marion scribbled a note for me: *18 heures* written next to an address.

"Six o'clock this evening," I answered in elementary English, hoping we would continue speaking English no matter how poor her skills were. Her English had to be better than my lousy French.

It wasn't, so I'd have to step up. "*Oui, Marion, chez vous à dix-huit.*" I was impressed that I could pull out a real French sentence.

"And thank you for lunch, Régine, *merci beaucoup*. That was a wonderful treat. I am sorry for the embarrassing moment."

She laughed briefly before answering Marion's questions about the lunch. Marion covered her mouth. Her shoulders shook with laughter, and she cast an empathetic smile at me before disappearing around the corner.

I stopped for a bottle of wine on the half-hour walk to Marion's apartment in the Saint-Victor district, south of the Old Port, mentally preparing for the evening. Who might be there? How would I fit in? Would I understand any French? How could I be cool at dinner when I'd blown it so badly at lunch?

One thing I could do was remember everyone's name at the party. Those memory tricks from some guy on TV would be handy, had I paid attention. My mom was amazing at remembering names, reminding me at every party that the sweetest sound a human can hear is the sound of their own name.

I caught my breath from six flights of stairs and knocked on Marion's door. A gorgeous girl answered wearing skintight jeans and a sheer blouse. She greeted me by name, kissed my cheeks, and said the same thing Marion said when she met me, some version of "You must be Michael." How she kept from spilling her full martini while clopping around in sky-high heels was a secret forever locked in the vault of feminine mystique.

She introduced me around the cozy apartment. A mix of eclectic friends had gathered to drink, smoke, and enjoy the amazing views of the Old Port at sunset. I wasn't pronouncing the guests' names correctly—Hugh, Phil, and Genevieve—but I was careful and I tried. It was an amazing opportunity to party with the young and beautiful of Marseille, a perk not available to tourists and one no money could buy. And it kept getting better. Guests arrived speaking Russian, Spanish, French, and finally some English.

Though Marion's kitchen was the size of an apartment closet, she fed a dozen guests fine home-cooked meals from a single-burner stove and a suitcase-sized refrigerator. In a single pan, she sautéed sauces, added ingredients to the pan, plated those, then quickly washed the pan and returned it to the fire to cook the next thing. It was the hardest-working little sauté pan in France.

Miniature casseroles came out of a toaster oven next. Fresh bread loaves appeared from long paper bags tucked among the ceiling beams, and condiments went from jars to gourmet bowls before all was set on the table by friends who worked together like five-star staff. I watched in awe.

Marion winked my way, pausing to clink our wine glasses. After the meal, the pan and all the cooking tools were washed in a flurry, leaving the kitchen completely clean and ready for the next meal. She joined the group at a makeshift collection of tables and miscellaneous things to sit upon. So much from so little. I was forever impressed at how one could cook for so many and walk out of the kitchen as though nothing had ever happened there.

The evening paced up with Genevieve translating bits of conversations for me. I got invited to go dancing in Cassis. Fortunately, I had skated through Cassis the day before. Unfortunately, I was dressed like a hobo.

But Marion's neighbor Charles, pronounced Shar-lay, took me down the hall for a makeover. "Come along, *mon ami* Michel, I turn you into French fashion model."

In minutes, I was back with dance shoes too big, French jeans too tight, a silk shirt too flamboyant, plus a well-manicured beard and slicked-back hair. My return brought on *woos* of appreciation at my transformation. I smiled and gave the crowd a bow and compulsory modeling spin, but the giant loafer hit a basket of magazines, tripping me, which nearly spilled all the drinks off the coffee table.

"Are you *sure* you want to take me to Cassis?"

I wouldn't have guessed Sharlay's Citroën Deux Chevaux could carry four grown adults, especially in the back seat. Cramming me and three more sensationally stylish guys back there, Phil shoved from outside to get the door closed. After a few turns on the way out of town, my left arm went numb and Sharlay's shoes were getting scratched under the front seat. The back seat was full of groans, jokes, and giggling before he pulled over to give us a break, have a smoke, and let the poor little car recover from its hill-climbing torture.

I apologized to Sharlay for the scratches on his shoes.

He laughed. "That's okay. You can keep them."

"Thanks, Sharlay, but honestly, what the hell am I going to do with dress shoes on a roller-ski tour?"

"You wear them to the swinging beach clubs. You'll be *fantastique.*"

The group laughed.

At Le Big Ben nightclub in Cassis, dozens queued up behind velvet ropes. Our chances of getting into the club by 3 a.m. looked slim. I dragged my way toward the back of the line, but Marion put her arm around me and guided me to the front, where the bouncer and Sharlay exchanged cheek kisses and we all walked straight in. The doors opened like the cover of a high-fashion magazine, leading to a hallway of models with one-of-a-kind hairstyles, dazzling jewels, and vogue dresses that barely covered beach-bronzed skin.

Not a girl in the place was less than a nine; same for the guys. Men wore anything stunning, from neon blue silk suits to sequined leather overalls. My mates and I were the ugliest dudes in the crowd. The women would best be described as "in costume." To my left was an eccentric society girl with a twenty-inch, opera-length cigarette holder and white evening gloves, her hot-pink collar extended to the top of her head—but not past her vertical up-do. To my right, identical triplets wore matching black boots, lacy black underwear bottoms, and sparkly half-jackets barely covering large, unbridled breasts.

A battalion of tuxedo-tailed waiters carried champagne buckets everywhere, defending a regiment of thirsty supermodels bobbing to the club beat. It wasn't a strip club, but later in the night, two girls with perfect bodies danced on the bar completely naked. By that time, I wasn't even shocked.

We giggled our way out of Big Ben at what must have been three or four in the morning. Sevens and eights still waited in line. Once again, we crammed into the little car for the forty-minute drive back to Marseille.

The streets of Marseille were silent when the door of the Deux Chevaux opened at my hotel, tumbling me out of the car into sidewalk swill.

"You can have the shirt too, Michel, but those pants are coming home with me." Sharlay puffed a cigarette before pulling the shoes and pants off me as I giggled hysterically on the sidewalk.

I thanked them all, then watched them swerve down the quiet road like a slow speed skier through the darkness, their laughter echoing down the Canebiere.

CHAPTER 27

BREAK A LEG

If you fall, I'll be there.
—The Floor

I showed up early the next morning with my train ticket to Monaco, carrying a warm croissant across the expanse of slick marble flooring. The station was a roller heaven, but my only interest was the bench at midplatform where I'd take off my pack and enjoy breakfast.

Gare de Marseille Saint-Charles stood proud with its steel and glass atrium, Roman-arched brick windows, and clock so large you could set your watch from the beaches of Italy. A sign on the wall shows 1848, the year the station was built with only four tracks.

A handful of passengers awaited the train, which arrived two minutes late. Two minutes late? Oh, my! There must be a serious problem, I joked with Germanic sarcasm. We all stared down the rails to catch the first glimpse of the train, as if there were some prize for the first one to spot it. What first appeared to be an overfilled refugee train from India turned out to be far better: girls.

My eyes got wider as they approached: five or more railcars packed with French girls leaning through the windows. It was a scene from the sixties, like movies of the swarms when the Beatles first came to America: dozens of foxy French faces hanging out of the windows, taking in what Marseille had to offer.

What was this, a beauty pageant? A cheerleading convention? Some girl's college field trip? It was a fantasy guys woke up to, only to realize it was just a dream and the sheets now looked like a tent. Jackpot! Like fish in a barrel, like candy from babies, like the bank vault left open—a hundred more easy-pickings analogies flashed through my head. I sniggered, a villain plotting a caper.

The train squealed to a stop. My bench was at the center of this garden of women. I wiped my freshly trimmed beard, tongue aggressively looking for anything that might be in my teeth.

A curious hush came over the station as the girls took notice of the guy with skates and ski poles. William Shakespeare wrote "all the world's a stage." My humble bench didn't have the makings of a stage, but it did have an enthusiastic front-row audience. I had unintentionally become the show for an audience of one hundred girls.

I stood up from my bench and threw my backpack on—nothing fancy, aloof. I grabbed my ski poles and headed for the train door. I looked up to smile at the group, eliciting a couple of "woo" noises from my all-female fan club. A mere thirty feet to roll across marble flooring, and I was as nervous as if I were stepping up to sing the national anthem at the Super Bowl. They all smiled, batting their big, gorgeous eyelashes partially covered by thick, flowing hair, watching me glide effortlessly across the landing.

For some reason I'll regret my entire life, I leaned back just slightly. I must have had a fraction of a second to recover from what happened next. But I didn't recover.

Before one could say "total loser," my feet flew out from under me, arms and ski poles flailing in every direction. I went up and straight down, landing flat on my back.

"Le gasp! Le scream!" The girls all took a long, deep breath in unison, taking a silent moment to make sure I was okay.

I was ruined. As I untangled my poles, it was clear I wasn't hurt, and it was appropriate for them to let out *le gran laughter*. I'd landed perfectly on my pack without a hint of physical pain, but the agony of a hundred teenage girls roaring in hysterics was an agony worse than death. After three hundred kilometers of semi-safe travels over steep, rough roads in hair-raising situations in which only my superior skating skills saved my life, this was how I fell. These girls had no idea where I'd been or what I'd been through. They'd only witnessed the first time in my life I'd ever fallen on skates—without hitting a bicycle or something.

My reaction was to get up—just jump up and act cool—but there was zero chance of pulling that off. Maybe I'd just lay here until the train left. I wanted to roll underneath it. There was only one thing to do in that situation, only one way to overcome the devastation.

I stood and faced the crowd, and with a big smile, took a theatrical bow.

The laughter turned to applause.

On board, a few girls grabbed my arms, guiding me to a seat they'd cleared for me. They clamored for the honor of taking care of me, helping with my bag and poles and touching the back of my head for possible lumps from the fall. They lifted my skates to rest my feet on the seat opposite and poured me a Coca-Cola as the rest of the train's young female occupants pressed closer to get in on the action.

I sat facing backward, looking backward out the window as if going back in time. I showed the girls the routes I'd skated as the beaches and hills I'd worked so hard to overcome flew past in reverse. I shared skating stories and they took turns feeding, watering, and protecting me as though I were the last man on earth.

I had to leave my harem when the train arrived in Antibes. I waved goodbye as the train pulled away, the girls as excited as I'd found them.

I was excited for different reasons. I had a routine in Antibes, a favorite shop where I bought ingredients for my favorite dinner and a favorite place to cook and camp. I headed to my old haunt, the lighthouse, to settle in.

But even I was impressed the next morning at waking up to a white bag of pastries and a cup of steaming coffee on the concrete next to me. The wafting Gitane smoke and clickety-clack of a reel casting bait were as comforting as to me as a slice of American apple pie.

CHAPTER 28

MONACO GRAND PRIX

Just as courage is the danger of life, so is fear its safeguard.
—Leonardo da Vinci

The *plein air* Gare de Monaco bustled with race fans, turning my backpack into an annoyance as I pushed through the crowds. So I stuffed my worldly belongings into a locker and stared at the key in my hand, considering for a moment the significance it held. Not a sole person in the world knew my whereabouts; my whole life was in that locker. Up until Marseille, I'd left at least some paper trail through postcards and letters around the world to friends and family, an assurance that some investigator might find me if they worked hard enough. But I hadn't told anyone where I was going this time; I'd just hopped a cross-country train to go watch a car race, with no one to report to and no one to ask permission of.

It was so grown-up.

Loathing the fact that I was wasting a perfectly good skating hill, I put my shoes to work. Walking? What was this crap? This was foreign, mundane, downright pedestrian. My thumping pace across the slick marble plaza devolved me to a mere mortal.

192

Some picnic foods and a bottle of wine would go well with this day. I stopped at a market for bread, cheese, and wine, using the rehearsed the question I would ask the clerk: "*À quelle heure commencer le Grand Prix?*" I was so proud to ask what time the race started correctly.

"*Le parcours ouvrira à onze heures dix.*"

It does no good to ask a question in French if you won't understand the answer.

My frozen expression triggered kindness in the gent next to me.

"The race starts at eleven-ten this morning," he said, a hint of French patronizing in his manner.

"*Oh. Merci beaucoup, monsieur.*"

"Fa-get-a-bout-it." A line he mocks from some Chicago gangster movie, and by his cocky grin, one he's been waiting to deliver.

"May I help you?" asked the server at the deli counter. Precious time before the race couldn't be wasted practicing French with a random American.

"This salami, please."

"How much would you like?"

It looked so good. My eyes said I could eat it all. I looked in my wallet, then looked at him, asking how much with my eyes.

"Fifty-seven francs per kilogram," he said, awaiting my answer while lifting a heavy butcher's cleaver, ready to chop.

"Twenty francs' worth, please."

Let him figure it out. Brief math on an imaginary calculator above his head concluded with the solitary *whack* of what he considered a twenty-franc chunk.

"*Ça va,*" he mumbled, writing "20ff" on a bag in black crayon.

"*Ça va bien,*" I replied, with no idea if it was a good deal or a total rip-off.

Local business flyers littered an old table by the door. A flyer from some real estate company showed a cartoon map of the race course.

"Are the race maps free?" I asked the cashier.

"*Oui, monsieur, la merde de chien, c'est gratuit.*"

I understood "*gratuit*" but didn't understand was why the other patrons started laughing. I took my free *merde de chien,* or shit of dog, and headed to the race.

Everything around the harbor was closed off and reserved for ticket holders. Low-budget loners would need to get creative and find places to watch from afar. The crowds shoved along, faces-to-backs, cramming to get to their seats in time for the start. How could all these men be wearing suits? I was burning up in shorts and a T-shirt. The women kept cool with exposed skin, which had the opposite effect on men. The crowd respected the beautiful women, allowing them to glide through the masses as if they were in a bubble, while the men stood on top of one another's feet.

Just on the other side of a plywood wall, the high-pitched scream of a Formula One car sent the crowd's pulse into arrhythmia. Like a single living organism, the crowd's pace had a seizure with each passing car, then went back to chugging along in normal rhythm.

Finding a place to watch without a ticket wasn't easy. Going left toward the casino would put me among nothing but high rollers and people who'd staked out their free spots for days. To my right was a hill where the prince's palace overlooked the harbor. Others'd had this same idea, but I found a narrow footpath and worked my way up through the crowd high enough to spy the harbor and parts of the race. What a spectacular place to view the town and watch the race from the Avenida de la Porte Neuve.

Comforting American laughter and conversations nearby intrigued me. I introduced myself to two sisters, Janet and Amy, and their girlfriend Ann, all from Saint Augustine Beach, Florida. They were partying with their new friend Todd from Philadelphia.

I opened with a joke. "What's everyone looking at down there?"

Todd stepped up as the voice of the group, playing off my joke without a pause. "Some race, I guess. We're here to look at this wall—yo, Amy, quit lookin' down at that race! There's nothin' to see."

The trio of girls went along with the gag, facing the wall for a comic beat like mock prisoners.

"Got a view from here?" I asked, primarily so I could inch into their personal space to test my boundaries.

They nodded and welcomed me as a new friend. We shared our travel stories, Todd and I quickly finding we were of the same ilk in humor and class (or lack thereof). Camping, youth-hosteling, and couch-surfing anywhere we could crash for the night or catch a quick shower, we were brethren wayfarers living on the cheap, out for the adventure and free to experience whatever came along.

The girls, however, told lovely stories of fine hotels in big European cities. God help them if they lost Daddy's credit card. But good for them. It wasn't safe for females to travel like strays in places where men were rambunctious, randy pigs—and those places, and guys, were everywhere.

"The Beau Rivage in Geneva? Oh my god, it's sensational!" Janet said. It sounded to me like a place even Swiss bankers might flinch at the nightly rates.

"I *love* that hotel," Todd said, then sidebarred to me, "I snuck into the pool there and took a hot bath in their Jacuzzi. Janet's right—it's sensational."

Todd and I had no ambitions of tricking these girls into believing we were traveling in the first-class sections, so we fabricated outrageous stories, poking fun at ourselves, topping one another's adventures in the no-class section of life.

"How about that Fountain of Neptune in Florence?" he said. "Amazing Italian artistic history."

"Right you are. One of the greatest places to soak sweaty socks after a long day."

The girls chuckled.

"I scraped enough lire coins out of there to send my folks a postcard begging for money," Todd returned with a bigger laugh.

"... all while scrubbing your laundry on Neptune's abs, right?"

"Yeah, and how about those four-hundred-year-old tables at Hofbräuhaus? I got enough gum off the bottoms to make a new arm for the statue of Goethe I broke in the museum."

"And you could wash your hair in the vomitorium there. Decent people rinse the bowl first."

We started getting gross, losing the girls with our toilet humor but bonding in brotherhood. I opened my wine and poured for everyone in their little collapsible travel cups, unsurprised that Todd was prepared with a huge travel mug.

A wave of cheering burst from the crowd below, quickly pierced by the shriek of thousand-horsepower V-10 engines spinning at eighteen thousand rpm. Even high on our wall, we had to yell to overcome the deafening echoes through the Monaco hills, an entire country afflicted with race fever. We only had a clear view of the southernmost hairpin turn, *La Rascasse*, but the girls pointed out that our eardrums weren't bursting from being down there in the center of the action.

I offered up my chunk of salami for the group, slicing odd-sized circles and wedges with my giant Swiss Army Champion, a folding red toolbox that barely fit in your hand and boasted every gadget and blade the Swiss could possibly invent. I carried it everywhere, keeping it protected in a soft leather harmonica pouch. I used every blade in that thing for tweezing, magnifying, sewing, sawing, wiring, canning, and scaling—a tool no traveler should be without.

"What a knife!" Amy was finally impressed by something other than the depth of our bedraggled exploits. She pulled a bottle of wine from her backpack. "Does it have a corkscrew?"

We shared picnic lunches and ran out of wine early; such is the case, typically, for budget travelers. By the end of the day, French driver Gilles Villeneuve had taken the cup, France's champagne reserves had been depleted—sprayed from the backs of yachts— and the overworked yacht horns were scheduled for overhauls.

Buying the fancy souvenir hat, which I couldn't live without, obliterated any remaining vestige of my budget.

The race had been thrilling, but the camaraderie with fans and friends was the real champion of the day.

CHAPTER 29

THE LAST ROOM IN NICE

I thought how unpleasant it is to be locked out; and I thought
how it is worse, perhaps, to be locked in.
—Virginia Woolf

I had no plan for what to do next. My ticket to Monaco had been
one way, leaving my options open. Perhaps I'd find Antony and
Nico on the *Sylvia* and bum another free night with them? The *Sylvia*
bobbed on anchor in the distance, her crimson hull glistening like
nail polish across the sea. But I had a one-in-three-million chance
of finding my mates on shore for the chance that they'd invite me
on board again.

Another option was to follow the girls to Nice and party with
my new friends there. Ultimately, I was headed that direction, back
to Marseille to continue skating to Spain. Nice was my town as
much as any town on the Côte d'Azur, and maybe the girls were
staying in a swanky hotel with a fountain Todd and I could bathe
in.

"There's a darling little Italian restaurant a couple of blocks over.
Chianti, candles, cheap spaghetti. Anyone?" I wouldn't normally

198

have used the term "darling," but this back-alley, string-lit, and bougainvillea-covered patio was exactly that. For my part, cheap spaghetti was all the romance my stomach needed.

Todd took command of his little harem. "Sounds great, Mike. We'll stop at the hotel first."

He had already arranged a night on their sofa, but I was on my own with urban camping or my own hotel.

They cleaned up for dinner while I stopped by my favorite Nice hotel. On my last visit, I'd crashed into a cyclist on their sidewalk; it was unlikely they'd forgotten it.

"Marcel! Jolie! How are you?"

"Monsieur Michel, comment ça va? Where are your roller skates?"

"In a train station locker here in Nice."

The people in our lives, the people who light up in your presence, love to tell funny stories about you, stories of how you messed up. These people were becoming part of my Riviera family, and this was as close to coming home as it got.

"Have you made it to Spain already?" Marcel asked with a smirk, obviously dubious I'd ever made it out of Nice.

I was proud to tell him otherwise. "I made it as far as Marseille, and I came back by train for the Grand Prix. It's been an interesting trip, yes, wonderfully interesting. But hard. Really hard. Impossible, some days. Yeah, it's been hard."

"Marseille? *Non...*" Marcel was testing me.

"Mais oui—Marseille." My French flowed more naturally, yet I still lost hope of understanding more than a word or two.

Marcel carried on with guests, telling the tale of my departure from their hotel. Their laughter quieted as all eyes turned to me.

"Yeah, that was me." I waved sheepishly.

Jolie sized me up from toe to head, smiling as she came from around the counter to greet me with a hug. "Michel, you have lost weight." She squeezed and pawed my new biceps as handles of affection. "And you've been working very hard. Do you need a bed to sleep in tonight?"

I must have turned red, because she continued quickly. "I'm sorry, we are sold out tonight. Race fans. We're booked sometimes years in advance."

"That's okay." But of course I was lying. It wasn't. I'd have nowhere to sleep, but my ego was desperate to maintain my facade of self-reliance.

My discomfort extended to dinner that night with my new friends. Being the one to ask for separate checks suggested that you didn't care about the folks you were breaking bread with. Splitting the bill after the fact was equally loathsome, a cold squabble among warm friends in which someone usually took charge and became a ruthless tax collector or buckled under the pressure and ate the remainder of the bill, since no one ever threw in enough.

"Let's just split it five ways," Todd said.

The girls pulled out their coin pouches.

I'd ordered the cheapest plate on the menu with all-you-can eat bread, exactly what I could afford after a big-ticket day in Monaco. But now I was paying for one-fifth of their quadruple-priced veal and a nice bottle of wine I purposely hadn't touched. Squirming for an invitation to sleep on their hotel floor, I threw down for my lavish plate of noodles.

Exhausted from a day of drinking in the sun and dropping hints that I was overextended for the day's budget, I had confidence their magical invitation would come my way.

"So yeah, hey," Todd said uncomfortably. "The thing is we don't have any space in the room, and the girls are kinda weird about having too many people in there, what with that hotel people and all."

Exactly the opposite of my plan. I should have told them the hotels were all booked, and I'd be in a sleeping bag on the train station floor in twenty minutes. Where was the shame in that, big shot?

"Oh, that's okay." I'd said it again. It wasn't okay. I smiled through the lie. "I know a little hotel right up the street here. I've stayed there before. It's nice."

I started wandering, looking for an affordable hotel. It was just me, the crickets, and the stars at that hour in Nice. I walked to the train station for my pack, searching for a place to camp out somewhere the police wouldn't find me and the muggers wouldn't kill me. It couldn't stink of urine, couldn't be muddy, should be bug- and critter-free, and should be dark enough in the morning to allow me to sleep in past daybreak without being arrested. Such high expectations were hard to come by so late at night.

But eventually, I found a suitable area under a park bush that made a nice tent for a few hours of hobo slumber—and hardly any bugs. I had a plan, and I was happy. But then I arrived at the train station to a detail I hadn't considered earlier: locked doors and darkness. The train station was sealed up tight. Damn!

I looked around for a fence to climb, a hole to crawl through, or any way get in. I was now forced to find and pay for a hotel with nothing but the shirt on my back, a little cash, a passport, and a locker key. I tried using a pay phone to call the hotel, but I lost the only coins I had by fiddling with the dial. After that, I walked the dark streets for hours, searching in vain for the vacancy I would never find.

I headed toward the seedy area of town, desperate. Headlights from a car reminded me to stop stumbling down the center of the dark streets and walk the cobbled sidewalks. Tree roots pushed the through the cobblestones, but better to trip there than get run over. The headlights belonged to a little white Mercedes that slowed, stalking me on the sidewalk. I got creeped out and unconsciously reached for my knife, which was in my backpack.

Why might this car be following me? It wasn't a police car; they didn't drive classics. Muggers didn't drive convertible Mercedes either. I recognized the unmistakable sound of an early-seventies, six-cylinder 280SL engine—the same car Mom drove, the car I used to drive Carrie to high school formals.

"Hey, Mike! Look who— It's side-surfin' Mike. What the heck are you doing?"

Who the hell knew me in Nice? I recognized the voice but couldn't place it.

"It's me, Ted the skater."

I couldn't believe someone had recognized me. Then again, I'd run into Marsha, Ted Nugent, Tom, Jolie… I guess it wasn't such a stretch to be recognized in Nice, after all. I would have been far too lucky if it were Rachelle.

"Hey Ted, yeah, how the hell are ya? What are you doing out so late?"

"Jazz club. God I love jazz—no, hear me clearly, I really love, love, looove jazz," he said with a full-body wiggle. "There's a little club up the street. Just out boogeyin' the night away." He clearly had no fear of driving drunk in his town. "Yep, out all night. It's Saturday night, baby, yeah!"

"Actually, it's Sunday now."

"Right. So like what the hell are *you* doing out here? Last we met, you were skating to Morocco or Colombia or wherever the hell." His clumsy hand pointed toward some far away land, knocking his rear-view mirror out of line.

I had vowed to tell no more lies in the name of pride. "I got locked out. All my camping gear's in a locker. I was looking for a hotel, but all the race fans have them booked for months."

"Bastards! Why, I ought to—locked out of what?"

"The train station. My backpack, skates—everything's in a train station locker. They lock it down after midnight."

"So where are you staying?"

In hindsight, this would have been a good time to lie in the name of pride. "That's the thing, Ted—nowhere. I'm looking for a hotel." I gave a brief account of how the day's events landed me in this mess. "I was going to camp in the park over that way, but my gear's all locked up at the station."

"Sleep in the park? Like some indigent dirtbag? What the fuck? What's wrong with you, camping with the bums?"

That was the reaction I feared most, the very words that kept me lying to people to maintain my dignity. I was petrified someone would find out my honest situation. But I'd just told Ted, and it wasn't that bad. The truth set me free—for a while.

"Well, I'm not exactly camping with bums. Even that's too nice without my gear. I'm heading this way to find a cheap hotel. Or I'll grab some coffee and walk around all night until the station opens at six. The bakeries probably open in a few hours. I'll get a croissant soon. It's okay."

"Oh, come on, that's horse shit. I'll have no part of that!" He slammed his hand on the dashboard. "You're coming with me and staying at my apartment up on the hill. And that's that."

I looked around, embarrassed that he might be waking people up.

He continued just as loudly. "I have the best view in Nice. I have a guest room with a balcony and—well, you just have to say yes. Come on, hop in. We'll get your bag in the morning."

Finally, something was going my way. The price was right, and it had to be more comfortable than mud without a sleeping bag.

Ted brushed his stuff from the passenger seat, and away we rolled down to the Promenade des Anglias.

The moon had devoured the stars. Only twinkling lights lining the trees down the Prom guided our lone car rumbling through the otherwise silent city.

"Mike, I have to tell you I've practiced your side surfing thing since you left and still can't get it. That day you came by—remember that day?—I worked on it all day long. I was so mad at you. Well, mad at me, really, that I couldn't do your stupid move on skates. It was driving me crazy. *I'm the one* who's supposed to do the skate tricks."

Too late to reconsider jumping into a car with a drunk at the wheel. He was doing okay, driving far too slow, but I made sure my belt was buckled tightly.

"Did you stretch out first?" I asked. "That's really the key, 'cause your legs just aren't meant to do that. It took a while to get mine to move that way. It's just practice, I guess."

He told me how he practiced side surfing every day and how it made him useless on the dance floor at the jazz club. He sounded like a real swinger. We laughed through a maze of streets up the hill to the west, the city lights and Mediterranean Sea glistening below.

True to his word, his apartment building was fantastic. A security gate opened, and he parked in a cliffhanger garage supported by stilts on the side of the hill. He left the keys in the ignition and the top down; the secure gate wouldn't let anyone in or out of the garage to mess with the car.

An elevator code took us up a few floors, where the doors opened directly into his apartment, decorated by a pro in swinging '80s lounge décor: white carpet, orange lamp shades, the works.

"You check out the balcony," he said. "I'll fix up some drinks."

I'd have a polite nightcap and indulge his incessant chatter for a little while. After all, he had kept me from wandering the streets all night. And he was right about the balcony; it truly was the most spectacular view of Nice. What the hell—if I had to have another drink and enjoy the view, so be it. This was some amazing life I was living. This had all worked out quite well tonight. What was I worried about? Things always work out for me.

Ted joined me on the balcony with some sweet cocktails. He clinked our glasses and stared into the distance. I drank quickly and practically passed out.

He asked if I wanted to sleep there on the double-wide chaise. It looked comfortable, and I really didn't care at that point other than needing a blanket to keep the sun out of my eyes in a few hours. I was a grateful rescue, and if that was what he called his guest room, I was happy to face-plant into the cushions and call it a night.

"Might be a little cold for me," I hinted.

Ted's next words—more accurately, the single word in the flurry of excited conversation my request provoked—was a life-changer: "Us."

Holy. Living. Mother of all hell. What had I gotten myself into?

Ted was gay. I'd said I would spend the night.

Oh shit, I was in big trouble.

Once he dropped the "us" bomb, he looked at me in a way that made me nervous. I'd never had a man approach me that way. I feared he would try to make a move on me and shutting him down could make things awkward, or worse, shift his amorous intentions into high gear.

The right thing to do would have been to stop worrying about being polite, tell him no, tell him to stop, express myself, push him away, move away. But hazy judgment from the cocktail panicked me and I proceeded directly to the final step: run.

Some survival instinct told me to get off the balcony, to stay clear of anything dangerous. Backing slowly off the balcony, I scanned the room for potential weapons, anything to use if it came to defense. "I'll just sleep on the sofa here. Me, by myself. Alone."

He approached me slowly, carefully...skillfully closing in. I caught a hint of persuasion in his smile, which told me he was still selling. I walked to the sofa, putting the glass coffee table between us.

I needed a diversion, something that would let me make a run for it. Still being polite, without a weapon in my hands, I asked him to refresh my drink. I assumed I was acting casual, but I was smashed after just a few sips.

Behind the bar, he leaned over to fetch ice. That was my chance.

I jumped into the elevator and slammed Close Door a hundred times as it closed slowly.

Ted ran for the elevator. "What are you doing? Don't go. You have to stay here!"

The elevator door closed.

Now what?

CHAPTER 30

BREAKOUT

You will never be free until you free yourself from your own false thoughts.
—Philip Arnold

I didn't hit the down button; the garage would be sealed up tight with no way to escape. The other floors led directly into other apartments, requiring a keypad code. Only the top floor button was available. Ted pounded on the door below as I went up somewhere—anywhere else. I'd figure it out when the doors opened. I'd be running into a labyrinth of apartments, lost with no idea where I was going. But Ted would know.

The elevator doors finally opened to reveal a swimming pool, lounge chairs, and a five-story drop down the side of the building. I was a mouse in a maze, and the cat was on his way. I ran around the pool deck, looking over the side for a way down. The lights from Ted's apartment below were the only sign of life.

Across the deck was an exit sign, a stairway that led me down the side of the building as quickly as I could run. I stopped at each floor, listening for footsteps. At the bottom of the stairs was the door back into the garage. I knew I'd be trapped there.

Footsteps at the top of the stairs alerted me that Ted was running down. I peered over the rail. Still a two-story drop to the ground below. A drainpipe on the outer wall looked sturdy enough to climb down, but it was out of reach from the garage level. I'd have to go up a level, toward Ted running down, to reach it.

I raced up a flight and hopped the rail, clinging to the pipe in silent desperation. I held my breath and prayed that my clenched hand wasn't showing.

He passed by.

I waited to hear the door to the garage below close before climbing down. Ted's Mercedes roared to life as I free-climbed the vertical pipe, jamming and camming bloody knuckles into off-widths behind the pipe and other holds. The Sierra Club would have rated this a class 5.13 on the Yosemite Decimal System, a level once compared to "climbing upside down on a glass window"—that is, if I'd had ropes.

The last of the pipe left me at a drop into blackness. I estimated a six-foot drop onto an unknown bushy slope. I took a deep breath and let go. The shrubs were thick with sharp stickers, making it impossible to get to the fence without looking as though I'd been caged with an angry cat. I found a hole in the wooden fence and squeezed my way underneath, pinched like a rabbit between spider webs and mushy, wet shrubbery that pressed into each bloody slash on my arms and legs.

Outside the fence was another drop. I rolled down some rocks and fell onto the street—inches behind Ted's car as he roared past.

He would come back to find me, of that I was certain. How to get down the labyrinth of neighborhood streets without being spotted was a mystery. On the way up, Ted had made several turns, and I'd paid little attention. I walked a terrace road, turning inland, then down, then up. Should I have stayed high on the last turn and dropped down later? Oh, hell. I'd walked half a mile without drawing one step closer to the beach.

Confused, exhausted, and intoxicated from whatever Ted had given me, I was driven by fear with nowhere to hide. I should've been sober after skipping the wine at dinner, but half a rum punch had done me in. My head spun, I was having trouble walking straight, and I couldn't make any sense of where I was going or what I was seeing. That a-hole had drugged my drink.

That's when I turned the wrong way—and here came Ted.

The deep-throated German engine approached slowly. Its high beams reminded me of Nazi searchlights on the wall. I leaped over a guardrail into thick bushes and held still, eyes wide, like a diver in a shark cage. The Great White Car drifted slowly by.

The bushes seemed safe, so I decided to wait it out. Maybe I'd close my eyes a moment. But just for a moment…

Something bit my neck in the darkness and I awoke in a jolt of cold panic, wondering where I was. Another bug was wiggling in my shoe, and itchy lumps all over my body came into awareness as I tried to recall the events that had gotten me there. Flashes of a white car, sounds of the Mercedes, remnants of exhaust, and the ache of my skinned knuckles brought back my climb on the side of the building. Had I gotten whipped by a thorn bush? It was coming back, vaguely. I had to stay down, figure this out before I got up. Danger loomed. I feared something, but I wasn't sure what. I fought a powerful urge to sleep, but I needed to get somewhere safe. I had to fight sleep, fight to remember. I had to get up and walk—carefully.

It was the middle of the night, beyond late, a decisive time when no one was either coming or going. It was a time when the night air lay still and cold. This hour was no stranger. I recognized this hour from my long nights in Avalon, waiting for the sun, cursing the decisions that had gotten me there. I found my way down the hill, hiding from anything that moved, too buzzed to defend myself. What kind of man was I, hiding in the bushes? I had become the quintessential horror movie actress, running and falling as the monster kept pace behind her.

Halfway across the Prom, I was back in familiar territory. Safe. By then, I recalled most of the night except the part when my brain had disconnected and I'd hopped into Ted's car. What an idiot. I could be in handcuffs, in a cave, or dead. Should I go to the police? I had no tangible evidence of any wrongdoing. Ted would tell the police I was a drifter, that I must have taken some bad drugs.

I decided to let it go, taking up a new cadence, "What-a-more-on," on my march to the train station. I still had hours to kill before the station opened at sunrise. I found a park bench I could sit on until the sun rose. When a police car drove by, I ducked into the bushes so he wouldn't ask questions. The bench wasn't going to work for a nap, so I dragged over some cardboard boxes from an alley and made a mattress under those bushes. My next postcard home would read "Mom and Dad, it's official. Your son is a homeless, box-dwelling derelict."

***

The morning dew made my bare legs shiver. I scrambled under the cardboard into the warmth of the dirt. Safety, the level below love and belonging on Maslow's hierarchy of needs, had disappeared.

I'd started my journey at the top of Maslow's pyramid, wearing my self-actualized crown and looking down at basics like safety. I had no worries of security of body, employment, resources, morality, family, health, or property. But lying there under the reeking cardboard, too tired to stay awake and too scared to sleep, ashamed, lonely, and disgraced, I surrendered. My safety had vanished. All of it.

I struggled to find a positive angle, anything to take the edge off the depressing facts of the situation. A mantra, a glimmer of hope. Finally, it came to me: with any luck, this moment would be the lowest point of my life. That made me smile.

That was when the automatic sprinklers turned on and soaked me.

It was time to get back on track: on the train tracks back to Marseille, and on track to get to Spain on skates. Soon I would be back with a good friends—but not in Marseille. I hopped off the train in Antibes and reached my fisherman buddy just as he cast his last bait into the sunset.

"*Bonjour, monsieur.*"

Our handshake was charged by enthusiasm; genuine smiles were exchanged. I waited until he looked away to wipe off the guano from my hand.

He lit another Gitane, perhaps unable to talk out of the side of his mouth without it, before blathering excitedly, indecipherably. This time he told happy, funny stories that made himself laugh. I didn't understand a word he said, but the joy of a happy friend brought me out of my funk enough to talk about my experience with Ted. I could see he understood my fears without understanding my words.

"I just feel so...violated," I said, questioning my own terms. I continued as he cast bait, balancing his focus between me and the tackle.

"The thing is, the guy didn't do anything—I mean, the big crime was saying "us" with a hint that we might sleep in the same bed. I just freaked out and ran. But being chased, hunted down like that, scared me most. Maybe he wasn't hunting me. Maybe he just wanted me to be safe, not get lost in the building, or the hills?"

A tiny fish splashed the surface, powerless against the line attached to his mouth, soon to be released by the fisherman's caring hands. I really wanted to understand the slow and methodical advice he was speaking while removing the small hook with the finesse of some sort of fish lip surgeon. He kept looking at me, and at the fish, and even removed the cigarette from his mouth to say his truth with clarity. Unintelligible sentences put me into deeper introspection, which by his tone, is what I believed to be his goal.

"An apology?" I said as if these were his words. "I didn't think about that. True, he might have been trying to apologize."

He shot me a glance to keep talking.

"Or," I paused, disbelieving what I might say next. "Did you mean an apology *by me?* Apologize, or did you mean forgive?"

"Oui, oui, oui," he said while gently releasing the fish to the sea. That word I understood. What I didn't understand was which one of us he was talking to; me or the fish. Maybe both.

I unpacked my bag on the lighthouse, preparing for a cold night of camping. Before he left, we exchanged grins and a bond beyond language. His name and his words were all a mystery, and still he had become my best friend in France. How could I show him?

I watched him walk away with a spring in his step, wearing a brand-new Monaco Grand Prix cap. A glance at my watch told me it was "now"—the perfect time to move on, like a saved fish.

CHAPTER 31

CHEZ BLANCHE

The quality of your life is the quality of your relationships.
—Anthony Robbins

We were passing through Cannes by the time I felt truly awake. My internal clock was set to catch the early train out of Antibes, departing even before my fishing friend arrived. I had a lunch date in Marseille with Marion, which would be a family lunch at the home of Régine and her husband, Monsieur Blanche.

I arrived a few minutes early. A woman in a classic French maid's outfit greeted me at the door of the posh Prado Parc apartment. Her Halloween costume in June caught me off guard until I computed: I was in France, and she was the maid. Duh. She was also the greeter, chef, and server, and from the disrespect they showed her, she was either bad at her jobs or they were simply rude to the help. I introduced myself and she showed me to the dining room.

M. Blanche sat at the table in suit and tie, contemplating his soup with suspicion. He must have been in a hurry on his lunch break, for he forgot to say hello when I walked in.

Marion lit up with excitement, affectionately guiding me to meet her father. "Papa, I want you to meet Michel from California."

M. Blanche lifted his head out of his soup to wipe his face but made no eye contact. He nodded while holding up his hand as if to pause whatever delicate situation he was in. After awkward silence, his first words were in a gruff tone.

"So," he said gruffly after an awkward silence, "you don't even know Freddie?"

Dear god, did I have to go through all this again? I explained to Régine how Freddie had arrived in America just as I had left for Europe.

"So you have never met Frederique. Is that right or is that wrong? Which is it?" He kept shoveling food into his mouth.

I kept my fat sausage fingers under the table and proceeded with caution. "No sir, I have not met Freddie. As I explained to your wife Régine, I was leaving California—"

"Okay, so your sister, that Julie, she knows Frederique but you do not. I am right, *oui?*"

Okay, that did it. Impressive home and suit or no, nobody called my sister "that Julie." I answered his questions. I remained polite. But I wasn't going to be bullied. I didn't care how delicious the hollandaise covered asparagus was.

"Yes, my *sister Julie* and my brother-in-law *Sean.*" I pronounced their names clearly, loudly. "They took your daughter *Freddie* into their home, where she lived and was welcomed as *family* for many months. That's just how we are in America, cordial and polite."

"So what are you doing here?" His knife screeched the dish as he cut his lunch meat as though it were the enemy.

"What am I doing here? As in here in Marseille? Or here in your house?"

He didn't answer, certainly not because he was chewing food.

"I'm here *in Marseille* because I'm roller-skating from Italy to Spain. Marseille is about halfway between."

"I live in Marseille. I know where Marseille is." His temper flared but it didn't rattle me at all.

Régine and Marion focused on their lunch plates, head down like inmates, habitually avoiding engagement in the latest of a long history of his tirades.

"I'm here *at your house* because your lovely *wife Régine* invited me. I had a wonderful time at your beautiful *daughter Marion's* dinner party."

"More coffee," he barked for the maid's quick response.

"Yes, please. Me too," I asked the maid—more with a smile, eye contact, and a gesture toward my cup.

The maid poured my coffee first, trying not to smirk at the tension I was causing.

"*Merci beaucoup.*" I asked her name.

"*Enchanté, Madeleine,*" I replied and turned to M. Blanche. "Her name is Madeleine."

He didn't care.

"Thank you for having me today, Monsieur Blanche. I welcomed your invitation to a family lunch."

"But you are not family."

With exception of his occasional grunts, that was the end of mealtime conversation. He slurped his coffee like a jet engine and bumped the table with his gut as he stood, wiping yellow sauce off his face and tossing the white cloth on top of his plate. He walked out the front door without a goodbye to anyone.

Marion's giggles broke the mood, but she wasn't giggling at her father.

Régine translated: "Marion thinks you're not supposed to eat the chewy end. This is the good end." She lifted a forkful of asparagus.

I mimicked her. "This end is what—the handle?"

She smiled at my joke. "*Oui, c'est la poignée.*"

That made Marion laugh again.

Tossing my manners aside, I picked up a spear with my fingers and bit the good end. We all needed a moment of comic relief.

When Régine left the table, Marion leaned close to whisper, "I did not know her name either."

"Is she new?" I asked.

"New? We don't have a maid. We've never had a maid. He must have hired her to impress you."

CHAPTER 32

BAD CONNECTION

Freedom is what you do with what's been done to you.
—Jean-Paul Sartre

The post offices were the best places for long distance calls. The postal clerks would connect the international line, provide a quiet booth with a door and a seat, and let you pay after the call. When you called from the post office, there was never an operator interrupting for additional coins.

I grabbed the receiver like a slot machine handle, trying my luck again at connecting with Carrie. The odds were with the house, but this time I hit the jackpot. Carrie's sweet voice played like my favorite song, live on the other end of the six-thousand-mile wire.

"Hi, Michael." She sounded tired. Sentimental. Downright sad.

The poor dear must be missing me something fierce.

We chatted a few minutes. How was France? Was the weather nice? It didn't matter what she said. I relaxed and enjoyed her voice, the melody I longed for.

But the lyrics that had tugged my heart over the hills of France now changed dramatically.

I repeated my question in bewilderment. "So you're not coming to Spain?"

I sat in silence as she enumerated the reasons her trip to Barcelona was canceled. The sorrow in her tone was heavy—too heavy. There was more. I listened in stunned silence.

"So you're dating someone else?"

I surrendered, softly hanging the receiver on the hook and clinging to it with both hands. Eventually I left the phone booth and rolled to the postal counter like a trash can on wheels, where I paid the clerk a ridiculous amount of money for the privilege of holding the phone in several painfully long minutes of silence. I'd just wasted a bundle of money as we listened to each other breathe, both afraid to say anything wrong and both afraid to be the first to say the final goodbye. Silence was a bargain compared to rehashing how it wasn't supposed to end this way, how she never meant to hurt me...the usual bullshit. Had I wanted nothing more than her pure happiness in life—as they say true love should be—I could have been supportive than sarcastic. Great, she found her Hollywood hairdo–band rock star to give her the glamorous life she's always wanted. *Yay, you.*

I was a long way from supportive. Fractured would have been more accurate, and cashing out with a wad of French francs at the postal window was insult upon injury.

I touched my backpack straps as I rolled out the door, not to adjust them but to ensure that the behemoth was still hanging there. The dead weight hung in apathy, like my arms. I stood there for ten, maybe twenty minutes, staring at the asphalt without noticing the street. No anger or pain or awareness. Something important was now gone, ripped from my chest and discarded on the phone booth floor.

Should I yell? Cry? Punch a wall? Jump in front of this bus? Standing like a sidewalk statue was all I could do. I was completely paralyzed, noticing only that I was still breathing. Involuntary muscles wrenched two words from my gut: *now what?*

Like the Tin Man from *The Wizard of Oz,* I slowly moved my joints, painfully turning my head, struggling to take a simple step forward. But why move? I had zero reason to move.

A ray of sunlight shot through a break in the buildings across the street, blinding me, a mustard seed of motivation to adjust my hat or put on sunglasses. I checked my backpack again; still there.

No, really. I couldn't just stand there for the rest of my life. I must do something. Anything. *Move, Michael.* Just a simple movement.

I pointed my skates down the hill, wallowing in the fact that I could stand still yet begin traveling. Some decisions were unavoidable, like whether to stop for traffic or just roll through a light and get plowed. But I wasn't suicidal, just numb.

Barcelona was another six or seven hundred kilometers away, but now I had no conceivable reason to go there. My motivation had been unplugged. Barcelona. I now had a hatred for the city. Barcelona: the mere name fired contempt, as if the city had anything to do with getting dumped.

It started to sink in that every step I'd taken on this stupid roller journey had been for nothing, an absolute waste of time and effort. Should I go back to a hotel? That wouldn't do any good. I'd probably sit drinking wine all day, growing even more mad or sad. I could do that for free. Better to be out in the sun doing what I loved—or what I once loved.

What did I love?

I kept rolling down the Canebiere. The gentle slope dragged me to the edge of the Old Port.

Maybe I should go somewhere else. I'd be even more pissed off if I'd skated all the way here for nothing. As if my voice could carry halfway around the world, I had to speak it out. I had to vent the despair, or it would explode through the lump in my throat.

"You don't even care," I said, heedless of the looks from passing pedestrians. "And I've been here writing you every week, skating my ass off every day to get to you."

I'm not well versed in the stages of grief, but clearly I was in the step they call anger. Yelling "FUCK YOU!" to the sea at the top of your lungs was one of the more therapeutic experiences I've had toward a full and healthy recovery.

The pain of her cheating on me was quickly replaced by the pain of me cheating on her with Carla. I wanted so badly to be mad at Carrie, to make it all her fault, but that argument didn't have a leg to stand on. It did get lonely, so far away, so many months. And Carrie'd had no idea when I would be coming home. Come to think of it, neither did I.

So where was I going?

My arms were day-old spaghetti, lifeless, dragging my pole tips. I didn't bother fighting the city traffic and rolled through the stop signs without looking.

It would be easy enough to go back up the hill and get on a train to…Paris? Rome? Prague? Maybe London, where I could buy a flight home and run back to Carrie, beat up her Hollywood rock star, and win her back. The possibilities were endless.

But no, I was free. Free to go anywhere in Europe—anywhere in the world, for that matter.

I could go back to the Kleins and crash there for a little while, but effortless family freeloading wouldn't solve anything. Considering easy things made me uneasy. I burned with a need, a drive to do the harder thing that would build more character, generate bigger adventures, change my life for the better. Indecisiveness was no choice at all. Where was the reward in taking the easy route? What could I possibly learn or experience from just getting by?

Character wasn't gained by avoiding adversity but by the pursuit of it. This moment, when I was at my worst, was a critical opportunity for making my best choice.

"It doesn't matter where I am or where I go," I said aloud, as if speaking in tongues. "I am my attitude. And I will travel with myself forever."

I would get away from the big city. I chose the route closest to the water; cargo ships were prettier than trains or oil refineries. Almost immediately, I ran across a section of old road that had once been paved but only showed historical patches of pavement with dirt and sand between. Like jumping rocks to cross a river, I tried jumping between pavement islands to make any forward motion. From my map, I had three miles of this until I was out of the area.

I considered putting on shoes and walking. I made only a few inches of forward motion with every stride, but I figured it had to be temporary. Like my bad attitude. I forced myself to look around with fresh eyes. What an amazing day it was. I was free, I was alive, and I had so much to be grateful for. My attitude improved, which changed everything—except the road.

After hours of scant headway, I made it back to normal streets with lunch on my mind. My map showed Martigues ahead, and the bridge there could be a good place to watch boats go by, maybe find some shade under a tree. I'd been drinking tons of water, all of it going right through my sunburned pores, soaking everything I was wearing. My Avalon Seafood visor could not soak up another drop, dripping sweat like rain off its saturated brim.

I stopped at another gas station to fill my bota bag with tap water and treat myself to a cold Orangina. The days of saving every penny for future dates with Carrie were over.

I proved my point by buying a second Orangina, the bottle of sweet bachelorhood even more delicious than the first.

CHAPTER 33

LEND ME YOUR EAR

If someone breaks your heart just punch them in the face. Seriously.
Punch them in the face and go get some ice cream.
—Frank Ocean

I was catching my breath under a tree at the Grand Canal at Martigues when my pathetic, broken heart finally caught up with me. The last of my happy endorphins drained away, and the weight of negativity tugged like a boat on anchor on a windy night. Far from cooling off, my feet told my attitude to get moving. My body got up on autopilot—a wiser, less dejected autopilot than the one controlling my emotions.

"Oh, you are some smart feet, making me get back on the road," I murmured. "Let's treat you with fresh socks."

Talking to my feet like puppies helped me separate mind from body. It was self-preservation. I was under attack. The negativity and sadness flooding my mind would have destroyed me had I stayed focused on them. Instead, exercise, endorphins, and good music in my headphones made for healthy therapy.

Still, I worried that every time I stopped, the pain would always catch up.

A short trek from my tree took me out into the country again, but not the same lovely, tree-shaded, winding roads through cool, dark forests. Hot, dry farmland drew arid mirages in the distance as tractors crawled through dusty waves of heat. This country ran flat, straight, and unchanging for hours. This was the stretch on my map I had dreaded ever since Régine Blanche had attempted to teach me how to properly say "Arles," the town waiting on the other side of this stretch of highway.

The highway had nothing to offer: nothing of visual interest, nothing in the distance to set a goal, and nothing to eat or drink. A road sign said "Arles 32 km," and then not another sign until I arrived. The road had a nice shoulder, which I used to avoid the eighteen-wheelers whose mass occasionally whooshed a compassionate cooling breeze my way. Other than those infrequent joys, it was my arms and my legs and my dread for hours.

Two hours brought me to a lonely gas station in the middle of this beeline span, the only stop for hours in either direction. By some miracle, their old drinking fountain poured chilled, filtered water into my mouth until I could swallow no more. I'd been drinking plenty of water along the way, but when I tried to pee, I found that all the liquid in my body had evaporated through my pores, into my clothes, into the torrid air. The stop was brief—long enough to tank up on water and short enough to keep sadness at bay.

I was back on the road, fighting heat and heartbreak with mind tricks, when the motorcycle cop pulled over and parked his bike ahead of me. He removed his helmet and gloves and reached for a ticket book in his saddlebag. I was nervous as he approached. I was probably getting a ticket.

"*Bonjour, monsieur. Comment allez-vous?*" I greeted him with feigned cheerful respect, though he would never believe I was French or fluent or cheerful. I took off my backpack and leaned it on a milestone, uneasy about surrendering my passport.

He launched into a French lawman's ass-chewing. On and on he ranted about— I guessed laws of the road. He'd stop and take deep breaths through his nose, practically snorting his whole mustache into his head while walking circles around me, checking my gear, and slapping his gloves on his palm.

I caught the occasional word, bit by bit collecting hints on his lecture topic. He was upset that I was roller-skating on the highway. If he was going to do something harsh, like slap me with his gloves, he'd have already done it. But I couldn't take the yelling anymore, and cooled off with some water from my bota bag.

"Maybe if you yelled at me with that bullhorn on your bike I'd understand." My snarky smirk likely revealed I was messing with him.

Words were lost on his French ears, but he pulled his mirror sunglasses off—slowly—to show me the squint in his eyes meant business. He wasn't about to let some antagonistic punk mess with his authority. He continued to wave his ticket book around in a threatening manner.

"So how is that book coming along? Is that your life story in ten pages there?" I should have feared an expensive ticket or even arrest, but I was too hot, exhausted, and emotionally drained to say anything short of cocky. "Shot any roller skaters today, crime fighter?"

He looked at me in wonder.

"If you handcuff me to the back of your bike, you can drag me to Arles. Or call a real cop with a car."

If he'd been serious, he would have written me a ticket right then, some heinous "pedestrian on the highway" offense. But he just kept threatening me with his ticket pad and ranting in French, loudly, to overcome the passing truck noise.

"What's the problem—a guy can't walk on the side of the road? Maybe I skate in the middle of the road."

I rolled out into the middle of the lane where a truck had just passed. The next truck was approaching quickly.

He looked at the fast-approaching truck, then at me, and then at the fast-approaching truck.

I took a swig of water from my bota bag.

"Looks like you got yourself a stalemate here, *frère Jacques*. A Mexican standoff, if you've ever heard of Mexico. Whatcha gonna do, Jack, haul me in on the back of your bike? Have me hang onto your cheesy handlebar mustache for the next thirty k?"

The oncoming truck blasted its air horn. The cop's squint morphed into wide-eyed horror.

Did I want to die? Did I want to scare him? Did I want to scare myself? Yes to all of the above, but he and the truck driver were the only ones alarmed. That fact alarmed me.

I stepped off.

The air horn dissipated as two trailers passed inches from my back, wind vortices whipping my hair and cooling the bead of sweat on the cop's forehead.

His tone changed now that he was talking with a madman; compassionate, empathetic. Still he was mad about something, but perhaps it wasn't me. Maybe his girlfriend had dumped him too? If he was going to air out his problems in the desert, I was going to join the party.

"The part that gets me most is that she didn't tell me she wasn't coming. I could have died on the way to Barcelona while she was off with her boyfriend trashing hotel rooms."

It didn't matter what either of us said. I was openly discussing my problems with this cop, and it was empowering to talk with a human about it, even if he didn't follow a word.

I shifted to a calmer, more sensitive voice. "Yeah, it really sucks, man. Women—what are ya gonna do? I mean, me too. I hold out for her for a year, and this is what I get? Does she have any idea how bad this hurts inside? Truth is, I saw it coming. She hadn't written in months. And if I'm honest, I've been no saint here in Europe."

I paused for him to interrupt. He didn't.

"I've been in denial," I said. "I didn't want to read between the lines and face the ugly truth that I was losing her. More painful, though, is to find out so abruptly, at such a bad time. The difference is choosing pain or having pain delivered to you. It's worse if it's delivered. How about your woman?"

His face was deadpan. I still had the floor.

"But you can't go through your whole life choosing pain. So maybe a little denial now and then is a good thing?"

He just looked at me. Something I said, or more likely the way I said it, calmed his harangue. He continued to vent, looking to the sky for answers, and his expression transformed from anger to pain. With a deep sigh between sentences, he bit his lower lip and put his mirrored sunglasses back on.

Unexpectedly, he presented his hand to shake. *"Merci beaucoup, monsieur."* And with that, he put his motorcycle gloves back on.

Mildly stunned, I rose from the mile marker I'd been leaning on, put my own gloves back on, and simply skated past him and his motorcycle with some confidence that he wasn't going to shoot me in the back. I kept on skating, waiting for him to shoot or pass me by. I looked back a few times. He sat by his motorcycle for another ten minutes before finally speeding past without so much as a finger wave.

"I'M GLAD WE HAD THIS TALK!" I yelled, but my words were lost against the deafening roar of his motorcycle.

It was good medicine to talk things out. Being understood is irrelevant, but you can heal yourself talking to a dog, a lizard, the ocean, or even a plant. It doesn't work with cats. I talked to myself all the time—not that I needed therapy like some homeless guy babbling to himself on the side of the road. On roller skates.

Maybe I really was starting to crack. I just wanted to be home. But home was strapped to my back, and every step forward reminded me that no matter how my address might change, the only home I would ever have was right here and right now. The home I craved was in Carrie's heart. But that home had an eviction sign on the door, the locks had been changed, and a new dog snarled on the porch.

I truly was that babbling homeless guy on the side of the road. I feared the people of Arles might have me committed to an insane asylum, just as they did with poor old Vincent Van Gogh. The homeless lunatic on wheels was coming to town, arguing with mirages, with some unexplainable urge to steal a grocery cart and cover my head with an aluminum foil hat.

***

Arles, at last. A quiet town, downright silent in comparison to Marseille and Monaco, perhaps even eerie with only a few souls walking the streets. Maybe it was Sunday night and everyone was in church? I took it as a further sign of my abandonment. Now the whole country was out to leave me. But Arles was unique, set apart from everything else on this trip. I'd left the Côte d'Azur and entered Provence-Alpes-Côte d'Azur, almost as if I'd crossed into a new country.

I skated past the ancient coliseum on my way to a hotel room that fit my balance between clean and cheap. Next to room prices, the hotel window displayed a poster advertising the weekend bullfights. I gazed into the poster, a part of me wanting to be the matador. An equal part of me wanted to be the bull.

The twenty-thousand-spectator Arles Arena was built for chariot races and bloodletting gladiator battles. At half the size of Rome's coliseum, the Arles Arena was inspired by its fifty-thousand-seat Roman twin. Built in 90 AD, this two-thousand-year-old arena was a mere ten years newer than Rome's.

"Funny, it doesn't look a day older than nineteen centuries," I joked with the hotel clerk, but he didn't laugh. Likely he didn't understand. More likely it was a stupid joke. But it was my dad's joke, so it couldn't be that stupid. It made me laugh every time, even if I was the one telling it and the only one laughing.

After skating one hundred grueling kilometers in a single day, unloading my backpack and putting my feet up on the bed had never brought such relief. Vincent Van Gogh would have loved my room. The pale lilac walls, tattered butter-colored chair, faded red floors, and cracking green window seemed tired, as if the bedroom were last painted in the late 1800s by Van Gogh himself.

Through the window, bedazzling stars and a great crescent moon cast awe and wonder upon the city's cathedral spires and flamelike cypress. I imagined the artist's isolated life so long ago, his dream of reaching the interminable stars. I imagined him in this room with a paint roller, sipping turpentine, eating paste, and going completely insane as he painted these walls.

"I get it, Vincent. Pass the turpentine, please." Now I was talking to walls.

I headed down the hall, where I found a private shower and separate toilet rooms, one with only a bidet. I had some business to do, and not in a bidet. Then there was the other room, the "what the hell is that hole in the floor?" room. At first I thought someone had stolen the toilet. The hole was surrounded by tiles—a "squatter." The idea was to squat over the open hole in the floor and do your business, at least that's what I thought. There was a hose and a couple of starting blocks to place your feet on; that part was clear. Some sort of ladle hung on the wall, conjuring up some gag-reflex-inducing questions about a soup. There were no instructions, no one to ask. You were supposed to just know, and I was beyond clueless.

"Story of my life," I sighed. "I can't even take a shit right."

Contemplation time destroyed my window of opportunity to find somewhere else to go, and pressing needs forced the learning curve in ancient plumbing.

If I squatted over my shorts, I'd go right on them. Then there was the door—not even a lock on it. What if I was wrong and this was a mop bucket? I wedged my shorts in the crack under the closed door and did my business in record time, ignored the hose and ladle, and ran straight to the hot shower.

***

The cobbled streets of Arles were designed three thousand years before the advent of the automobile. I would have to check my history books, but by the look of things, the wheel may not have been invented by then.

"Jesus Christ, this town is old… Eight hundred years older than you."

Reproductions and prints of Van Gogh paintings lined the sidewalks and gift shops. Photographs compared modern landscapes and his paintings, showing that little had changed in Arles over the past century. I passed the Place de Forum, where a café terrace had inspired Van Gogh to paint one of his most famous works, *Café Terrace at Night*. A gift shop postcard noted that he "...tried to express the idea that the café is a place where one can ruin oneself, go mad, or commit a crime."

"Charming. Sounds like my kind of place," I said aloud to no one.

I took a seat, ordered a glass of wine, and caught up on the next steps of my grieving process. Perhaps at the very same dinner table, I sat despondent like Van Gogh. Even after one hundred kilometers of skating, I ate without an appetite, wondering what I would do next.

Walking back to my hotel room and sitting alone was a dreary notion. I might get tempted to cut off an ear or something. I wanted to be out, but not out in the open; I wanted to be around people, but not people that talk. I wandered Arles's dark and narrow labyrinth until the stairs of Saint-Trophime Cathedral found me, and I dropped for a seat in the shadows to stare at the yellow lights of the plaza.

I found solace in my old friend the harmonica, blowing blues into the Place de la République. I played from a tortured soul. I shed tears. I aired my pain through the instrument.

A couple walked by, arm in arm, and dropped a couple of francs at my tired feet. This, by definition, made me a paid, professional musician. Yay, me. I kept on playing because it felt like the thing to do—like it was the only thing I *could* do. The rich tonal warmth of the harmonica reeds vocalized my very breath. My tongue bent the notes, and my choked-up throat magnified the strain of whatever I was playing. I didn't have songs to play; the music just came like I'd swallowed something evil.

Footsteps passed and more coins clinked at my feet as I closed my eyes and wailed—through my eyes and through the harp—filling the plaza like an opera house. When I could blow no more, the coins at my feet covered my dinner and half the hotel bill.

But I still wanted to cut my own ear off.

CHAPTER 34

THE CAMARGUE

*Even the knowledge of my own fallibility cannot keep me from
making mistakes. Only when I fall do I get up again.*
—Vincent Van Gogh

The *Côte d'Azur* and Provence were behind me. The Catalan dialects
and hot Spanish romance of Languedoc filled the air, the beaches
replaced with bullfights and Bordeaux. Bright canary sunflowers
were picked by hand, and grapes were stomped by foot. A
comfortable adjustment at worst.

Not only had the country changed in a blink, but a universe that
didn't revolve around Carrie awaited my exploration. I geared up
and rolled out to the Arles post office, where I was surprised to find
a letter from Guy, which I read over breakfast. He told of their
beautiful wedding and how ecstatic he was when she said yes. But
after the reception, he got really drunk and admitted how I'd
introduced them—my "she's so dumb" line—and that he got
engaged because he felt sorry for her. Now they both hate my guts.

And it had been such a lovely, promising morning.

I read Camargue pamphlets and browsed photos of the region I was entering. Most scenes promised wild white horses running through beach grasses, with a flamboyance of hot-pink flamingos in the background. The Camargue is touted as the ultimate *National Geographic* photographer's canvas, but thus far I'd only passed a few gas stations and fruit stands on the way out of Arles.

I'd expected a King Kong gate or a sign or something that told me I was entering the Camargue, but the change was gradual and unannounced. Then again, everything changes gradually when traversing a country on foot. Kilometers of countryside and winery gift shops packed with tour buses added up behind me. They say bus drivers on these trips often make twenty percent of everything sold at the shops in exchange for bringing in a huge group of fat wallets and trophy wives.

Weathered wooden signs in English and German told me no proper Frenchman would set foot in these "dishwater bottling factories," as these wineries were once described to me. And so I rolled past the tourist traps, overdone with driftwood tree stumps and old ropes from ships, on my focused mission to get wherever the hell I was going.

I was still undecided. As long as I continued skating in some direction, I didn't have to decide where I was going, what I would do when I got there, or how I would continue with the rest of my life. Skating was the only thing. The rest of those decisions would work themselves out somewhere down the road.

Deeper into the Camargue, rain-battered roads painted a distant black horizon separating sky from sea. Peppered with blowing debris, the roads were a wino's path of sand traps that could quickly stop a roller skate wheel. Slim marsh reeds sang in the light breeze, their songs whispered softly to the feathery clouds above. I was officially in the Camargue, and not one white horse in sight. The postcards were a lie, a representation of what one guy with a camera and a great deal of luck captured on the alluvial plains. Yeah, that happened once. Like the casino marketing posters where the guy's winning a million dollars from a slot machine, perhaps Camargue marketing stretched things too.

I skated past a gray dapple hitched to a lonely shade tree by a fruit stand. Antiqued beams patiently supported the brave tin-and-vine-covered roof over vestiges of paint that had once displayed the proprietor's name. Without a farmhouse in sight, the forlorn girl at the stand had no fruit to display. My curiosity broke a sweat. How far had she ridden her horse to get out there? How much would a glass of ice water from her cooler cost? And how did a girl get so gorgeous in only twenty years?

She looked lonely, bored. She read a book leaning over the counter, twirling her chocolate silk hair. I told myself I should stop and take a break from the heat, but that was only half the truth. The other half was overshadowed in denial, grappling with guilt about approaching this girl so quickly after breaking up with Carrie.

"Breaking up?" Ha! That was no breakup. That was getting thrown off a moving bus at the Dumpsville depot, population: me. Guilt be damned.

Pea gravel in the parking lot crunched under my wheels, the only sound in the stagnant heat. She lifted the brim of her straw hat to look, cocking her head like a curious pup. I sat at her bar and took a huge gulp of the ice water she handed. Her naturally faded denim and thin white blouse buoyed her femininity. Her cosmetic kit was salt air and trail dust. Sunlight and passion provided a blush.

I drank so fast the ice water ran down my front. I considered covering up with a T-shirt out of respect, but her hungry lioness's stare at my torso brought a sexy smirk to her lips.

"*Salut, je m'appelle Brigitte. Enchantée de te rencontrer.*" Her lips projected halfway across the bar, pronouncing her name in such a slur: bru-zheet.

I paused, hoping she might say her name again. And again.

"I am Michael. *Je suis Michel. Bonjour.*"

"*Bonjour*, Michel."

I tried a little French, Brigitte a little English, but our words became lost in what our eyes were saying. Not that I cared what she was selling. It occurred to me that this was not a fruit stand but a wine bar.

"You rode here by the horse? *À cheval?* What are you doing here? Where did you ride from?" I could see nothing but country shacks and barns in the area, and I hadn't passed one in well over an hour of skating.

She answered with champagne, finishing her pour with a drop of raspberry. I cupped the shallow, broad-bowled glass with Madame de Pompadour's breast in mind, such as King Louis XV had designed the glass. Brigitte enjoyed a berry for herself, almost as much as I enjoyed watching the delicious red fruit pass her lips as a thunder of stallions led a herd of wild white horses across the sands behind us. Her dapple reared up, pulling at his rope around the tree. Her loud whistle and dominating commands calmed the horse but had the opposite effect on me.

For a moment I considered that I'd been hit by a tour bus and was dying on the side of the desolate road, hallucinating in the heat. Reality was weird. What good thing had I done in my life to deserve this moment? I sipped and considered the possibilities, but romantic rebound kept me off my A-game of being smooth with the ladies. Had I ever really been smooth? Dad was smooth, a fun gentleman with a confidence that made the ladies smile. Oh, to be that smooth.

But I did have a smokin'-hot girlfriend, which counted for something—"did have" being the key term in the imaginary thought bubble over my head, which I popped with my physical finger. Way out here, alone in the Camargue, single, free, and with Brigitte… Anything could happen.

We sat at the bar, Brigitte spinning my skate wheels with the toe of her boot and a kittenish grin. What would a guy much smoother than me do? What would James Bond do? Well, he'd finish this champagne. But he'd probably have rocket-powered roller skates, or probably a car. And he'd speak in perfect French. But those were mere words. Maybe my American English was better than Bond's French? Maybe this champagne was *fantastique.*

By the third glass of champagne and raspberry tongue tease, my sordid fantasy of making love on Brigitte's horse reared like a *Penthouse* forum column, but the alcohol acted as an antiseptic. How would I even climb on a horse with roller skates? I began to laugh at myself. I tried the drunken daydream again, this time in white socks, worrying about my sad, swollen feet getting stepped on by the horse.

Damn! Why couldn't I enjoy a simple fantasy? Analyzing body mechanics, considering safety issues—what the hell was wrong with me? I was agonizing about leaving stinky skates sitting on the bar, dream-walking across the dirt lot on my heels to avoid getting dirt in my blisters. This was *so* not sexy.

The fantasy ended with Brigitte tending my sprained ankle in the champagne bucket, just as a pair of real-life buses entered the parking lot.

I nodded toward the buses, pantomiming a sad face. "You must work. I must go."

"*Oui, les buses sont ici.*"

"Yes, the buses are here. Thank you. *Merci beaucoup.*"

"*Merci, mon amour.*" Softly holding my face, she air-kissed my cheeks in quick French fashion, paused, then planted a glorious full-mouthed kiss on my lips that left me dizzy.

I twisted for one last look as she welcomed the buses, waving her cowboy hat at the tourists in feigned excitement. She cast me a secret wave as I rounded the bend into a flight of flamingos, creating a midday sunset under a cloud of hot-pink feathers.

I had found the perfect woman and remained a gentleman. Furthermore, I'd soon be over my heartache; I'd find love again. I knew this now. But mostly I felt liberated from the small diamond ring I'd carried for so long across France. I smiled. It had found a good home at the bottom of Brigitte's champagne glass.

I was pleasantly surprised to find it was all true about the wild horses. The Camarguais weren't everywhere, but they were out there, galloping limitlessly against a magnificent backdrop of bright sea lavender, flowing tamarisks, and estuaries flocked with seabirds. It was all so beautiful.

But I couldn't get Brigitte off my mind.

Maybe I should have stayed? No… Better to live with one perfect experience, simple memories that would last a lifetime. In Montpellier, I'd check if she left lipstick on my cheeks, but two gallons of sweat would have passed through the pores in my face by then.

I wasn't hallucinating: more wild white horses were running across the dunes. Flamingos, bulls—the Camargue had every living species, and one skater representing humanity. The road stretched flat for miles between any tree or farm. I missed the hills, but not the knee and elbow pads. The rest of the day would be nothing but hot, flat cruising with the wind at my back.

At the next minimarket I repacked my backpack for the change in road and climate. I laid out my backpack as if prepping for surgery, tossing knee and elbow pads in the trash and making room for more water. My body would need every drop over the remaining course of the journey.

Yeah, and what about that journey? Where the hell was I going, anyway? I had plenty of time for contemplation as I hit the road again in a southerly direction, practically on autopilot. Drinking in the countryside, getting an endorphin high from the exercise, recovering from heartbreak…

In that moment, my new commitment came together. I was going to skate to the Spanish border.

I had to continue, but not for Carrie. I had to continue because I'd told so many people along the journey that I was skating to Spain. I had to keep my word to total strangers I'd never see again. I had to keep my word to myself. I had no reason to continue another two hundred kilometers to the border, but I had no reason not to. Stopping would have been quitting, and quitting would have been a direct result of getting dumped. I would not let getting dumped make me a quitter. A victim. A loser. I needed these challenges to become the man I was meant to be.

And the first thing I would do was ignite the positive energy by not labeling my experience "getting dumped" anymore.

My road trip serenity was disrupted by a police van screeching to a stop just ahead of me. This did *not* look good. Didn't they usually pull up behind you? The policemen inside the van frantically prepared for something, and then four cops in tactical vests burst onto the street. Maybe they were preparing to pick me up and throw me into the van. One of the men was assembling some sort of apparatus while the others huddled around him. A machine gun? A portable guillotine? A bazooka?

The enforcer stood up from the huddle, twisted to face me, and shouldered a television camera in time to film me approaching the van. The other policemen started taking snapshots, yelling comments to me in French as they laughed and cheered and mimicked my cross-country skiing motions with their arms.

I barely missed a stride passing them with no more than a nod toward the camera.

Heading inland in the heat would be miserable, so I chose the longer beach route. The road changed to hardpack dirt. It wasn't much further to the bridge, where I could walk across and get back on the main roads again. About an hour ahead was an ancient, stone-walled cathedral on a small island, surrounded by estuaries and the bridge that would take me back to the main road. The international symbol for a church on my map was easy to recognize, but my map lacked the "bridge out" symbol which I found when I got there. I had just skated five kilometers down a dead-end road.

It would do no good to get mad. I'd find a shady spot and get over the loss of time, put my mental game back together. I let it go and enjoyed a moment of gratitude for the opportunity to get out of the sun.

I was probably the only guy in a thousand years to have roller-skated to this church. I parked my backpack in the shade of the three-, maybe four-story church. I walked around its two-meter-thick walls, peering through the unglazed Romanesque windows and testing the narrow doorways, seeking any sign of life. Even the palm fronds were fixed like statues in the still, hot air.

A thousand years of weather and war had not been kind to Maguelone Cathedral. I slid down the ground against a wall, catching up on my water, when a man appeared from around the corner. We both startled. At first, I thought it was Ted Nugent.

"Bonjour," I said.

He took the conversation from there, slurring in what could have been a Southern French dialect, drunken locution, or a sign that maybe he was just plain nuts. Not dangerous, by my intuition, and not drunk, based on his ability to bend and to pick rocks and shells from the dirt, spin, and throw them into the exact same place each time. Not a threat, but I'd still keep one eye on him; I'd been wrong about weirdos before.

He carried on a conversation with either me or the stones of the church for five minutes or so; the stones and I seemed to share an equal comprehension.

I finally got up and joined him. "Who ya talkin' to up there, old man?"

It was as if he had a beef with someone in the tower window. I wouldn't have been surprised if the ghost of the sword-carrying guy carved into the wall materialized.

"Is there someone up there?" I called out. "Hey Rapunzel, is that you up there? Saint Peter? Paul? Mary?"

He carried on as if trying to explain something to me, but I didn't understand any of it until he mumbled something that sounded like "Carrie's up there."

My wide eyes immediately met with his squinty ones. "Wait. Did you say Carrie's up there?"

"*Oui!*" he cried out, then continued mumbling French gibberish.

I stared curiously at the window as the old guy insistently gestured for me to either yell at or perhaps levitate myself up through the tower window. Oh, what the hell. It was just me and Crazy Pierre here.

"Uh, hey Carrie, are you up there?"

We waited, watching the black, lifeless window opening in air so silent her voice whispered from America.

Pierre pantomimed for me to try again.

I laughed a bit. "This is crazy, old man. Okay… Yoohoo, Carrie, can ya hear me up there? Come on out and meet Crazy Pierre."

Pierre smiled when the palm fronds swayed, but there was no breeze. A little spooked, I looked for his reaction; his eyes closed, head down, holding up a finger to wait.

A fragrance wafted by—floral and familiar, utterly out of context on a hot, dusty island. Not a perfume, more like a soap, a shampoo. Carrie's shampoo—I'd have recognized it anywhere.

Pierre turned when I gasped.

"*Qui est fou maintenant*—now who is crazy?"

Had he just spoken in English? Couldn't be.

Had Carrie's hair just flown across my face? Couldn't be; there was no breeze.

Obviously, I'd been in the sun too long.

Pierre persisted with motions for me to take flight, and I went along for the ride. I joined him in flapping arms as if I would fly up to the window.

He smiled at my ridiculous mannerisms, encouraging the performance. "*Oui, oui,*" he sang out.

I tried yelling instead.

"Carrie, I—" I gulped and looked to Pierre. "I don't have words."

"*Non, non, non.*" He shook his finger at me unhappily, crossed his arms, motioned toward the window, and waited.

"Maybe you're right, Pierre. I do have the words. I just don't—"

He held up his hand, stopping my explanation, and motioned toward the window once again.

"Carrie, honey, if you're up there, if you can hear me, I'm sorry." The palm fronds wavered again as a lump grew in my throat. "I'm sorry I hurt you. I'm sorry I left you waiting and wondering if I'd ever come home. I'm sorry you probably went through so many tears, wishing I had come home when I said I would. Wishing we'd been together. Wishing you didn't have to explain where your so-called loving and devoted boyfriend was to every guy you met."

My voice went soft, frail. Ashamed. "And wishing I'd been true to you."

Pierre slapped me on the back of the head, said something loud, and pointed to the window.

"Okay, okay! I was an asshole, honey. I cheated on you, ran off to Paris, and had an affair. I was such an asshole, and I'm so sorry. You deserve so much better."

Pierre nodded, pleased with my confession.

The sun shifted its way around the castle, bringing a glow so warm and intriguing to the window that I didn't even notice Pierre had walked away. I had to say thank you; I had to say goodbye. I walked around back where he must have gone, but all the doors were padlocked and there was nowhere else for him to have gone on this forsaken island. He had vanished.

When I returned to the front of the cathedral, a perfect scalloped shell with golden ribs and pearly tips rested atop my backpack. If the shell had a gold chain attached to it, it would have been an exact duplicate of the necklace Carrie wore around Avalon.

***

It was easier to walk the dirt road in shoes, although I dreaded the extra weight of my roller skates on my back. My feet were hypersensitive to each impact with the ground, and I had to stop occasionally to dump pebbles from my shoes. This pedestrian crap had to change. I tried to enjoy the situation I was given, for God hadn't given man wings or wheels, and this was the way things were supposed to be.

Once out of the dirt, I laced up the skates and headed south on a shortcut through Villeneuve-lès-Maguelone. Once again, I was overcome by ovations and photos from folks in sidewalk cafés. What an ego boost having total strangers applaud as I passed. My energy was renewed, and I was ready to put more road behind me. I pressed on.

Skating until 10 p.m. left me exhausted but satisfied to have made it all the way to Sète. I passed a group of outdoor restaurants and got another ovation from everyone at the bar, the outdoor tables, and those walking the sidewalk, as if they were having a party for my arrival. I smiled and waved and soaked up the positive energy. Forget the supermarket and cooking in my camp stove; this would be a fun dinner stop in town with a fan club.

Though I sat alone, dozens of people came to talk with the kid on wheels, take snapshots, and listen to my story. "Yes, I'm going to roller-skate all the way to Spain" left some folks in quizzical shock. Once I told them I'd started in Italy, their jaws dropped. Someone bought me one beer, then another, and then another. The party went on with me as the accidental guest of honor, and I loved every minute of it; of course I did, after three beers.

After midnight I headed off to the Sète lighthouse, giving a last side surfing show for the fans on my way out. The high of those final cheers was soon doused by the high price of the hotels, each affirming the reality of my short-lived star status. When the stage went dark, I was still a homeless, jobless, loveless eight-wheeled hobo.

CHAPTER 35

MASSACRE AT BÉZIERS

You never know what you have till it's gone.
I wanted to know what I had so I got rid of everything.
—Steven Wright

The Sète lighthouse was miserably cold. Whipping winds flapped the space blanket in my face and chilled the moist terry cloth of the sleeping bag to wick every speck of heat from my skin. Sleeping in a French flag beach towel might have looked cool, but that didn't matter because I camped out of sight. The ostensible plan for its design also included sleeping in warm places.

My legs had become stronger than they'd ever been in my life. My biceps bulged from constantly pushing the ski poles for speed, and there wasn't a speck of fat under my browned skin. But when my skates came off to change socks, a crisp tan line exposed feet so pale you'd have thought I'd stepped in buckets of white paint.

I lay there watching the stars, realizing most of my plans for this trip had already crashed down. None of it was working.

It was four in the morning, and the beer buzz that helped me sleep through the night cold had turned to a pounding hangover. A ski hat would have been nice, but where would I buy one of those by the beach? I only had a visor, which did the exact opposite of a ski hat, so I stuffed my head inside the backpack. Nearly gagging on the stench of old socks and sweaty T-shirts, I found a breath of warmth.

Hot tea after sunrise warmed my insides until I eventually stopped shivering. My little stove flame was too small to warm my hands, and cupping the hot pot with my hands just brought me at risk for third-degree burns. As eggs fried in the pan, I warmed up by doing jumping jacks around the lighthouse, looking like a baboon that just discovered fire. Never will I judge homeless people for acting batshit crazy; you do what you must, and you just don't care.

Maybe it's the effort that goes into the meal, but nothing makes your mouth water like a camp breakfast. A Denver omelet, French toast, and hot tea—ha, let's see a schizoid baboon make a breakfast like that. I rubbed my stuffed belly before leaving the lighthouse down the cobblestones.

The day's fifty-kilometer slog would take me along the beaches of Cap d'Agde to the bullfights of Béziers. I crossed the old bridge that had once led a million spectators into the walled city for the annual Feria de Béziers, a four-day massacre of bulls and Bordeaux wines established half a century before Christ.

An even bloodier massacre had struck in 1209 during the Cathar Crusade, when Pope Innocent III ordered that the neo-Gnostic antimaterialist Cathars be exterminated. The Catholics of Béziers refused to give up the Cathars to the crusaders, thereby sharing their fate and perishing with them. Not even the Catholic priests were spared, and they sought refuge in the original Béziers cathedral, which was burned and collapsed upon hundreds of innocents. When the Crusaders asked their commander how they would recognize a Catholic life to spare, he replied "Kill them all, for the Lord knoweth them that are his." Twenty thousand civilians, both Catholic and Cathar, died by the sword in a matter of hours.

With plenty of daylight left, I checked in to a reasonably priced hotel and then went to investigate a hand-painted sign on plywood: *Skate Park*. Skate parks were a new thing. *Surfer* magazine had just published photos of California guys roller-skating in the dry swimming pools of Dogtown. Intrigued, I left my backpack in the hotel room and skated to what I hoped would be a cool skate park.

Not cool. What used to be a school had become a teenage hangout with thrashed sofas, graffiti-covered walls, and some young girls coughing on their first cigarettes. The park turned out to be a busted-up empty swimming pool with square corners. It was only a couple of meters deep, with cracks so large it couldn't hold water. Some kids had set up a plywood ramp at the bottom of the pool, which defeated the purpose of skating around the smooth, plastered walls like the Venice Beach guys in *Surfer*. I was no park skater, but this was a lame attempt to turn a crumbled concrete box into a smooth, flowing bowl. Still, some skateboarders were getting air at the top, doing skateboard tricks and grinding back down the plywood ramp.

By the time I got into the pool, everyone had gathered at the edge as the roller skater—me— prepared to do his thing. But I didn't have a thing to do. It was my first time on a ramp, in a pool, or at a park. My thing was vague memories of magazine photo spreads showing some guy on roller skates in a pool, and those stunts looked horrifying.

Side surfing brought some smiles from the crowd. My first pass up the ramp was a mulligan, testing whether I could roll smoothly over the lip where plaster met plywood. The supports, engineered by children, creaked under the ramp like a condemned roller coaster. One of my feet could go right through the thin plywood.

I rolled up the ramp, made a nice backside cutback at the top, and headed back down. Nothing spectacular or showy. Nothing to change the disappointed faces in the crowd. I'd have to be more daring to gain any respect.

After my third pass, most of the kids went back to skating and smoking and making wisecracks about me. I built confidence, and each pass became more daring than the last. I tried to hit the ramp at full speed and catch some air, but my chickenshit meter brought me back to reality. I was no circus performer. Still, I pushed it with a good approach, my footwork fast and smooth. I unweighted to clear the ramp lip with ease. The plywood bent a little and up I flew, light as a feather, before gravity signaled my feet back into position to stick a perfect eight-point, heel-to-heel landing.

My back leg collapsed and in an instant, my lovely air show became a bloody crash and burn.

I reacted with a tuck to slide through the fall, but my right foot wasn't on board. It skidded off the side of the ramp, dragging my shin across the sharp plywood ramp edge, with all my weight and acrobatic G-forces upon it. The ramp was a plywood knife, its ninety-degree bevel slicing the meat of my shin with brute crudity and jagged splinters. Nails and knots shredded the thin skin, ripping it down to the bone with the kind of pain you remember for the rest of your life.

I skidded onto the pool floor on one shoulder and curled up in a ball, then rolled out onto my back and lay there as torn nerve endings in my leg reported the damage to my brain. My left wrist and elbow throbbed; I may have broken something. My hip was screaming, and my shoulder was grated like Parmesan cheese. I'd have a lump on the back of my head, if the galaxy of stars flying out of it was any indication. But all these sensations were mere discomforts, pale in comparison to blood draining out of my leg.

An older guy, maybe someone's dad, came running down into the pool.

"*Est-ce que ça va?*" he asked, which I assumed meant "Are you okay?"

He got his answer from my expression. I wanted to ask him how bad it was, but his expression told me the truth. Panic washed over his face, and he began yelling orders to the crowd around the pool.

I didn't understand a word, but everyone understood my urgent bellowing.

I grabbed my leg, as if holding it might ease the pain. I guess I was curling into the fetal position at point, my lizard brain acting out some primitive survival instinct. I kept pressure on the wound with my filthy bare hand, watching blood ooze through my fingers, enduring pain that surged with each throbbing heartbeat.

A flurry of French didn't indicate if help was on the way or if I was on my own. Someone tossed down a white T-shirt, the best they had as a medical kit. It fell into some green ooze by the drain, rendered useless. I lay back and elevated my leg up the ramp, back upon the very spot that ripped it apart. That brought the pain level down from a ten to a nine. It was obviously going to be up to me to stop the bleeding. These kids would probably watch until I died. No one here was going to save my ass. What should I do? How long could I lay there? Was help coming? Could I move?

A skateboarder took a run up and down the ramp, passing close by.

"Really, jackass? I'm dying here!"

The other skaters yelled too, which engaged a little more compassion and support for my situation. Dad returned with a roll of brown paper towels, the crunchy kind you get from gas station bathrooms, but the unpleasant task of blotting the blood to clean it out was all mine.

The nerves in a deep section of the leg had been cut through close to the bone. I reached in and felt two shards of wood, each the size of a sixteen-penny nail. I braced myself and pulled one out with a roar I'd never made before. Cold sweat beaded on my forehead as I placed the bloodied shard on a paper towel and went in after the second shard.

Several pads of paper towels later, I crawled my way out of the pool, still on skates, still bleeding. More skaters came by to stare at the gash, asking questions in their best attempts at English. After a while, the bloody paper pads stopped piling up so quickly. My plan was to wrap a bunch of paper towels around my leg and skate back to the hotel.

A grinning young man showed up with a roll of masking tape, as excited as if he'd found a missing element from a medical kit. He wrapped my leg with brown paper and taped it up as tightly as possible. I looked ready to be spray-painted, with lots of red overspray.

When I tried standing up, a rush of pain shot up my leg, collapsing me to my hands and knees. I breathed heavily, bent in a cold sweat. I was in real trouble.

Then I told myself I could do it. I had to. I'd be okay. It was just a gash halfway through my leg. I'd make it.

Still, I desperately needed to get back to my hotel. All the skaters were young and not even Dad had a car, so I forced myself to get up and glide down the gentle hills on one foot, holding my right leg up as blood soaked the paper. Then the road began to rise, and my skating motions began ripping the stiff paper off my leg. The masking tape and paper bandage wouldn't stay in place; it slid down to my ankle, creating a stiff cuff that chafed the wound. I tore the bandage away, allowing blood to trickle down onto the clean white athletic sock cuffed neatly over the top of my boot. After a couple of blocks, the sock was completely saturated. Further movement was like squeezing a red sponge onto the boot leather. I stopped at a bus bench and put my leg up to take a break from the pain, waving the bus on.

The last stretch to the hotel was a smooth, gentle downhill. I tried an old roller-rink trick called "shoot the duck" where you squat and roll on one foot with the other leg held straight out in front of you. I simply followed my own bloody leg down the hill and shot that duck right into the lobby.

From there, I had to figure out how to climb the stairs to the third floor. Fortunately, I could climb the narrow staircase by hopping backward on one skate, bracing myself on both rails with my arms and dragging the lame leg behind.

The desk clerk caught the awkward scene from across the lobby and ran to the stairwell. "*Monsieur*, oh my gosh. Are you okay?" Hearing my language was comforting. "Do you need help?"

Did I need help? I wanted to say no, to be polite, to assure him with confidence that I was fine. I didn't want to be a burden. For god's sake, I was out here to prove I didn't need anybody, to show myself I could be self-reliant, to claim my independence as my own. Asking for help would be an admission, a surrender, an agonizing self-confession of the impoverished, destitute condition of my poor broke dumb ass. It would be a cry to the universe that I had failed.

I sighed heavily. This was no time for do-or-die heroics. I'd plummeted from the self-actualized, all-that-and-a-bag-of-chips kid at the top of Germany's highest mountain to a beaten beach drifter, a needy indigent wrestling his lifeless leg up the stairs like a fisherman dragging the day's catch. I was just an injured guy trying to climb the stairs and making a royal mess. Now was as good a time as any to evolve.

The hotelier stood there, his offer to help floating in a voice bubble up the narrow stairway. I began to form the word "no" with my mouth, the word I wanted to say so badly. My mind was clinging desperately to the bottom rung of emancipation, and letting my fingers slip with a "yes" would send me plummeting to the very bottom of Maslow's hierarchy.

I took a breath for bravery. "Yes."

It was a grenade in my gut. Pulling that pin blew my "need is weakness" philosophy to smithereens.

"Yes sir, I'm injured—quite badly, to be honest. It's my leg. I've ripped it open. I'm terribly sorry about all the blood on your stairs. And in your lobby. And on your streets."

"Do not worry about the lobby, *monsieur*." His words were kind, and he had no problem asking for help himself. "Monique, get the medical kit, please. We have a patient." He put a handkerchief under my dripping leg. "We will to take care of you, *monsieur*. Do not you to worry."

It was the worst thing he could have said. I half expected—secretly wanted—for him to wave me off with his hand and say, "Man up, you'll be fine." After all, isn't that what real men did? Instead, he treated me like a human in need, comforted me with confidence, and acted quickly with kindness and care.

How could he do this to me? I was supposed to be a man by now—I didn't need anyone. My body had given up, but my belligerent pride wasn't surrendering so quickly. I kept climbing the stairs, then dragged my leg across the wooden hallway to my room, where that grenade in my gut detonated a lifetime of stockpiled emotions.

Sputum-filled sobs erupted from my throat. Decades of pressurized denial shattered the last vestiges of the wall of pride around my heart. I let them flow, no longer embarrassed. The great pain was from the fortress wall collapsing inside me; the agony in my leg paled in comparison.

I sat on the floor with my back to the door until composure found me.

"*Monsieur*? Are you all right?" It must be Monique, the hotelier's wife.

"I'm okay, considering. I should take a bath."

"*Oui, monsieur*, I have some extra towels here for you. I will put them on the chair in the hallway."

"Thank you. Are you Monique?"

"*Oui*."

"Thank you, Monique, it's nice to meet you—hear you."

"*Oui, monsieur*. I will come back after your bathing and check on you."

"*Merci*, Monique." I grabbed the white bath towels, wiped my pink eyes, and dragged my red leg down the hall.

The leg slipped slowly into the warm water with a little vocal pain management. There was no relaxing in this bath, only the grisly task of debridement: bits of plywood and small shreds of skin. I hobbled back to my room, where I found another stack of fresh towels next to my little first aid kit. I squeezed every last bit of anti-bacterial goop I had on the wound, swallowed five aspirin, drank half a bottle of wine, and then collapsed on the bed with the leg propped as high as I could get it. I passed out quickly, vaguely acknowledging the sounds of someone messing about the room.

Hours later, consciousness intruded. I thought I'd been pretty smart to use a dresser drawer and a chair pillow to prop my leg up high. I hadn't been quite so smart at pulling the bed sheets over my leg, where they were now embedded in my blood-clotted leg.

The sheet was embedded in my leg—ha, em-bedded! Even through the pain of delicately plucking the sheet out of deep, dried blood, I cracked myself up.

But this sheet wasn't coming out without a tug-of-war with my severed nerves—fragile nerves that were losing the battle. So back to the tub I went, sheets and all. Actually, there was no "and all," since I hadn't been able to pull my shorts over the bed sheet to walk down the hall. I bunched the sheet around my privates, my butt exposed, looking both ways before doing some sort of bloody-toga, grabbing-the-crotch limping thing down the hall. If the Bloody Toga Grab the Crotch Limping Thing ever became something people did, I wanted full credit as the inventor. I was perfecting the BTGTCL Thing.

When I got down the hall, the bath door was locked; someone was up even earlier than me. I did the BTGTCL Thing back to my room to wait, but just as I reached my room, the bath door opened and footsteps walked away. I turned around and did the Thing back toward the bath, but this time a lady in a robe cut me off and whisked her way into the bath. I leaned on a wall a moment before honing my Thing technique once more back to my room. No sooner did I shut my door than the bath door hinges creaked again, footsteps pattered down the hall, and the robed lady returned to her room. Standing meant throbbing and bleeding; maybe I would simply bleed the sheet out of my leg. But once again I did the Thing toward the bath.

The lady in the robe found me halfway down the hall, hands bunched in a white sheet over my privates, a red sheet hanging from my leg, and my white ass hanging out the back. Her eyes bugged out; she might go back into her room and slam the door, maybe even scream. Instead, she looked me up and down, stepped into the hall, and composedly greeted me with a nod.

"*Bonjour.*" She scurried down the hall and hopped in the bath.

I'd had enough of the Thing. Would she be in the bath for a while, or would she come out again quickly? Could I even do the Thing a few more times? Should I wipe up the drops of blood on the hallway floor? Ultimately, I needed to get the sheet out of my leg, so I sat on the floor outside the bath to wait in line.

"A watched pot never boils," and one should never wait for a woman to finish bathing. The water ran on and on. My leg throbbed. I sat. I waited. I covered myself as nicely as possible, hoping no hotel guests would walk by. The throbbing was unbearable without the leg elevated, so I fashioned a bedsheet sling from the utility closet door handle, lay on my back, and waited, wondering if a man could bleed out in the time a woman takes to bathe.

I awoke to steam wafting from the open bath door. It wasn't the lady in the robe. Different lady, same mortified expression.

"Is this the line for the bath?" I asked before she ran down the hall.

How many guests had showered while I slept in the hall would forever be a mystery. But there was no mystery in how the guests must have reacted at the sight of a naked kid with his bloody leg tied to a door handle passed out in the hallway.

***

Soaking the leg in warm bathwater released the embedded sheet from the coagulated blood. Doing one last Thing back to my room startled the chambermaid, who was gathering blood-soaked sheets and towels, likely wondering if the room guest was a murderer or a victim. Either way, she screamed when I entered.

I was far beyond maintaining dignity, standing there with my butt still reflecting sunlight. After a few moments of staring, she went back to cleaning blood out of the dresser drawer as I apathetically dropped my wet red toga to put on shorts.

The hotelier came in to check on me. "*Bonjour*, it is *Henri*." His face went pale when he caught a look at my leg and all the blood in the room. "Do not worry about blood on the towels, *monsieur*, or the blood in the hall. Or on the sheets." He paused in confusion. "Or…in the drawer?"

I explained what had happened to me and asked to stay another night to recover.

"Michel, you cannot travel like this until you are healed. You will stay at half price, a guest of my wife and myself. We will care for you."

And just like that, I had people again. Someone cared about me, and it changed everything. I had surrendered, admitted I had reached rock bottom. I'd dropped to the lowest point of Maslow's hierarchy of needs and was struggling to meet my most basic physiological requirements.

And it was okay.

I gave Henri some cash. "Could someone bring me something to eat?"

While he was gone, I stared out the window, recalling how I had fallen—not at the skate park, but from the top of Maslow's hierarchy. Esteem had been lost in San Remo when I couldn't gain acceptance by showing Joel my achievements. Love and belonging had been shattered in Marseille by the loss of Carrie's love and M. Blanche's family. Safety clearly fell out of my realm when I had to run from Ted the Skater. Down here on the bottom rung, basic physiological needs were slipping away as I tried to keep myself alive.

Rock. Freaking. Bottom.

An hour or so later, Henri knocked at my door. "*Monsieur*, I have some food for you."

"*Oui*—come in, Henri."

He pulled the cigarette from his mouth as an appropriate gesture to introduce his wife, Monique. She held a basket of sandwiches, baguettes, cheese, salami, roasted chicken, and grapes.

"Hello, Monique. It's a pleasure to meet the face behind the voice."

She smiled from beneath a perky blond bob with pink highlights and laid the food out on my table. Assuming she was fluent in English like her husband, I rambled excitedly about how this was the nicest thing anyone had ever done for me, where I'd been, what I'd done, what a kind and generous person she was, and what a blessing she was in a cold, cruel world of absolute strangers.

She smiled at me, then looked to Henri for translation. He translated minutes of my babble in three words: "*Il dit merci*," meaning "He says thanks."

I gave her hand a squeeze with as much fondness as I could give without hurting her tiny fingers. "*Merci*, Monique, *merci beaucoup*."

I began to appreciate how amazing life can be, bringing the perfect people into your sphere at the perfect time. A brother, a mother, a friend, or a lover, they were all over the world, wearing different faces and name tags, showing up when we need them most.

The warmth of introspection fell away as I realized I was seriously hurt and lying in bed. The pull to talk with Mom was strong. I wanted to tell her and Dad I'd been hurt, where I was, how bad it was, how I was drowning at the bottom of my emotional sea. She'd say the right things, cheer me up, maybe even cry if I told her everything. Mom would make it all better.

"Can I get you anything else, Monsieur Michel?" Henri asked.

"How would I make a telephone call to America?"

He brought up a dial telephone and plugged it into the wall next to my bed, then explained which numbers to use to begin the call.

I stared at the phone. Perhaps it might tell me what I should say and how I should act once the call connected. I dialed for the French operator, who initiated the connection to America, and the American operator would ask to reverse the charges.

My excitement grew, staring at the open gash in my leg and knowing Mom would make it all okay. She'd probably be making dinner when the pale mustard phone on her kitchen wall rang. She'd call Dad over, and they'd hold their ears next to the receiver, listening as I told my story. She'd cry. Dad would have encouraging words, and my needs would be met. And then we'd say goodbye.

And exactly how would this help Mom and Dad?

I paled, considering my intentions. Like Dad flying his B-24 in WWII, I was making a bomb run by telephone, an attack from overseas that would destroy their freedom from worrying about me. Mom wouldn't sleep for days. Dad's work day would now include the stress of helpless emotion. And after the blitzkrieg, I would hang up, leaving a tearful aftermath in the cold darkness behind me.

I couldn't do that to them.

"Yes, operator, of course we'll accept the charges, thank you, uh-huh, thanks…Michael? Hello, Michael, are you there?"

Mom's voice was warm maple syrup, but I closed my eyes heavily, stiffened my upper lip, and gently laid the phone back on the hook.

I opened my eyes to the silent judgment of the blank wall. I could have lied and told them everything was fine, but that was a horrible plan. Instead, I'd write a long letter with a positive attitude, tell them everything, and be back on my feet long before they even got it. No sense being a whiny little bitch over the phone.

My phone rang. The French operator did his best with English. "*Oui, monsieur*, I am sorry, telephone, uh, broken call to United States, is. I have operator, uh, USA connection in maintain. You like, uh, restore to call?"

"No. No thank you." It was easier to have the operator hang up on them. "But the US operator is still on the line, connected, *oui*?"

"*Oui, monsieur*. I have USA connection still."

"Then I would like to make a new call, *s'il vous plaît*. But this will not be reverse charges." I unzipped the pouch in my backpack where I carried maps and letters. Without looking, I grabbed the air mail envelope I'd read a dozen times, unfolded it, and found the place where Carla had written her phone number. "I would like to place a call to San Francisco."

This time, the connections clicked and hummed in a relaxing way. I smiled, sat back in my pillows, and pulled the sheet over my bandaged leg.

Carla answered, cheery and bright. Her smile filled my room. Our giddy laughter eventually calmed to the point that I could tell her where I'd been, where I was, where I was going. I told her about the accident and my leg.

"It still hurts like hell and it's a bloody mess, and that not in the British sense of bloody. The folks at this hotel are loving me up like family. Well, the chambermaid isn't so fond of cleaning blood out of the drawers; the whole place reeks of bleach. But it'll heal. I'll be back on the road after a little R and R."

It was a telling free of drama, absent of sympathetic prompts. She cared, but she wasn't worried. She was tickled with my accomplishments and ecstatic with her own. We could have talked for days, and I wished I'd called her more often. The only thing better than her letters was her voice on the phone.

"So you call me from the land of brie and Burgundy, out of the blue?" she asked. "A call and not a letter? Okay, lay it on me—did you lose your pen? They have pens in France. It's true, I bought one once. Do you need a pen to write me? Don't make me hop on a jet and bring you a pen."

I was breaking our pen-and-paper protocol. This was the first time we had talked on a telephone, despite many impulses to dial her number along the journey; I'd foolishly squandered my overseas phone budget on a different phone number. But I loved the way Carla wrote, and I loved writing back to her. Still, after so many black-and-white letters, her voice painted things in rich, vivid color.

"I tried calling my folks," I explained, "but there was a disconnect there. Actually, I hung up before the call went through. And then called you."

The pause on the other end of the line told me she was adding up the situation. "So you're all laid up making prank calls from France. Did you give that girlfriend of yours a call too?"

"Actually, that number has been disconnected and is no longer in service. At least not for me."

"Interesting." I could hear her tongue in cheek across an ocean and two continents.

We gabbed tirelessly about San Francisco and Europe, summer plans, stories from my adventures I'd already told her on paper.

"I've got about nine days of skating left until I reach Portbou. That's the first town in Spain across the border. That'll give me the border-to-border status of getting all the way across France by roller skates, since Barcelona's no longer on the tour."

"And then what?"

There was the big question.

I paused so long I could hear cash sliding through the silent phone connection.

"You still there?" she asked.

"Yeah, I'm here. I just…"

"Hey, don't worry about it. When you get there, you'll know. You'll be fine. You've got a full nine days to figure out the rest of your life. No pressure."

She got me. She got me good. As though she'd dumped a bucket of water on my head, all I could do was laugh.

"Well, my dear, you've got some things to think about over there," she said, "and this phone call is costing you a few hotel nights, so I'll say *au revoir, mon amour*. I don't want you blaming me for freezing your ass off on some lighthouse tomorrow night."

I hung up the phone gently, my other hand clutching her letter. I smiled for a long time, at least until time replaced the afterglow with pain in my leg and the anticipation of a crippling phone bill.

It was worth every friggin' franc I had.

CHAPTER 36

RED, WHITE, AND BLUE

Particularly with the blues, it's not just about bad times.
It's about the healing spirit.
—Taj Mahal

Long, tedious days were spent healing in my room, hours of looking at pictures in French magazines, writing in my journal, and drinking wine to sleep the uncomfortable, bedridden days away. Eventually the leg became tolerable enough to hobble my way to a pharmacy on a wooden crutch Monique found in the hotel basement. On the way to the store, I rehearsed what I might ask the pharmacist. Medical terms were beyond my pocket translation dictionary, and I had to look up the words for "cut" and "hole" and "leg." The chambermaid had already taught me how to say "lots of blood."

I limped a couple blocks to a pharmacy where, unlike American pharmacies, they would be able to offer some basic health care. I stepped up to the counter, the crutch caught the pharmacist's eye. I didn't have the right words to begin, but stretching several times each day had given me the flexibility of a ballerina to throw my shredded leg up on his counter.

"*S'il vous plaît?*"

With some excitement, the pharmacist shifted me to a table in the back. He called in his young, attractive female assistant. Honestly, were there no ordinary girls in this country? They donned plastic gloves, brought an assortment of bandages, pads, and wraps to their makeshift OR, and got to work.

"It's just a scratch," I joked with the assistant, who giggled at everything I said. I was sure she didn't understand a word.

Later I hobbled back to the hotel with a huge bag of bandages, ointments, pain pills, and socks. Monique greeted me in the lobby, where she sat me in a comfortable chair, brought me a cup of tea on a tray with a flower, and settled in to inspect the pharmacist's handiwork.

Carla was right. I'd heal up just fine.

The leg continued to throb, but after four night in the hotel, I was pretty sure I could continue skating…with great caution. After hugs and snapping photos with Henri and Monique, I waved goodbye and skated out the hotel door—watching for cyclists on the sidewalk, of course. The tight bandage on my leg and pain-pill hangover meant I would have to take it slow. I rolled out with low aspirations of getting far. Twenty-five kilometers to Narbonne sounded like child's play after logging one hundred kilometers some days ago.

I made several stops to rinse off the road dust and rebandage my leg, budgeting each miserly dribble from the hydrogen peroxide bottle. The bleeding hadn't stopped completely. By midday, the escalating throbbing required frequent stops. I'd sit and elevate the leg on anything I could find. Even a few minutes of elevation plus a handful of aspirin helped manage the pain. Slowly, painfully, I made progress.

A grassy patch under a tree beside a quaint farmhouse in Nissan-lez-Enserune looked inviting. The lady of the house, watering her lawn in a flowery apron behind the low stone wall, gave a neighborly smile and watched me dismantle my pack to rest. Out of her sight,

I peeled off the saturated bandages and let the wound air out. Rather than rest the bloody leg on her wall, I hung the heel wheels of my skate in the crotch of a low tree branch. I snacked on a baguette and salami with my leg strung up for display like some roadside lemonade stand of torture. I relaxed on my back in the warm sun with a full stomach and fell into a deep sleep.

The afternoon sun found its way around the shade tree and into my eyes. My camping gear was still flung everywhere, ski poles carelessly cast where I'd dropped them, my arms sprawled in crucifixion and my bloody right leg lynched up the tree. I tried to sit up.

My leg had cramped while I was asleep. I was stuck.

I tugged and twisted and finally released the heel of my skate, sending me into a slow, rolling backflip through my gear. It would have been highly embarrassing if anyone had witnessed the bumbling maneuver.

And that's when I met English Russell, enjoying a picnic under the same tree.

"I do say, old chap, I was wondering how one might find his way out of such a precarious predicament," he said. "And by the by, dare I ask, if I may be so bold, however did you get yourself into this in the first place?"

Relaxed and cool, he'd been carving and munching apple slices, waiting for me to wake up so he could release all these questions.

"I stopped on me bike and here I've been wondering—apple?" He held out a slice, and I took it and chewed as he went on. "I was wondering, well, a goodly number of questions, ruminating over the perplexing array of gizmos and gadgets in your caboodle."

Coke-bottle glasses, black socks and bad teeth screamed "tourist" even louder than his rubicund face and cycling panniers. I munched another slice of apple as he continued.

"So here I am riding through the countryside, and there's a man—what *appeared* to be a man—strung up in a tree, quite literally beaten profusely and bleeding out. Dear god, such harsh punishment for roller-skating on the streets. What might they do to a cyclist, oh dear?"

He spread a slice of baguette with foie gras and stuffed it into his mouth as if it might help him speak.

"And then I pondered. Perhaps this bloke was a nutter? Perhaps he'd lost the plot and put himself arse over tits into this sapling by his own accord?" A pause as he chewed, a bit of pâté bouncing about his rust-colored mustache. "Nonetheless, this has been quite the thought-provoking picnic plot, undoubtedly the best show in Nissan le Lezzie-ville or wherever the hell we are, if I do say. So here I sit. Brie, mate?"

Self-powered travelers don't have much to offer. We have what we have, and we make the best of any chance for a communal meal. Russell had enough for a good spread, but my bottle of Bordeaux, white-rinded cheese, and half a baguette lifted the snack into a party. We exchanged travel stories over wine, bantering with similar dry wit. Neither of us laughed out loud, for such is the unwritten code of deadpan comedy; he who laughs first loses. I ended up losing, thanks to a couple of belly laughs.

Though we both spoke the king's English, I had to stop him frequently for translations.

"I was gutted when they made me redundant," Russell said.

"What does that even mean?"

He sipped his wine and continued as if I'd understood. "So I threw a spanner in the works on my way out the office door. They can't just toss a few quid at the ol' boy, and Bob's your uncle."

"Bob?"

"Your father's brother, Robert. Auntie Fanny's better half... That's not important. Nooo, not this scouser, I say to the Guv'na. A kip and a fortnight later I'm gobsmacked when the barrister gave us a bell and now I'm horses for courses. It's just me and me John Thomas on the pull in the south of France. Nothing but wine and strawberry creams."

"The south of France... I got that part."

Over the next cup of wine, he translated his story to American English, poking fun at me with a goofy American accent.

"So where're your friends now?" I asked when he finished. "John? Thomas? Uncle Bob? Your aunt? Are they down on the beach eating dessert?"

He broke the code of deadpan ethics with a long-winded belly laugh. I might have been the new winner of our deadpan contest if I'd been trying to be funny. That's what made it funny.

"Oh, my dear boy. There are no friends here. I'm out on a lark, stag. And if anyone's eating the creams, it's me."

"The creams?" I asked.

"Strawberry creams. Tarts. Girls! You like girls, right? Or what do the Yanks call them? Foxes? Dolls? Bettys? Honeys?"

"Chicks."

"Ah yes, chicks. British girls are titillating bakery treats. In America, they're pubescent poultry."

"And the French girls? What are they—birds?"

"I don't rightly care, as long as the wings are spread for bangers and mash."

We toasted to our similar differences, my aluminum camp cup against his wine glass.

"Of all the bits and bobs in that rucksack," he said, "you can't tote a decent glass for French wine? Good god, man, this is the south of France—Bordeaux, Beaujolais, Burgundy… They're all right here. Get yourself some bloody stemware if you know your onions."

He pondered the blank stare on my face and tried again, with painfully slow enunciation. "You. Should buy. A. Wine. Glass. Ya bloody plonker." The last words were mumbled under his breath.

I raised one eyebrow. "What was that last part?"

"Nothing. Didn't say a word, not I." He seemed embarrassed I'd caught him mumbling.

"I think you said something."

"You certainly heard not a thing. I wouldn't say such a thing about my fine host." Then, in softer mumble, "...even if he was a cheeky plonker."

"I heard somethin'."

In time we learned we were both headed to Narbonne, so we ventured out together with a good wine buzz and a mutual destination. Russell had a reservation at the youth hostel a mere sixteen kilometers ahead. With wine as my painkiller, I skated at a quick pace while Russell cruised alongside. He seemed happy with the pace.

"How's the leg?" he asked a few times.

My words told him I was fine, but the grimace on my face said I was lying.

"You can hang on the back of the bike if you'd like. I'll tow you along, ya ligger."

I understood that if I touched his bike, "Ligger" would become my new nickname. I reached out tentatively.

"There's plenty of daylight, chap," he said encouragingly. "Take it easy. We'll get there in due time."

On the flats, I drafted behind his bike and skated without wind resistance, nearly straddling his back tire in tight formation. On downhills, I side-surfed alongside him, often hanging onto the racks near his wheels. I strapped my ski poles to his bike rack, freeing my hands to attach myself to the bike like a sidecar. Russell pedaled in high gear, effortlessly picking up speed. Crazy, exciting, fun—and potentially deadly for fingers.

"Watch your fingers down there, mate!"

Gravity pulled us down the highway at a steady clip as I rolled along next to Russell, talking with him as casually as I might have standing next to him in a bar.

"Russell, I'm not sure if you noticed, but I don't actually have all my fingers on my right hand."

He twisted out of morbid curiosity to have a look at my hands.

I showed him—all ten fingers where they should be—and finished the joke "... 'cause five of them are on my left hand."

He fell silent, pedaling without a word, almost as if I'd upset him. For ten minutes, the only sounds were his bicycle wheels spinning like a fishing reel and my grumbling urethane wheels on the asphalt. When he could no longer restrain himself, he stopped the bicycle.

"That is indeed and without reservation by far the stupidest joke I have ever survived in my lifetime."

"Maybe so, but you'll be telling it later tonight."

He shook his head in disbelief. "Not to begrudge your enthusiasm, my fine young colleague, but fuck no."

After a couple of wine breaks to elevate my leg, Russell and his sidecar ligger arrived in Narbonne. The streets narrowed, forcing me to skate on my own. By this point, only one leg was useful in pushing me uphill. As usual, cars slowed for photos of the roller skater.

The laughter, cheers, and applause were a new experience for Russell. "Are you sure you're not from around here? You're like a celebrity."

I'd become blasé about my notoriety, especially with the throbbing in my leg. We were both exhausted and getting a little cantankerous as our buzz dried up. We swerved around a pair of little girls who ran out into the road to gawk and wave.

"I'm gobsmacked," he cried out.

"Translation, please." I had to raise my voice so he'd hear me from behind. The city was getting busier with each block.

"Gobsmacked;   adjective.   G-O-B-S-M-A-C-K-E-D. Gobsmacked. A perfectly sensible English word. Look it up."

"I only have a French dictionary, and I'm a little busy at the moment."

"Well then you're shite out of luck, ain't ya, wazzock."

"Ya know, if you had another brain in your head, it would be lonely. Now translate. Wazzock?"

"Wazzock; noun. W-A-Z-Z— ."

I interrupted his spelling bee.

"You are so full of shit, Russell. I'm getting jealous of the people who haven't met you yet."

We were headed up a slight hill when a group of French kids in a car no bigger than Russell's bike pulled alongside to ask questions and shoot photos.

"We go toward youth hostel," they called. "*Tirez?*"

"*Oui! Tirez.*" I wasn't going to let that word slip by again. I grabbed the open window and caught a free ride to the top of the hill, yelling back at Russell. "Hurry up, ya wobbly wazzock. Put your legs to work like yo mama."

***

We checked into the hostel for two nights and were promptly drawn into dinner plans with fellow travelers. They were headed out for Chinese food, so we tagged along without a clue what French Chinese food might be like. Another glass of wine wiped me out to the point that I wished I'd stayed in my bunk.

Our new friends include runner Gert-Jan from Netherlands, Ricardo (or Handsome Dick, as we dubbed him) from Spain, Gabi and Józef, the Polish lovers, and a goth couple without names who watched us in silent judgment. I ordered water, cheap rice, and a cheap entrée.

After dinner, Handsome Dick, who ordered shrimp and steak and wine, asked with a chummy smile. "Why don't we just split the check eight ways to make it easy on our server?"

He made it sound as though he was such a humanitarian. I snorted.

"Sounds great—but hang on, I might not be done. I didn't eat much so that I could try some desserts and a fine champagne. *Monsieur*, the dessert and wine list, please?"

"If we're going to be amalgamated, perhaps I'll enjoy a fancy whiskey or two," Russell chimed in.

Ricardo was taken aback. "Uh, well then, maybe we just split the check if you're going to order all that. What do you say, folks?"

He grinned his best salesman's smile, but the goths just stared through their black makeup.

"We ask for separate checks," Gert-Jan said. "Perhaps it's a little more work for our server, but at least we don't take up eight tables. Really it is no big deal."

Even the goths smiled at the suggestion, and I learned it's okay to ask for separate checks.

Russell and I checked in for two nights at the hostel so we could spend the entire next day exploring Narbonne's canal where tourists in rental boats dock to gather supplies. This seaboard, a sidewalk stretching the length of the canal, hosts a bazaar of Tunisian vendors selling jewelry, art pieces, musical instruments, henna tattoos, incense, and oddities, carefully displayed on blankets in blatant defiance of the multilingual signs prohibiting street vendors.

We were browsing a musical flea market with wooden flutes, guitars, and drums when the cool tribal beat in the shade of the riverside trees was interrupted by a French policemen strolling his beat. Word spread to the far end of the wharf in seconds. Like a shark swimming through a school of bait, the policeman eased along just out of reach, silently forcing each vendor to grab their blankets at the last second and run for safety. The savvy vendors calculated the exact distance they could safely allow the cop to approach before needing to bolt. Down the wharf, a happy couple was admiring a wooden carving. The salesman had one eye on his sale and one eye on the cop. When the cop drew too close, the salesman grabbed the carving and bolted.

Russell and I marveled as the predator slowly eliminated the impromptu mall with each step forward. But as quickly as the vendors ran, they came back, setting up their blankets behind the shark as though he had a force field around him. At one point, he surprised them with a one-hundred-and-eighty-degree turn, scattering those who had just set up again.

We sat on a bench along the wharf all day, leaving only for coffee, then tea, then sandwiches, then beer. We watched boats and cops and vendors and tourists, but mostly locked visually onto the girls walking back and forth. The day passed like a slow tennis match.

"Ya know, Russell, this is really nice," I said, "just sitting here like grown men discussing philosophy and world politics. I might make it to becoming a grown-up one day."

"Lest we forget our grand symposium of boobs and beer. And that, my eight-wheeled friend, is a part of manhood that never reaches maturity. God help me should I ever become so mature."

As the day progressed, Handsome Dick joined us with a bottle of wine, sharing with us in paper cups. "Why are you not talking with the girls?"

"We're enjoying the show."

For all our talk about girls, we really didn't care much to talk with the girls. The suave Latino could not help himself, delivering a pickup line for each lovely passerby. Russell and I sipped from our paper cups, spectators to Ricardo's masterful flirting with a dozen girls.

"There—she's the one," Ricardo declared, putting his cup down abruptly and walking straight toward a girl by the canal. In minutes, he was walking away with her in the opposite direction.

Russell seemed downright angry. "Did you see that? He just...and then he...holy hell."

"Gobsmacked," I said. "G-O-B-S—"

"I know how to spell it, for Pete's sake. How on god's green earth does he do that?"

"Russell, my dear boy, I don't have the time or the crayons to explain it to you."

He glared at me. "You do realize your birth certificate was really just an apology letter from the condom factory, don't you?"

"And you... you're so inbred, you might as well be a sandwich." I snipped back.

The women stopped looking our way once Handsome Dick left, but a good buzz kept us sparring. The sun had an hour or two to set when we ran into Gert-Jan from the hotel, stretching for a run as the day cooled off.

"Hey Gert-Jan," I called, "where ya headed?"

"For a run. Like to join me?"

The invitation sounded more like a joke or a challenge, but the idea of doing a little skating around the town intrigued me.

"Sure. Where to?" I asked.

He blinked soberly. "I do not jog, Michael. I run. I run very fast. Most people cannot keep up with me."

It was a challenge.

"Well, Gert-Jan, I do not run. I roller-skate. And I skate very fast. Most runners cannot keep up with me."

"Perhaps." His squint was nearly unreadable, but his body language screamed "bring it on."

"You stretch for five more minutes while I get my skates and meet you back here. Will you wait?"

"I will wait for you here, but I won't wait for you when we're out there."

"You won't have to unless I turn around to come get you."

"This will be interesting."

Turned out we both wore Adidas, although I had wheels on mine. Russell watched us puff up our chests in preparation for some sort of race. As it happened, Gert-Jan Wassink was an Olympic cross-country runner, and it was apparent that he was going to leave me in the dust, even with my wheels. Still, it would be fun to step up to the challenge in a race with no rules, no course, and no finish line.

"Where are you boys off to?" Russell asked.

"I'm just following Gert-Jan, if I can keep up. Where we goin', Gert-Jan?"

"Into the distance."

"I love that place! I hope there are lots of downhills so I can catch you."

Gabi and Józef showed up just as we headed out. Gabi did the honors: "Ready, set, GO."

I got a good start using my ski poles, like jumping out of the giant slalom gates. Gert-Jan began by running across the cobblestones of the Tunisian marketplace. I quickly caught him on the smooth streets paralleling the seaboard. Wow, was he fast! His legs were a blur before me. While he ran straight through the grass and flowerbeds of traffic circles, I had to go around and merge lanes with the cars to get through.

We kept the pace for some time before I casually pulled next to him with my ski poles. In response, he cut along the canal through a construction zone.

I caught him on the next smooth leg of asphalt only to find him smiling.

"I figured you were gone some time ago," he said.

"So you *are* trying to ditch me!"

He kept a steady pace, breathing through a smug smile. He continued to test me in places that were smooth for skating but filled with obstacles that would challenge me.

I looked ahead. He was heading for the Carrefour, an outdoor shopping mall filled with diners and shoppers enjoying the sunset. We zoomed between the pedestrians, two shirtless, air-chugging guys flying through the hordes of model-perfect pedestrians carrying miniature poodles as their husbands followed along lugging a booty of beauty in paper sacks.

Gert-Jan took a shortcut, hurdling across a concrete bench, hoping I wouldn't be able to jump it. Taking a technique from the slopes, I planted my poles and vaulted up and over the bench. My landing wasn't as smooth as his, but the chase was still on.

Then he cut the corner through a café serving diners at sidewalk tables, dashing directly between the tables to get around the bend. Not to be outdone, I made for a clear path directly through the restaurant interior itself where there were no diners. Cast iron chairs slid across the concrete and gasps filled my ears as I flew across the marble floor of the restaurant and popped out on the other side—and in front of the Dutch runner. I'd taken the lead.

We stopped by silent, mutual agreement a block later at a bench to laugh and catch our breath. I'd beaten his game, or at least gained his respect.

"I've been told I am crazy when I run," he said between heavy breaths, "but you, skating through the restaurant... Those poor people were gasping, your sticks flailing about... So brilliant. Right through the restaurant. *Briljant.*"

The evening wasn't going to get any better than that, so we parted ways, to meet back at the hostel after he ran several more miles. I stopped for a scoop of gelato, sporting a big winner's smile to go with my melting chocolate. Back at the hostel, I enjoyed a long, hot shower, steaming the road grime and dried blood from my leg before meeting Russell for dinner. We told jokes and watched girls over spaghetti, then returned to the hostel to share wine and stories with Gabi, Józef, and Handsome Dick until two in the morning.

I looked around at my friends from faraway places; I'd likely never see them again. I smiled, basking in gratitude at the amazing opportunity I had to do things like this, to learn how others live, to hear how they perceive Americans, and to find how we all shared common ground aboard Mother Earth.

It was hours later when Russell pushed back from the table with a yawn. "Well, it's off to Bedfordshire."

My puzzled expression forced him to explain himself once again.

"It means I'm going to bed." He tucked his socks into his shoes, wiggled his toes, and left, shooting one final comment over his shoulder from across the room. "Hey, Gabi—did you know I don't have all my toes on my left foot?"

CHAPTER 37

OPEN THE GATES

The traveler sees what he sees. The tourist sees what he has come to see.
—G.K. Chesterton

"Safe travels to you, old chum."

With a wave goodbye, Russell rolled slowly around the corner and off to distant relatives in the French countryside. Soon they'd be cooking five-hour French sauces in five-hundred-year-old kitchens, telling stories over dusty bottles of Bordeaux.

On the other hand, I was still a nineteen-year-old roller skater with no idea where I'd be that night, who I might be with, or what I might eat, And I had no particular reason to be there. Still, urgency smoldered within me. I felt a drive to leave so I wouldn't be late, an eagerness for adventure that drew me toward new landscapes. On with my travels.

At Port Barcarès I stopped for a lunch of sugar water and fruit in a can, a baguette, and some mystery meat that looked like baloney. It was only three in the afternoon, and though I was dead tired from the rough roads, I pressed onward. The border was too far off to make that day, but I wanted to get on deck so crossing the border would be easy the next day.

Blisters swelled on my feet again. In hindsight, using powdered borax hand soap to wash my socks in the gas station bathroom sink was not among my best ideas. It was time to call it a day at Canet-en-Roussilon, completing a sixty-eight-kilometer day.

But the next morning, the blisters told me I needed another day of recovery. I sat on the beach writing postcards, journal pages, and a long letter.

Dear Carla,

It feels like years since I started this journey—not the journey on roller skates, but the journey I've been on as a human, as a kid and as a man. I was at the peak of my game when I started this adventure, but the game changed along the way. This journey has taken me from the top to rock bottom, to a place beyond my physical or imaginative reach. This place is where people need people. Independence, autonomy, self-sufficiency—everyone strives for these things, but they're all illusions.

I'll cross the Spanish border tomorrow and finish this adventure. John Wayne once said, "A man's gotta have a code, a creed to live by." I've been searching for my code this entire journey, and I wasn't even aware of it. Men like Dieter, Der Spiegel, Der Meehee, and of course my dad have theirs. I'm getting mine, but it's still incomplete. It's theoretical, made up of experiences I don't completely understand and haven't fully deciphered. The character I've gained through Rollan, Joel, and Mitch bring me closer to cracking that code. Many great men, a bunch of women, but only one special girl have brought me this far. Thank you for being my guiding light of purpose.

And through all the miles skated, I realize that I haven't found myself on this journey; I've created myself. I've learned that humans do not thrive when isolated from others, I expected to learn the opposite about real men.

Individualism can only be viable up to the point that reliance on others allows growth.

These changes in my life seemed as strange as the hundred-meter ship parked in sand next to me. I couldn't imagine how this cruise ship, *Lydia,* got so far up on the beach. A few other tourists also stared, dumbfounded. The city of Le Barcarès had made her a casino on the sand, the "Eiffel Tower of the Mediterranean Landscape." Through some investigation, I found they had dug out a harbor for her, dragged her in and sealed up the harbor with sand. An amazing feat of engineering, and a reminder of what men can do when they put their minds to a goal.

With healed feet and a high drive to get to the finish line, my immediate goal was to leave the hotel early so I'd have the whole day to enjoy the coves and mountains ahead. I had no desire to stop for breakfast in Argelès Plage after an hour of skating. The border was so close.

I dreaded the mountain roads after so much flat land, but climbing up and slaloming down the winding coastline brought back the thrill of downhill speed. Postcard-perfect vistas waited to be unwrapped like visual gifts around each point. Each cove was a sparkling gem hidden from the vast sprawl of tourism, too small to support more than a few vacationing families yet among perhaps the most prized, intimate coves of France.

These hills weren't as tough as some of the others I'd done. I'd gone up and down some Doozies, like the downhill drop-in to Monaco. I hated them for trying to kill me but loved them for how they had shaped me. They were just roads and I was just a man, simple as that. I was just a man on wheels.

The coastal road ran right along the beach, low and close to the shore, guiding me through Banyuls-sur-Mer with plenty of time for a midday swim. The beaches and cafés were at maximum capacity on this summer Sunday. Crowds filled the plaza, dancing to street music and celebrating life. I cruised past, staying on the Route de Cerbère until I found a little cove just south of town. I hiked down for a dip off the pristine Plage du Troc.

Only ten kilometers to go. Nothing to do but dry off with the French flag sleeping bag and hit the road.

The ridge of the Pyrénées climbed across Spain and France to Mount Aneto at 3,400 meters, then back down to the Atlantic Ocean. Somewhere in those mountains was El Camino de Santiago or The Way of Saint James, a trail across the Pyrénées of Northern Spain. Long before Jesus Christ was born, *pellegrinos*, or pilgrim hikers, would trek to Fisterra, the end of the world, burn their clothes, and watch the sun set into the sea next to La Costa de Morta, the Coast of Death. This ritual symbolized a pilgrim's death and rebirth.

Tourists continue the ritual, hiking the Camino, stamping their passports, and passing out in hostel bunk beds after drinking with fellow *pellegrinos*. I've read the journey is physically and piously demanding, both romantic and enlightening, and numerous books have been written about the metamorphosis of souls. As alluring as it sounded, I preferred the journey I'd taken, living the difference between traveler and tourist.

My low coastal road abruptly turned inland to become a thirteen-percent incline. This was the road I'd feared when considering the Pyrénées from afar. Ugh… It was all uphill from here. The road turned inland and upward, hotter and higher. It would surely be even steeper coming down. A few distant coastal points reached out to sea; one of them must be the border.

The cove at Cerbère was blocked by homes capitalizing on the spectacular sea views. Between every few houses were glimpses of water—way, way down there. Somewhere up ahead was the left turn that would get me down to lunch and a final celebration on this sublime bay before crossing the border. Narrow, charming streets guided my wheels past architecture weathered by centuries of sea air and wind. Some say the name of Cerbère comes from the giant dog Cerberus of Greek mythology. Cerberus, the three-headed pit bull with a fang-toothed snake for a tail, guards the gates of hell. I had a bad feeling I was about to get chased by that dog.

Rue Watteau—"What-O' Street," as I dubbed it—was lined with pictograms of train tracks, arrows pointed to the right. I wanted a pictogram of a roller skater drinking an enormous beer with his feet on a table, arrows pointed to the left. As the road grew a little steeper, I blew past the signs directing me to go right. The beach was to the left. There had to be a left turn up there somewhere.

The town's buildings may have told a seventeenth-century tale of guarding the Franco-Spanish border, but the streets were paved in fresh black asphalt, immaculate for twentieth-century transcontinental roller skaters. After a block of tight slalom on a one-lane road against traffic, I decided one of the French signs behind me must have said "one-way street, do not enter." But I still had a skinny old sidewalk to skate on. I could swap into pedestrian mode when a car came up the hill. Skinny little What-O' Street was so narrow that homeowners had to look both ways for traffic before stepping out their front doors. I worried a door might swing outward and flatten me.

There it was, the left I'd been looking for. A sign pointed left to La Ville, where I turned down a wall-lined street as though I'd been dropped out of a helicopter, on skis, into a chasm. The left wall was chunked stone; the sidewalk on the right became stair steps with a few gates to homes.

A gate under an ancient brick archway swung open into the street from a house—whammy number one in my loss of concentration. From the gate came three bursting bikini tops— whammy number two. Then a car struggling to climb the one-way road blasted its horn at me, forcing me up against the jagged rock wall—a bona fide triple whammy.

I side-surfed past the car, dragging my backpack across the rock wall as a brake. Once the car had passed, I was going too fast to regain speed control with tight slalom turns down this rocky crevasse of a street, a double black diamond, "expert skiers only" run. I did my best, but it was no use. I was committed to speed. My choices were crash into the wall and splatter myself in front of the girls, or blindly banzai to the bottom of whatever came next.

Death or humiliation—those were my choices. Humiliation would have been the wise choice, and I really should have been wiser at that moment. I was quite familiar with humiliation's agony—after all, I'd fallen in front of a hundred girls on a train— but I was still unclear how painful death by blind banzai might be.

So banzai it was.

I regretted my choice an instant later. Splattering face first into jagged rocks as bikinied girls laughed would have been a party with balloons and clowns compared to the street ahead. The street on which I now had to skate for my life.

A ninety-degree right turn lay dead ahead. If I didn't make the right turn, a ninety-degree drop down a ninety-foot cliff would ensure I didn't live more than ninety seconds longer. This was no time for bare knees and elbows. Why had I gotten rid of my pads? For that matter, why hadn't I chosen the wall? I could have smashed my face into those soft bikini tops instead of the jagged rock.

There was no escaping the reality that a man has a sexual thought every seven seconds, even when he was face-to-face with death.

I cut as hard as I could into the right turn. My left foot slid into the dirt edge of the road, four wheels skidding and plinking pebbles off the cliff. I would have to complete the high-speed turn on my inside right foot, a maneuver skiers dread as the hardest way to make a cut. Nearly all my weight was on my outside left leg, using every bit of traction on the road to keep my feet from skidding out from under me. Shifting all my weight to my right leg so I could lift my left out of the dirt went against all the physics and kinesthetics of making such a turn.

If I'd been skiing, I could have taken the fall and slid down the hill, covered in snow. In the street, the ditch at the bottom of the hill would leave me covered in blood. But there was no other option.

I could do this. I yelled out a fake-it-till-you-make-it affirmation with zero confidence. I yelled it again. And again.

"You'll make it, Jarvis, you can do this!" I shouted.

But my frightened, bugged-out eyes were windows to the perjurious truth within.

CHAPTER 38

SIT, CERBERUS. STAY.

It is vain for the coward to flee; death follows close behind;
it is only by defying it that the brave escape.
—Voltaire

Strategies raced through my head as another car confronted me
head-on. The only way to pass him was to side-surf along the cliff.
The driver leaned on his horn as he approached. Timing this
maneuver correctly would be a life-or-death difference.

Practice and instinct transitioned my feet flawlessly to the side-
surfing position. I cut in front of the moving car with barely an inch
to spare, my right leg twisting into the heel-to-heel maneuver I'd
perfected. An aluminum *clink* jarred my hand as my ski pole hit the
car's bumper.

Now I had to finish the turn around the car on only a couple of
feet of space on the cliffside. Like a high-wire artist, I reminded
myself not to look off the cliff just inches to my left. I couldn't
glance at the jagged rocks below. Heel-to-heel alongside the car, I
caught a glimpse of the passenger's wide eyes as my chest left a

streak of sweat across the window. It was possibly the longest two seconds of my life.

I prepared for the hardest surf-style bottom turn I could crank, as close to the car's rear bumper as I could pull it. Leaning hard, I made the turn at fifty kilometers per hour, sideways and straight toward another wall of rock.

And that was the easy turn.

Backside turns on roller skates are much different than in surfing. In skating, both feet need to contort beyond the heel-to-heel formation and so that your toes are pointing behind your body, an ass-backward, inverse pigeon-toed stance that makes ballerinas and orthopedic surgeons cringe. Normally I could have made the smooth backside turn with my heels together, but I was using the trucks on my skates to make the turn.

Again, instinct from months of skating spoke to me. Instinct told me there was no way I'd pull off this backside turn. As my back leg came around to reconfigure into parallel skiing, the sidewalk came up too quickly. I hopped up the curb using only my shaky left leg; my still-bloodied right leg was now airborne.

My brain began to parse tactics to each body part, each seeming to take on a mind of its own. Right leg understood it was about to hit the wall and instinctively reacted by kicking forward and sideways in some pseudo-one-legged, off-the-wall turn back onto and off the sidewalk, an extreme skate park maneuver that brilliant leg must have dreamed up while the rest of my body was freezing on some lighthouse.

Arms, legs, wheels, and all the other parts, piloted from my subconscious, flew past a speed limit sign: thirty kilometers per hour.

"Thirty?" I shouted in shock. "I wish!"

On the twenty-three-percent grade, I would have been ecstatic with a mere thirty kilometers per hour.

My yell disrupted the tranquility in the village below, further disquieted by the sound of cast iron chairs screeching across sidewalks as people stood to watch what was coming down the hill.

I was still gaining speed. Bombing from steep-and-smooth onto flat-and-rough could have locked up my wheels and put me flat on my face. A huge pothole sank in the old concrete ahead—and by "old," I mean that this concrete had probably been poured by Louis the First's great-grandfather when he was my age. I'd have to leap the pothole to set up for the big turn, a ninety-degree left at the bottom at full speed.

I approached the street crater, planted my ski poles, and leaped over it, landing and bumping the safety rail with my knee. The irony of this so-called safety rail on the cliff was that it was no more than a trip wire for anyone on skates, ensuring I would transition into a lovely swan dive for the tourists as I plunged into the rocks below.

"*Not today!*" screamed a voice from within.

There were more gasps from below, and a woman's scream filled the cove.

At the bottom of this hill was a dead-end wall, at least from my perspective. The sharp left turn I'd have to make was like expecting Cerberus to open the gates for me. If that wasn't enough to worry about, I was approaching a section of corrugated concrete that helps cars maintain their traction up the hill. My feet did an amazing job of skating the ridges parallel to their forty-five-degree angle. An edge in the pavement forced me to leap from the old concrete onto new asphalt and lean left, as though I was making an Olympic giant slalom turn at the bottom.

The last shred of road was a one-foot section of sidewalk. My right foot finished off the turn, springing back on the road just inches away from a telephone pole. I was on flat, solid ground.

I'd made it. I was at the bottom. I was alive.

It was over.

My heart was trying to pound its way out of my chest. I coasted along the center line of the road into the village, head hanging, catching my breath and quietly thanking God for my life and my fine motor skills. As bodily control came back, I began shaking, scared out of my wits, utterly astonished I'd made it without a scratch. Tears formed in my eyes. Stressed laughter leaked from my mouth, eventually overcoming the silence. I buried my face in my hands, ski pole grips dangling, still bent over, still rolling. Total comprehension sank in of how close I'd come to rolling along here in an ambulance or hearse.

But I'd done it.

When I stood back up, I stretched my arms wide, reached for the sky, and stared at the heavens. Uncontrollable bursts of words, between gasps for air, increased in volume with each breath.

"I MADE IT! I'M ALIVE. I'M ALIVE, GOD. WE DID IT."

I jumped and yelled as loud as I could, oblivious to the world around me.

***

A crowd gathered in the street ahead. Every sidewalk café seat emptied, not a single beach towel occupied. And then the first few people began to applaud. The applause spread across the small town until everyone was standing in the streets in ovation.

The applause, outcry, and whistles brought out the a smile I never knew I had. I let the tears flow as I shook about seventy-five hands and waved to the other half of the crowd.

One man acted as impromptu reporter and translator, asking me questions and yelling my responses back to the crowd in French. Reaction and chatter ensued.

The crowd quieted for the next question: "Where did you skate from?"

When I told the man, he looked at me with a deadpan expression. "*Noooon.*"

"*Mais oui!*" I replied, beaming.

When he told the crowd that I'd skated across France from Italy, their reaction was more animated than his. But my story appeared to be in question, so I dropped my backpack and pulled out the maps that journaled each day. The man seized the papers, scrutinizing them before bounding to his feet again, shouting out in French that I really had skated across their entire glorious nation.

The crowd went wild, at least in my head. I pulled out my sleeping bag, my big French flag, and skated around the street.

At the end of my fifteen minutes of fame, the crowd returned to the chairs, towels, and cars that had been put on pause. They honked their way along, trying to get past the scene in the middle of the main road, as the crowd dissipated.

I accepted a frosty liter of beer from a couple of Dutch guys begging me to join them and lifted my tired feet, skates and all, right up onto the table. I smiled for the photographers in the crowd, a tired, shirtless American in my Adidas shorts, skates on the table and a joyous soul within.

The Dutch guys and I shared a few laughs, but when they asked me about skating across France, I was surprised to find I wasn't much of a conversationalist. With so many memories of rolling across every inch of the Riviera, meeting so many new friends, and surviving so many near-death experiences, I couldn't begin to describe it all in a few words. I stared at a wall across the street in a state of shock. I was here. The last cove.

But there was more work to be done before this day was over. The border waited at the top of the next hill. I thanked my new friends for the beer and prepared to cross the border.

CHAPTER 39

OVER THE LINE

There is nothing noble in being superior to your fellow men. True nobility lies in being superior to your former self.
——Ernest Hemingway

Only four kilometers to go, and all straight uphill.

I schussed my way out of town while waving goodbye, cherishing every step of the last miles of the journey as I climbed through the switchbacks. The last few cliffhanger hotels and restaurants were familiar sights. The blistering street air was broken up by cool breezes from the Mediterranean Sea between each building, like a cool fan oscillating every few moments. In those moments, those times when life presented an on-off switch of pleasure and pain, one gained a fundamental appreciation of how good life could be and how quickly it could all be taken away.

Each parcel away from town became less touristy, more rural. Each step away from the cove brought a visible reduction in land value, until finally the mansions and hotels became abandoned weed farms on empty lots.

I stared at the road like an old friend, a pure soul of asphalt and center line curving ahead. Once again I was in my element, at one with the road, at home on the highway. Last turn inland; it was up, up, and away to the finish line.

A stone distance marker, weathered and pitted by centuries of salty air, displayed a simple "1." One more hairpin turn. One more kilometer.

Paint on the street was set up for lines of cars, but I was the only one around. This must be it.

The first guard shack was no larger than one you might find at a gated neighborhood. The sign read *Douane*—customs. Still climbing a steep uphill, I put my arms and legs into a sprint to the finish, crossing the line out of breath and with an ear-to-ear grin.

I rolled up to the stop sign painted on the road and removed my backpack. A woman in the first shack slid open a window and asked if I would like to exchange my French francs. I shook my head and proceeded to the next shack, where guards in French and Spanish uniforms waited to inspect me.

I still hadn't caught my breath and my heart was racing, mostly with excitement. I had one foot on the painted finish line of my journey, leaning on the wooden lift gate to Spain.

Officer Pasar of Spain, tall and tan with a mustache you could sweep the floor with, requested my passport. I showed him my date of entry into France and watched as he attempted to figure me out. He handed my passport to the French guard, opening their conversation with both French and Spanish.

"How did you get here, Señor Jarvis," Officer Pasar asked. "On the roller skates?"

"That's correct. I skated from Italy."

He paused, puzzled, and translated for the other guard.

I took a swig of water from my bota bag as they inspected my backpack.

"You say you skated from where?" Pasar asked again dubiously.

I answered by pointing: "From Italy. To Spain. On roller skates. *Oui. Sí.* Yessiree."

The other guard circled. Was there some trouble? They discussed me further in their languages.

"*No no, señor. No comprende.* From where you roller-skated? From Cerbère?"

"Yes, from Cerbère just now. But weeks ago, I started skating from Italy. And I skated all the way across France. From Italy to Spain."

I guess I could have simply told him I'd skated up the street, but I was excited to say the words I had nearly died for.

"And *señor*, you have traveled all this way by roller skate to come into Spain?"

Was this guy dense?

"Yes. Yes, I have. And if you open that gate for me, I can make the journey all the way into Spain."

Pasar went back into the shack with my passport while the French guard poked around my backpack in an unofficial, curious inspection. I stood at the door of the shack, wondering what Pasar was doing in there. Something was wrong. This was too dramatic for a pedestrian crossing a border.

Pasar exited the shack with no indication of acceptance until he handed me my passport and showed me the *España* stamp. Then he pushed down on the counterweight, raised the wooden gate, and motioned for me to pass the yellow line painted across the road.

"You have made it, Señor Jarvis," he said, throwing one hand out to shake mine. "*Bienvenido a España.*"

And so on June 14, 1981, I became the first person to ever roller-skate, street ski, roller-ski——whatever you wanted to call it— across France. The French guard shook my hand and took photos with his camera and mine. They too wanted to memorialize the day that crazy Californian crossed into Spain on roller skates.

I skated to the top of the next hill to take in some cool breezes. Now what? It was over. I won. But victory, no matter how one defined it, is not found at the top of the mountain. My victory was found in the climb, in the process, in the daily struggle of doing what was needed when it was needed, not just when I felt like it.

I stood at the Pyrénées, a natural divide with Spain to the south and France to the north, the world at my feet—and I still had nowhere to go. Though I'd been living on the road, doing whatever I wanted whenever I wanted and however I wanted to do it, an entirely new independence came over me. How could I get any freer than this? I had nothing to do and nowhere to go after rolling down that hill. And so I rolled, enjoying the long, gentle slopes into Portbou. The infinite horizon beyond the Mediterranean gently reminded that I could go anywhere, do anything. I spread my arms in emancipation, and exhaled the last of bit of a breath I had been holding in since I left Zugspitze.

I was nineteen. I had a year's worth of savings in a bank and most of the things I needed on my back. I had families I could go to in America and Germany and invitations to visit friends throughout the world.

It was otherworldly and a bit frightening. I was starting all over again with an understanding that it was better to work toward a goal than to go through life without one.

The Portbou train station had a huge map of Europe. I stared at it for a good long while. The next train would leave in two hours. It was a train to everywhere, since there was only one way out of this town: out of the station and directly into a long tunnel to France. I had my wallet in hand and I was near the ticket window, but I didn't want to look like an idiot when the clerk asked where I wanted to go.

The fact of the matter was that I was that idiot. I'd had weeks to figure this out. Maybe I'd never believed I would make it, but whatever happened next in my life, I had completed this major accomplishment.

And now that was all behind me. And for what really? Had anyone benefited from my selfish travels? Had I done it to cure cancer or feed hungry children? Had I done it to make someone smile? I hadn't done any of those things.

A case of post-transcontinental roller skater depression set in.

I put on my espadrilles and let my poor blistered feet air out. Though I could ski eight hundred miles of street slopes, I could barely walk a sidewalk. I packed up for pedestrian travel, collapsing my ski poles and strapping them to my pack along with my steaming skates. Then I sat down with a beer in the train station garden, a perfect place for unwinding and figuring out my life. Which I had two hours to resolve.

I took a long pull on my beer and looked around. The Spanish girls were cute, but there was a clear shift in natural beauty on this side of the border. Besides, I wasn't interested in the girls. I was enjoying my lonely, isolated, empty moment of selfish triumph—without a soul to share it with.

Travelers had already formed a tangled mess outside the ticket window. I'd better buy my ticket to somewhere while I had the chance. When I got to the window, I nervously handed my passport to the clerk in anticipation of the next monumental crossroads of my life: the moment he asked—and I had to tell him—where I was going.

"*Un momento,*" he said.

And then he walked away with my passport.

Oh, thank god—maybe there was a problem with my passport and I'd have to go back to jail in Monaco or something. Anything. As long as I didn't have to decide. As long as someone would tell me what to do so I didn't have to be responsible for messing up my own life.

The clerk returned with a small padded envelope covered with postage stamps, cancellation inks, customs stickers, and postal notifications. There was hardly any room left for my name, which had been transferred several times from the envelope to the stickers and stamps.

"A package for you, *de* general delivery. Please to sign for this."
He pulled off a ticket from the package, revealing my name written
by hand on the last sliver of visible manila.

I recognized that penmanship.

I tore open the envelope and dumped the contents on the
counter: a lovely ballpoint pen with a simple note card in its clip.

I don't expect another call until
you're done over there, but just in
case you lost your pen, I wanted to
ensure there's more writing. And
writing. And writing.
XO,
Carla

The clerk smirked at my obvious delight with such a simple
delivery. "Okay, *señor,* where would you like to go?"

"San Francisco!"

As if I'd grasped the lost ship's wheel in a storm, a new direction
and purpose came alive. Total clarity overcame me, unlike the poor
clerk trying to figure out how to sell me a ticket to California.

***

Settled comfortably a few hours later in front of the big window of
my rail cabin, I watched the Spanish train station clock tick endlessly
forward. Oh, how I now appreciated the German train system. The
4:15 from Portbou departed at a lazy 4:49. As quickly as I'd said
hello, I said goodbye to Spain, for in another moment I'd be in the
tunnel and through the Pyrénées.

On the cabin table, Carla's pen lay on a pad of paper,
shimmering in the sunlight like the mighty sword awaiting a literary
swordsman to conquer the blank page. The train lurched forward

toward the tunnel as I began to write before the whole train plunged into the darkness ahead.

My dear Carla,

The huge rucksack filled with dynamite tugged my shoulders, leather straps leaving bruises on my shoulders and the weight nearly buckling my legs with each step up the icy Alpen tunnel—

THE END

A NOTE ON THE TEXT

Like the story, the characters in this book are all real. Their dialog was mostly recreated—with the exception of verbatim quotes from a stack of letters and postcards Carla somehow saved for three decades. Details of the story came from daily entries in my journal, scribbles in the corners of paper maps I carried, on the backs of photos I took, and in an address book of friends I met along the way.

But I misplaced all those documents for thirty years. And with them, I lost the ability to write this book accurately for half a lifetime.

Immediately following the adventure in 1981, I mailed all the photos and maps and journals to my parents. When I returned home to write this book, they said they had received the package and put it "somewhere around here." For years, I looked everywhere until I finally gave up. It wasn't until my parents passed away and my sisters deep cleaned the house we all grew up in. The girls brought some cardboard boxes with yellowed tape to my garage; "Michael's stuff" labeled in thick black ink. Inside one of those boxes, amongst a flurry of moths and 1980's dust, I found the package. Moments later, I wiped the tears from my eyes, sat down at my keyboard and began writing French Roll.

Though I also found the address book, I had better luck contacting most of the characters through the Internet, and I've been able to thank them for their contribution to the story. Most of them I've reconnected with—via a chat on social media or a lunch when I made it to their town. A few I have yet to find. And then there are two young men who I'll never have the opportunity to reconnect with; Rollan tragically lost his life in a paraglider accident in 2009, and Mitch passed in his sleep in 2018. I've been in contact with their families, in hopes they'll be able to spend a few precious moments with them in the chapters.

I'd like to thank Carla, who kept me skating forward and writing back. Your prose was my number one inspiration for better writing and becoming a better man. To Carrie, who captured my teenage heart with a summer smile; there can only be one first love in a lifetime, and that is your title to keep. And to Joel who started all of this by giving me a journal and challenging me to write "just a few words a day for all to share someday."

Mom and Dad, you told me I could be a writer in the third grade and I'm sorry I waited too long to show you I could do it. To my kids, I'm glad you're all old enough to read this and maybe one day not be weirded-out by knowing that Dad thought like a teenage boy at one point.

And especially to my dear wife Tamerra who endured so many long nights and longer years of hearing me type and talk and research this book…and now you've read it and it's over—until I start the next book.

AUTHOR BIOGRAPHY

J. Michael Jarvis writes from his experiences as a professional jet pilot, yacht captain and global adventurer with thousands of true, remarkable and often hilarious stories of how he mucked things up. From roller-skating across France as a teen, to escaping pirates as a yacht captain in the Caribbean Sea[RJS1] [RJS2] , to flying Sir Richard Branson and Chuck Yeager from some of the world's most remote airports, Jarvis has lived a life even the most imaginative writers can only begin to fictionalize.

Jarvis is a graduate of Embry-Riddle Aeronautical University, receiving a Bachelor of Science degree in Aeronautics. He is a captain of both air and sea. He holds an Air Transport Pilot license and a Coast Guard Master License, allowing him to command yachts and airplanes through experiences from North and South America to most Caribbean island nations.

A surviving passenger of a 1986 airplane crash, Jarvis has lived by his twisted version of an old pilot's adage. "Any landing you can crawl away from with broken arms and legs—on fire—is a good one." Jarvis continues to fly and write about his adventures on the sea and in the sky. His humor is both inspirational and thought-provoking, with rare insight into the generosity we are given with each extended day of our fragile lives.

An active member of Southern California Writers Association, Jarvis lives in his birth town of Newport Beach, California, where he is happily married with four adult children. French Roll is his first book.

Connect with

J. Michael Jarvis

— visit —

JMichaelJarvis.com
Twitter.com/JMichaelJarvis
Facebook.com/Interseller
LinkedIn.com/in/Interseller
Instagram.com/JMichaelJarvis
GoodReads.com/JMichaelJarvis

Made in the USA
Las Vegas, NV
12 April 2023

70502823R00178